CW01023270

CULTURAL INTERACTIONS
Studies in the Relationship between the Arts

Edited by J.B. Bullen

Volume 40

PETER LANG

Oxford · Bern · Berlin · Bruxelles · Frankfurt am Main · New York · Wien

Antony Buxton, Linda Hulin
and Jane Anderson (eds)

InHabit

People, Places and Possessions

PETER LANG

Oxford · Bern · Berlin · Bruxelles · Frankfurt am Main · New York · Wien

Bibliographic information published by Die Deutsche Nationalbibliothek.
Die Deutsche Nationalbibliothek lists this publication in the Deutsche
Nationalbibliografie; detailed bibliographic data is available on the
Internet at http://dnb.d-nb.de.

A catalogue record for this book is available from the British Library.

Library of Congress Control Number: 2016958019

ISSN 1662-0364
ISBN 978-3-0343-1866-2 (print) • ISBN 978-1-78707-231-2 (ePDF)
ISBN 978-1-78707-232-9 (ePub) • ISBN 978-1-78707-233-6 (mobi)

Cover image: Paul Klee, *Temple Gardens* (1920). The Metropolitan
Museum of Art, The Berggruen Klee Collection, 1987
[www.metmuseum.org].

© Peter Lang AG, International Academic Publishers, Bern 2017
Hochfeldstrasse 32, CH-3012 Bern, Switzerland
info@peterlang.com, www.peterlang.com, www.peterlang.net

All rights reserved.
All parts of this publication are protected by copyright.
Any utilisation outside the strict limits of the copyright law, without the
permission of the publisher, is forbidden and liable to prosecution.
This applies in particular to reproductions, translations, microfilming, and
storage and processing in electronic retrieval systems.

This publication has been peer reviewed.

Printed in Germany

Contents

Figures

ANTONY BUXTON, LINDA HULIN AND JANE ANDERSON

Introduction

This volume emerged from a shared sense of limited perspectives. As editors, and as contributors we are all interested in the human condition – arguably universal across place and time – of habitation. But disciplinary parameters being what they are, we became aware of the fact that our own methodologies and contexts could only ever reveal so much of a broad ranging and complex totality. No matter how comprehensive our own enquiries might be, they could only ever hope to be part of a much richer and more revealing narrative. Encountering, often by chance, others whose perspectives could enrich our own, and vice versa, we created a setting for conversations between scholars in different disciplines, sharing the same interest in habitation: The Oxford Research Centre in the Humanities (TORCH) seminar series of which the editors of this volume were convenors, entitled 'inHabit' [*sic*].[1] The title for such an enterprise, engaging with such a multifaceted condition – structural and spatial, material, social and ideological – was problematic. The choice of inHabit was chosen as one which hopefully embraced this complexity, with the subtitle 'People, Places and Possessions' indicating an emphasis on social and spatial properties. As a totality 'inHabit' indicates the spatial process of dwelling in place and structure, but the deliberate capitalisation of 'Habit' seeks to emphasise the root meaning of dwelling (Latin *habitare*) and possession (Latin *habere*, to possess or to hold). Habit also forms a connection with, to us, an important theoretical strand relating to habitation, Bourdieu's theory of practice (1977, 1990) and his concept of *habitus* as habitual actions in place which order knowledge of the world and social relationships. Suitably

---

1   Dr Oliver Cox also convened the inHabit Seminar series and runs (2016) the Thames Valley Country House Partnership at TORCH.

then 'habit' also possesses connotations of custom, and also of attire, the 'dressing' of person and place.

Other words which are associated with the state of habitation – domesticity, dwelling and home, for example, all carry other connotations. Whilst the term 'domestic' is certainly commonly used to describe elements of human habitation and associated activities – often with significant gender connotations – as a concept domesticity is applied far wider. Archaeologically domestication is viewed as a critical state of cultural transition of the human species to a settled and more controlling engagement with the environment implicit in the etymology of the Indo-European root 'dom', connected with forms of control (Hodder 1990; Benveniste 1973: 249–51). Similarly the concept of 'dwelling' has been extended philosophically from simple habitation to the sense of engagement with every aspect of being in the world (Heidegger 1971: 145, 150–1; Ingold 2011: 9–12). And the word 'home', now with highly affective and personal associations, originating from old German and Norse becomes in old English 'ham', a designation of a settlement of origin, or homeplace, thus implying a place and importantly a community of origin and belonging (Liberman 2015). The range and associations of terms employed in connection with human habitation thus indicate the many facets of this condition and possible strands of interpretation, and 'habitation' was selected as the unifying theme of this volume, emphasising the elements of space and time, relatively neutral in relation to social status, gender and affections, but nevertheless embracing the combination of structures, actions, social relationships and values.

Deliberately interdisciplinary, the conversations which took place at TORCH provided a context for sharing of various perspectives on habitation, an awareness of disciplinary limitations and the possibility of mutually enriching our methodologies. We do not suggest here the dilution of the strengths brought by disciplines – specialism in evidence and contexts, and rigorous methodologies – but rather recognition of their limitations and the possibility of learning from others. Archaeologists, anthropologists, social and cultural historians, geographers, art and design historians all contributed to these sessions and many are represented in this volume, intended as a continuation of this conversation.

This volume was thus inspired by the series of seminars convened by the authors and held under the auspices of TORCH, which was established to foster interdisciplinary research. The theme of human habitation seemed a highly suitable focus for an interdisciplinary discourse, pertinent to scholars in diverse fields. As seminar convenors and as editors we individually represent ethno-historical, archaeological and architectural perspectives, and have sought in this volume to bring together other scholars with an interest in habitation derived from textual and aesthetic perspectives and from understanding gained in the field and in practice.

Human habitation – or dwelling – is a condition central to human existence and experience, the complexity of which spreads beyond disciplinary boundaries, consisting of the provision of shelter and subsistence, biological and cultural reproduction, group and individual identity, and attendant values. We approach habitation primarily from a phenomenological perspective – the knowledge of the world acquired through being in the world (Husserl 1900, Merleau-Ponty 1965, Heidegger 1971) – and also employ structuralist concepts of *praxis* and *habitus* (Bourdieu 1977, Bourdieu 1990). But we recognise that habitation is conceptualised in its structuring, in varied responses to the physical environment and the variety of material registers (Buchli 2013: 71–88), and to the affective and the social dynamic which takes place within (Douglas 1973).

How might a phenomenological emphasis inform an understanding of the complexity of habitation? Where the Cartesian dichotomy posits the internal world of mind and culture as distinct from and superior to the external world of body and nature – and thus the person distinct from their habitation – Edmund Husserl argues that it is the conscious registration of external phenomena through the senses that constitutes human experience (Husserl 1973/1900). His pupil Heidegger carried the significance of physically external phenomena further, seeing human life as inextricably enmeshed in its material environment, with no division between the material and the conceptual. For Heidegger, the human being, *Dasein*, is part of the material world and its conceptual universe is drawn from its experiences in that world, from the objects and people around it (Heidegger 1927/1962: 78–86). As well as temporal, the experience of being is spatial; location and the physical structuring of location thus gives context to our being: 'The spaces through which we go daily are provided for by locations; their nature is grounded in things of the type of buildings' (Heidegger 1971: 156). Being in the world is to dwell in the world, and habitation locates dwelling; 'We attain to dwelling, so it seems, only by means of building' and 'building as dwelling, that is, as being on the earth … remains for man's everyday experience that which is from the outset "habitual" – we inhabit it' (Heidegger 1971: 145, 147). Thus for Heidegger the notion of dwelling is a way of locating ourselves in the world that we experience, both conceptually and physically: 'We do not dwell because we have built, but we build and have built because we dwell, that is, because we are dwellers' (Heidegger 1971: 148).

Habitation is however more than building. In his analysis of the society of the Kabyle of North Africa Pierre Bourdieu observed that the arrangement of the furnishings in the domestic interior clearly articulated the conceptualisation of social relationships. He therefore concluded that it was in repeated actions around objects in the home that members were inculcated with its values; a process Bourdieu terms *habitus* (Bourdieu 1990: 52–5). The individual generally acts in accordance with learnt norms, only occasionally choosing to act of their own volition. Social relationships and cultural values are thereby inextricably linked to human actions, or 'practice', in the material world (Bourdieu 1990: 54). Habitual actions underpin both physical and social existence, and the concepts which link these states. In the words of Gosden (1994: 16), 'It is the mass of habitual actions and the referential structure they form which carries the main burden of our lives, giving them shape and direction'. Thus if built structures, differentiated space and actions are the framework for social relationships, agency may also be said to reside in buildings and objects (Knappett and Malafouris 2008).

Habitation thus consists of occupation of place and of human actions, objects and relationships: 'House, body and mind are in continuous interaction, the physical structure, furnishing, social conventions and mental images of the house at once enabling, moulding, informing and constraining the ideas and activities which unfold within its bounds' (Carsten and Hugh-Jones 1995: 2). In his structural analysis however, Amos Rapoport's distinguishes within the domestic domain fixed features (buildings), semi-fixed features (furnishings) and latent features (people and meanings).

Domestic activities thus range from the instrumental and manifest to the latent and conceptual, with increasing cultural specificity; for example cooking is a universal manifest activity, but the social contexts of food consumption and the symbolism of food preparation and consumption are conceptual, varying widely between and within cultures (Rapoport 1990: 11). The organisation of domestic life is thus culture specific and domestic building formed by the wider cultural context. Just as architecture encloses behaviour, so activities – and culture – shape architecture (Rapoport 1990: 9, 16). The *latent* qualities or meanings of activities are often hard to deduce in the past, and the semi fixed features of buildings – or furnishings – may provide more indications of activities than the fixed structures of the buildings themselves (Rapoport 1990: 13).

Extending and emphasising their social significance Douglas and Isherwood see commodities – including those of habitation – not primarily as functional objects, but (because human beings engage most effectively with their environment collaboratively) as the material expressions of the relationships and attendant values constituting a culture; 'Instead of supposing that goods are primarily needed for subsistence plus competitive display let us assume that they are needed for making visible and stable the categories of culture. This approach to goods emphasising their double roles in providing subsistence and in drawing lines of social relationships [is] ... the way to a proper understanding of why people need goods' (Douglas, Isherwood 1979: 59). Indeed Rapaport suggests that – built structures being relatively permanent – changes in the conduct of habitus – the domestic culture – can often be most effectively expressed by changes in the semi-permanent furnishings, and their attendant actions, adaptation to the structure of buildings often following thereafter (Rapoport 1990: 13).

The perspective adopted by Bourdieu and fellow structuralists suggests that human relationships are largely predetermined by the social and physical structures in which they are situated. However, for Anthony Giddens humans act both with 'practical' unconsciousness, and 'discursive' consciousness. The individual is self aware and reflective, therefore capable of knowledgeable interaction with the world s/he inhabits, but routines, and the daily face to face encounters which they involve, provide individuals with a sense of ontological security. Importantly, in terms of domestic life, Giddens sees this day to day interaction with its spatial and temporal considerations (albeit without specific reference to the role of materiality apart from inclusion in 'allocative' resources) as central to human experience of life and the formation of social structures (Giddens 1984: 5–6, 34–7). The predominance of structure in the exercise of human life and habitation is however questioned by Bruno Latour (2005: 23–43, 63–74), asserting that structures, social and physical, are primarily the traces and expressions of relationships, without which they would have no validity and existence. To this extent habitation then can be viewed as a physical manifestation of the ordering of social life, and the extent to which the individual identity is situated in relation to the group has been usefully modelled by Mary Douglas (1992) in her group-grid framework, expressing the extent to which individuals choices and group solidarity interact.

The engagement with habitation by various disciplines

Unsurprisingly, as part of a condition which encompasses so much of human life, elements of habitation form the evidence for enquiry in many disciplines; archaeology, social and economic history, geography, sociology, design and art history, and architecture. A brief survey such as this can refer to only a representative fraction of this multi-disciplined work. The anthropologist is perhaps concerned most comprehensively with the totality of domesticity, from the formation of the social group (Fortes 1958) and community to the nature of the dwelling and domestic practice (Carsten and Hugh-Jones 1995). For archaeologists (Buchli 2013: 47–8) the habitation, or dwelling, constitutes some of the most enduring evidence of human culture in the remote past. Adopting a diachronic view of architecture, archaeologists are able to narrate the long development of habitation, and attempt to interpret the wider culture from the built record and other material artefacts.

Originally mostly concerned with the evidence of wider settlement, individual habitations have become the focus of specific study; household archaeology, a distinct sub discipline credited to Wilk and Rathje (1982). Households are recognised as elemental units which organise the economic, political and social activities of the community, distributing resources of production, reproduction and shared ownership (Rice 1993: 66–7). Remains of human habitation have been a central concern since the inception of archaeology – for example Roman Herculaneum and Pompeii from the mid-eighteenth century – and have provided evidence of the earliest human culture. Habitation associated with cave shelter at Zhoukoudian in China (670,000 and 470,000 years ago) was excavated by Otto Zdansky in the 1920s (Beeman 1959), and also at Shanìdar in Iraq (65,000 to 35,000 years ago) (Solecki 1954). In Western Europe the Upper Palaeolithic Magdalenian culture (17,000 to 12,000 years ago) has been subjected to household analysis (Zubrow et al. 2010), and in his *Domestication of Europe* Ian Hodder (1990) suggests that domestication was foremost a conceptual shift, an attempt to master nature. Excavations at Lepenski Vir (circa 6000 BCE) have provided evidence of created dwelling structures (Srejović 1972). Household remains have been employed to explore the development of Mesopotamian cities and towns from the fourth to second millennia BC (Stone 1996), and in the Near East Bronze Age domestic life has been interpreted through household furnishings (Daviau 1993). Some of the best preserved Neolithic habitations in Europe were discovered at Skara Brae in the Orkneys (circa 3180–2500 BCE), systematically excavated by Vere Gordon Childe in the mid-twentieth century (Childe 1952).

The exploration of settlement in pre-Columbian Americas was pioneered by Gordon Willey (1953) in the Viru Valley in Peru in the 1950s. The term household archaeology originated (Wilk and Rathje 1982) during the 'post-processual' re-evaluation – influenced by anthropological and neo Marxist perceptions of ambiguities of the social discourse – of the 'processual' assertion of an objective, empirical interpretation of the data, William Rathje developing household archaeological studies in the Mayan region. Similarly, in central Mexico household archaeology focused on habitation in the great city of Teotihuacan, Cynthia Robin and Elizabeth Brumfiel (2010) focusing particularly on the role of gender (De Lucia 2010). Richard Blanton (1994) has also engaged in comparative work on Mesoamerican households. In North America the development of Anasazi

(Pueblo) habitations from rock shelters to elaborate stone and mud dwellings has been well documented (Cordell 1994). The study of these dwellings has also been adopted by modern architects (Morrow and Price 1997). Household archaeology is now the subject of studies by a wide range of specialist scholars (Parker and Foster 2012).

In the modern period 'historical' archaeologists have sought to analyse the material remains of habitation through other contemporary sources, primarily documentary (Glassie 1975, Alcock 1993, Johnson 1993, Tarlow and West 1999, Deetz and Deetz 2000) and focused (Fogle, Nyman and Beaudry 2015). Historians also have widely employed habitation and life in the home as evidence for social and economic studies (Houlbrooke 1984, Tadmoor 1996, Overton, Whittle, Dean and Hann 2004, Buxton 2015 inter alia). Pictorial representation of the home, in particular the domestic interior, also serves as evidence for historical studies (Aynsley, Grant 2006). Architectural historians are very much engaged with the built structure of the dwelling and concepts governing its design (Barley 1961, Brunskill 1997), sometimes combining architecture with the social culture within (Johnson 1993, Girouard 1978). Interior decor and furnishing has also formed the subject for studies (Thornton 1984). Geographers have also focused on the home as an essential element in human settlement (Blunt and Dowling, *Home*, 2006).

Besides those who are examining, from various perspectives the phenomenon of habitation, there are also those – architects and interior designers – who theorise and conceptualise habitation in the abstract and materialise this thinking in the practical and physical act of building and furnishing. Architects use these concepts in the process of design, in their observations of everyday life, in their predictions of future change and in their development of project briefs with clients. Architects have long recognised the intimate relationship between the human body and building. Indeed, in laying out the correct principles for the construction of a temple the Roman Vitruvius (first century BC) asserted that the relationship between its parts should ideally correspond to the proportions of the human body. In Europe in the early modern era the Venetian architect Andrea Palladio (second half of the sixteenth century) adapted Vitruvian principles to the elite dwelling. Humanist principles have continued to echo that ideal, promoting a rational, ordered structure which became the expression of education and taste. Sir Henry Wotton (1624–72: 6) paraphrased Vitruvian building requirements as 'firmness, commodity, and delight', and Sir Francis Bacon (1627–69: 193–200) argued the need for the correct planning of dwelling to facilitate day to day living but also to enhance social status. In the eighteenth century a number of British writers opined on the correct principles of architecture (Langley 1727, Ware 1756, Adam and Adam 1773–1822), continuing to assert the primacy of classical style and principles. In the nineteenth century also Robert Kerr (1864) provided a manual for correct design – now referring to a number of historically sourced styles – and complex planning of the elite house, whilst others authors catered for the dwellings of the middle class (Wickes 1859–62). In the later part of the century, in response to uncontrolled urbanisation, a growing link was made with living conditions and social well-being for all social classes, a concern expressed in various acts of housing legislation, and also in a desire to design buildings and furnishings that expressed an honest 'fitness for purpose'. Significantly this quality of authenticity and unadorned and appropriate functionality was identified in vernacular architecture and artefacts. The designers and architects associated with the British Arts and Crafts movement (William Morris, C. F. A. Voysey, Hugh Baillie Scott, Charles Rennie Mackintosh and others) provided an example adopted in America (Gustav Stickley, Greene and Greene, Frank Lloyd Wright and others), and also through Herman Muthesius (1904–5) in the German Werstätte movement. After the First World War, the Bauhaus (1919–33) proved to be the focus of an evolving debate on the correct principles to govern the design of objects and of buildings, one which according to Adolf Loos (1908) should be devoid of meretricious decoration. An emphasis on functionality and simple form became the defining characteristics of international twentieth-century Modernism. The Swiss architect Le Corbusier formulated rational principles for building habitation, viewed as 'a machine for living in' and furnishings as 'equipment' (1923/1931), whilst Scandinavian Modernism – Alvar Aalto a leading figure – sought to soften functionality with organic forms and materials. In America after the Second World War the concept of the 'ideal home' – architects Charles and Ray Eames, Richard Neutra, Eero Saarinen inter alia – was formulated for returning servicemen. But the latter part of the twentieth century saw a stylistic reaction to pure functionality expressed philosophically as the holistic experience of 'dwelling' argued by Martin Heidegger (1971), and the Post Modern reintroduction of historically sourced symbolic elements (Venturi 1977).

More recent architectural theorists, borrowing from anthropology, have sought to re-emphasise the need for biulding design to comprehend the social dynamic of structures; the manner in which space is an expression of, and structures 'practice' and social relationships, producing and reproducing human culture (Le Febvre 1991, Hiller and Hanson 1984, Samson 1990, Low and Lawrence-Zúñiga 2003). Kent (1990) draws together a range of disciplinary perpsectives to explore domestic spatiality, and Melhuish and Toy (1996) and Buchli (2013) both employ anthropological and archaeological perspectives to achieve a better understanding of human habitation. McCarter and Pallasma (2012) return once again to an elaboration of the fundamental principles of architecture in key themes with a phenomenological bias, including space and time, materiality, and conceptual values of dwelling, memory and place. Thus during the sixteenth to the eighteenth centuries architectural theory concerned itself primarily with elite expressions in the classical trope, and in the nineteenth century diverse historical references, but an increasing concern for the quality of living conditions. The practical problems of decently housing a rising population have been addressed with functional solutions in the twentieth century. The architecture of habitation now turns increasingly towards an anthropological and environmental understanding of the condition for all of humanity (Oliver 1997).

Inter- or pluridisciplinary approaches to habitation

Elements of human habitation or domesticity are thus the evidential foci of and subject of study from a broad range of disciplinary perspectives. But the multifaceted nature of these elements – structure and spatial differentiation, material culture and activities, social relationships and attendant values – suggest the benefit of studies which look beyond disciplinary limitations in order to better comprehend their complexity and interrelatedness. The human search for understanding has tended towards compartmentalisation, the Greek philosopher Aristotle for example responsible for the creation of an influential hierarchy of knowledge, theoretical deliberations considered to have higher value than those of a more practical nature. The methodology of enquiry was altered by increasing emphasis on empirical proof – there is no innate knowledge but only that which must be ascertained (Locke 1689) – and abstraction challenged by the greater applicability and certifiable nature of scientific enquiry (Moran 2002: 3–5, 5–8).

Driven by the search for critical understanding, academic enquiry has tended towards circumscribed fields determined by types of evidence and effective methodologies (Turner 2000: 52). Such focus is a necessary condition of the pursuit of the most refined interpretation through specialist skills and knowledge. The very term 'discipline' denotes a degree of control and ordering of knowledge (Moran 2002: 2). A broad consensus thus develops on relevant areas of enquiry – the questions asked, the evidence employed and bodies of theory – and the resultant disciplines are thus 'each characterised by [their] own body of concepts, methods and fundamental aims' (Toulmin 1972: 139). However, in the development of such specialism – and the academic structures within which they reside – useful complimentary perspectives from other disciplines can be either unknown or ignored. Various disciplines identify specific and diverse forms of evidence and contexts in a multifaceted field of enquiry such as habitation, and the effective methodology for their interpretation. In the latter part of the twentieth century a desire to embrace the accessible totality of the historical context emerged, influenced by Marxist notions of 'total history' (Moran 2002: 14–15). Foucault argues against 'the unquestioned continuities by which we organise, *in advance*, the discourse that we are to analyse' as inhibiting a comprehension of a reality of 'dispersed events'; 'those readymade syntheses, those groupings that we normally accept before any examination' (Foucault 1972: 22, 25). Venturing beyond such disciplinary parameters can reveal 'an active field ... set free ... made up of the totality of all effective statements' (Foucault 1972: 26–7). Seeking out theoretical

perspectives beyond and between disciplines can be a transformative process, in historical enquiry, and more broadly in the comprehension of the
complexity of the human condition (Barthes 1977: 155) A useful concept
here is hermeneutic interpretation (or circle) where habitation in its entirety
constitutes a narrative and its many facets – material, social, conceptual –
the individual elements of evidence, or text. A fuller comprehension of
the various parts is gained by understanding their context, and of the
whole through a better understanding of the parts. However, abandon-
ing disciplinary specialism would be to deny valuable and necessary skills
in interpretation, and Readings (1996: 176) suggests a *reflexive* form of
interdisciplinarity that recognises disciplinary limitations. Arguably then
the aim of interdisciplinary discourse is to employ disciplinary specialisms
in evidence and methodology, but to be open to and engaged with those of
other disciplines; a 'trans-disciplinary' process in which we have engaged
in this volume. In the words of Moran (2002: 187): 'We can seek to transform the disciplines, encourage communication between them or use them
to create new intellectual configurations and alliances, but we can never
entirely dispense with them as a way of organizing knowledge'. As much
pluridisciplinary as interdisciplinary, we seek here to employ disciplinary
specialisms in evidence and methodology, but to be open to and engaged
with those of other disciplines who are engaged in parallel studies into the
same condition, and with whom, crucially, we share or develop a common
theme; a process and discussion in which we have engaged in this volume.

Developing themes and discourse

The aim of this volume was thus to create conversations between disciplines in a shared context of enquiry: habitation. The chapters are broadly
arranged around developing emphases on that theme, although it should
be emphasised that, habitation being as complex and multifaceted as it is,
there are elements in every chapter which could 'correspond' with those in
any other chapter. The first three chapters focus on the conceptualisation

of habitation. Linda Hulin explores the tension between the idea of 'home' and its material expression, and surveys the common themes within habitation, its structures, spaces and artefacts which can – and should – be the subject of interdisciplinary conversation. Jane Anderson examines the 'subject–object' relationship between humans, architecture and the wider world, a challenging dichotomy to both archaeologists seeking to interpret habitation and architects in its creation. The theory and practice of Japanese architects Atelier Bow Wow are studied to explore how an awareness of these ambiguities can be beneficial to designer, occupant and built environment. Andrea Placidi explores the notion of 'furnitecture', challenging the historical dichotomy between architecture and furniture, space and object.

The next four chapters focus on the complex inter-relationships of the *praxis* of habitation: place, objects, actions, relationships and values acting in concert. Employing Mary Douglas's matrix of cultural possibilities Wendy Morrison examines the worldview of the Late Iron Age and Early Roman inhabitants of southern Britain, revealed by their choice of utensils for food preparation, consumption, and disposal. Matthew Jenkins and Charlotte Newman bring together recovered artefacts and documentary evidence to narrate the complex social, economic and structural habitation of a London Georgian street. Antony Buxton examines the way in which habitation is structured and enacted through movements, as an overt expression of elite social status and its expression in the English country house, subject however to physical alterations which can be related to changing notions of power in the modern period. Rebecca Devers reviews both advisory text and fiction in 1950s editions of the *Playboy* magazine, narrating a new form of consumption – both material and social – in the American bachelor apartment.

The theme of 'diminished habitation' then explores habitation reduced to its bare essentials. Damian Robinson's chapter explores 'mobile' domesticity in the present day and through the evidence of artefacts on Tudor and Roman ships. Rachael Kiddey recounts the scant domesticity of the homeless in contemporary Bristol and York, both from accounts of the homeless and their own archaeology of their own temporary habitations. The last two chapters explore the theme of 'ruptured habitation'. Catherine Richardson explores the fragility of the social dimensions of habitation in an account drawn from documentary evidence of the rupture an early modern household through death, expressed in place, speech and in gesture. Stephen Walker examines the conceptual representation and dismantling of habitation in the work of the contemporary installation artists Rachel Whiteread, Dan Graham and Gordon Matta-Clark. To conclude Frances F. Berdan draws together the themes of the volume.

Although approaching habitation from a variety of contexts and disciplinary perspectives, shared themes flow between these contributions: the nature and structuring of habitable space, its enclosure or permeability controlling movement and directing social engagement; optic and haptic perceptions; the furnishing of habitation, *praxis* and *habitus*, possession and consumption; social structures, gender, conduct, affection and agency; ideologies and values. It is hoped that the implicit conversations between chapters in this volume will stimulate the reader in their own discourse on habitation. It is intended as a platform for the presentation of specialist and focused contributions on habitation in a wide range of contexts, and simultaneously the exploration of these wider shared themes, and the awareness of the manner in which multiple disciplinary perspectives can enrich our understanding of this fundamental human condition.

Bibliography

Adam, J., and Adam, R. (1773–1778, 1779, 1822). *Works in Architecture of Robert and James Adam*. London.

Alcock, N. W. (1993). *People at Home: Living in a Warwickshire Village 1500–1800*. Chichester: Phillimore.

Aynsley, J., and Grant, C. (2006). *Imagined Interiors: Representing the Domestic Interior since the Renaissance*. London: Victoria and Albert Museum.

Bacon, Sir F. (1627/1669). *Essays of Francis Bacon or Counsels, Civil and Moral*. London.

Barley, M. W. (1961). *The English Farmhouse and Cottage*. London: Routledge and Kegan Paul.

Barthes, R. (1977). *Image, Music, Text*. London: Fontana.

Bauhaus Manifesto (1919). <http://bauhaus-online.de/en/atlas/das-bauhaus/idee/ manifest> accessed 20 May 2016.

Beeman, G. L. (1959). 'Peking Man', *Science*, 130(3372) (August): pp. 416.

Benveniste, E. (1973). *Indo-European Language and Society*. London: Faber.

Blanton, R. (1994). *Houses and Households: A Comparative Study*. London and New York: Plenum Press.

Blunt, A., and Dowling, R. (2006). *Home*. London: Routledge.

Bourdieu, P. (1977). *Outline of a Theory of Practice*, translated by R. Nice. Cambridge: Cambridge University Press.

Bourdieu, P. (1990). *The Logic of Practice*. Cambridge: Polity Press.

Brunskill, R. W. (1997). *Houses and Cottages of Britain: Origins and Development of Traditional Domestic Design*. London: Victor Gollancz.

Buchli, V. (2013). *An Anthropology of Architecture*. London and New York: Bloomsbury.

Buxton, A. (2015). *Domestic Culture in Early Modern England*. Woodbridge: The Boydell Press.

Carsten, J., and Hugh-Jones, S. (eds) (1995). *About the House: Lévi-Strauss and Beyond*. Cambridge: Cambridge University Press.

Carsten, J., and Hugh-Jones, S. (1995). 'Introduction'. In J. Carsten and S. Hugh-Jones (eds), *About the House: Lévi-Strauss and Beyond*. Cambridge: Cambridge University Press.

Childe, V. G., and Simpson, W. D. (1952). *Illustrated History of Ancient Monuments: Vol. VI Scotland*. Edinburgh: Her Majesty's Stationery Office.

Colomina, B. (ed.) (1992). *Sexuality and Space*. New York: Princeton Architectural Press.

Cordell, L. S. (1994). *Ancient Pueblo Peoples*. St Remy Press and Smithsonian Institution.

Daviau, P. M. M. (1993). *Houses and their Furnishings in Bronze Age Palestine: Domestic Activity Areas and Artefact Distribution in the Middle and Late Bronze Ages*. Sheffield: JSOT Press.

De Lucia, K. (2010). 'Looking Beyond Gender Hierarchy: Rethinking Gender at Teotihuacan, Mexico'. In Cynthia Robin and Elizabeth Brumfiel (eds), *Gender, Households, and Society: Unraveling the Threads of the Past and the Present. Archeological Papers of the American Anthropological Association*, No. 18.

Deetz, J. (1977). *In Small Things Forgotten: An Archaeology of Early American Life*. New York: Doubleday.

Deetz, J., and Deetz, P. S. (2000). *The Times of their Lives*. New York: Freeman.

Douglas, M. (1973). *Natural Symbols*. Harmondsworth: Penguin Books.

Douglas, M., and Isherwood, B. (1979). *The World of Goods: Towards an Anthropology of Consumption*. London: Allen Lane.

Fogle, K. R., Nyman, J. A., and Beaudry, M. C. (eds) (2015). *Beyond the Walls: New Perspectives on the Archaeology of Historical Households*. Gainesville, FL: University Press of Florida.

Fortes, M. (1958). 'Introduction'. In J. Goody (ed.). *The Developmental Cycle in Domestic Groups*. Cambridge: Cambridge University Press.

Foucault, M. (1972). *The Archaeology of Knowledge*. London: Tavistock Publications.

Giddens, A. (1984). *The Constitution of Society*. Cambridge: Polity.

Girouard, M. (1978). *Life in the English Country House*. New Haven, CT, and London: Yale University Press.

Glassie, H. H. (1975). *Folk Housing in Middle Virginia: A Structural Analysis of Historic Artifacts*. Tennessee: University of Tennessee Press.

Gosden, C. (1994). *Social Being and Time*. Oxford: Blackwell Publishers.

Hanson, J. (2003). *Decoding Homes and Houses*. Cambridge: Cambridge University Press.

Heidegger, M. (1927/1962). *On Being and Time*. Oxford: Blackwell.

Heidegger, M. (1971). 'Building Dwelling Thinking'. In M. Heidegger (ed.), *Poetry, Language, Thought*, translated by Albert Hofstadter. New York: Harper and Row.

Hillier, B. and Hanson, J. (1984). *The Social Logic of Space*. Cambridge: Cambridge University Press.

Hodder, I. (1990). *The Domestication of Europe*. Oxford: Blackwell.

Houlbrooke, R. A. (1984).*The English Family 1450–1700*. London: Longman.

Husserl, E. (1973). *Logical Investigations* [1900, 2nd revised edn 1913], translated by J. N. Findlay. London: Routledge.

Ingold, T. (2011). *Being Alive*. London and New York: Routledge.

Johnson, M. (1993). *Housing Culture: Traditional Architecture in an English Landscape*. London: UCL Press.

Kent, S. (ed.) (1990). *Domestic Architecture and the Use of Space: An Interdisciplinary Cross-cultural Study*. Cambridge: Cambridge University Press.

Kerr, R. (1864). *The Gentleman's House: Or, How to plan English Residences: from the Parsonage to the Palace*. London: J. Murray.

Knappett, C., and Malafouris, L. (eds) (2008). *Material Agency: Towards a Non-Anthropocentric Approach*. New York and London: Springer.

Langley, B. (1727). *The Builders Chest Book*. London.

Latour, B. (2005). *Reassembling the Social: An Introduction to Actor-Network Theory*. Oxford: Oxford University Press.

Le Corbusier, *Towards a New Architecture* (1923/1931), translated by Frederick Etchells. London: Rodker.

Lefebvre, H. (1991). *The Production of Space*. Oxford: Blackwell.

Liberman, A. (2015). 'Our Habitat: one more etymology brought "home"'. OUP blog <http://blog.oup.com/2015/02/home-word-origin-etymology/> accessed 20 March 2016.

Locke, J. (1689). *An Essay Concerning Human Understanding*.

Loos, A. (1908/1998). *Ornament and Crime: Selected Essays*. Riverside, CA: Ariadne Press.

Low, S. M, and Lawrence-Zúñiga, D. (2003). *The Anthropology of Space and Place: Locating Culture*. Malden, MA, and Oxford: Blackwell.

McCarter, R. and Pallasmaa, J. (2012). *Understanding Architecture: A Primer on Architecture as Experience*. London: Phaidon.

Melhuish, C. and Toy, M. (1996). *Architecture and Anthropology*. London: Academy Editions.

Merleau-Ponty, M. (1965). *Phenomenology of Perception*, translated by Colin Smith. London: Routledge and Kegan Paul.

Moran, J. (2002). *Interdisciplinarity*. London and New York: Routledge.

Morrow, B. H., and Price, V. B. (1997). *Anasazi Architecture and American Design*. Albuquerque, NM: UNM Press.

Muthesius, H. (1904, 1905). *Das Englische Haus*. Berlin: Ernst Wasmuth Verlag.

Oliver, P. (ed.) (1997). *Encyclopedia of Vernacular Architecture of the World*. Cambridge: Cambridge University Press.

Overton, M., Whittle, J., Dean, D., and Hann, A. (2004). *Production and Consumption in English Households, 1600–1750*. London: Routledge.

Parker, B. J., and Foster, C. P. (eds) (2012). *New Perspectives on Household Archaeology*. Winona Lake, IN: Eisenbrauns. <http://www.ameeri.org/foster/publications/Foster_Parker2012.pdf> accessed 20 May 2016.

Pearson, M. P., and Richards, C. (eds) (1994). *Architecture and Order: Approaches to Social Space*. Londona and New York: Routledge.

Rapoport, A. (1990). 'Systems of Activities and Systems of Settings'. In S. Kent (ed.), *Domestic Architecture and the Use of Space*. Cambridge: Cambridge University Press.

Readings, B. (1996). *The University in Ruins*. Cambridge, MA: Harvard University Press.

Rice, D. S. (1993). 'Late Intermediate Domestic Architecture and Residential Organisation at Yaral'. In M. S. Aldenderfer (ed.), *Domestic Architecture, Ethnicity, and Complementarity in the South-Central Andes*. Iowa: University of Iowa Press: pp. 66–82.

Robin, C., and Brumfiel, E. (2010). 'Gender, Households, and Society: An Introduction'. In C. Robin and E. Brumfiel (eds), *Gender, Households, and Society:*

Unraveling the Threads of the Past and the Present. Archeological Papers of the American Anthropological Association, No. 18.

Samson, R. (1990). *The Social Archaeology of Houses*. Edinburgh: Edinburgh University.

Solecki, R. S. (1954). 'Shanidar cave: a paleolithic site in northern Iraq'. *Annual Report of the Smithsonian Institution*. Smithsonian Institution: pp. 389–425.

Squires, G., Simons, H., Parlett, M., and Becher, T. (1975). *Interdisciplinary*. The Nuffield Foundation

Srejović, D. (1972). *Europe's First Monumental Sculpture: New Discoveries at Lepenski Vir*. London: Thames and Hudson.

Stone, E. (1996). 'Houses, Households and Neighborhoods in the Old Babylonian Period: The Role of Extended Families'. In K. R. Veenhof (ed.), *Houses and Households in Ancient Meso-potamia*. Istanbul: Nederlands Historisch-Archae-ologisch Instituut: pp. 229–35.

Tadmoor, N. (1996). 'The Concept of Household-Family in Eighteenth Century England'. *Past and Present*, 151 (May): pp. 111–40.

Tarlow, S., and West, S. (1999). *The Familiar Past: Archaeologies of Later Historical Britain*. London and New York: Routledge.

Thornton, Peter (1984). *Authentic Decor: The Domestic Interior, 1620–1920*. London: Weidenfeld and Nicolson.

Toulmin, S. (1972). *Human Understanding*, Vol. 1. Oxford: Clarendon Press.

Turner, S. (2000). 'What Are Disciplines? And How Is Interdisciplinarity Different?' In P. Weingart and N. Stehr (eds), *Practising Interdisciplinarity*. Toronto: University of Toronto Press: 46–65.

Venturi, R. (1977). *Complexity and Contradiction in Architecture*. London: Architectural Press, 2nd edn.

Ware, Sir I. (1756). *A Complete Body of Architecture*. London.

Weingart, P. (2000). 'Interdisciplinarity: The Paradoxical Discourse'. In P. Weingart and N. Stehr (eds), *Practising Interdisciplinarity*. Toronto: University of Toronto Press: pp. 25–41.

Wickes, C. (1862). *A Handy Book on Villa Architecture: Being a Series of Designs for Villa Residences in Various Styles*. London.

Wilk, R. R., and Rathje, W. L. (1982). 'Household Archaeology'. *The American Behavioral Scientist*, 25(6) (July/August): pp. 617–39.

Willey, G. (1953). *Prehistoric Settlement Patterns in Peru*. Washington, DC: US Govt Printing Office.

Wotton, Sir H. (1672). 'Elements of Architecture', in *Reliquiae Wottonianae*.

Zubrow, E. B. W., Audouze, F., and Enloe, J. G. (2010). *The Magdalenian Household: Unraveling Domesticity*. Albany, NY: State University of New York Press.

PART I

Conceptualising Habitation

LINDA HULIN

1   InHabiting Space: Archaeologists, Objects and Architecture

ABSTRACT

This paper seeks to outline the tension between the idea of home and its material expression. The argument moves from the ways in which archaeologists have shifted from narrative descriptions of the home to the household as an economic unit and shows how this has reflected changing interests in the discipline as a whole. The discussion then turns to architecture's view of buildings as agents of social transformation and the expression of domestic life, and in particular the way in which the contents of houses act in that process. This brings the argument back to the way in which archaeology can approach objects within houses and how they work with the space in which they are placed to support feelings of home.

House and home

Sir Edward Coke, writing in *The Institutes of the Laws of England* in 1628, declared 'an Englishman's house is his castle'. A house is not necessarily a home, however; rather, it is the material stage upon which private life – itself a highly variable concept – is set. A home, on the other hand, is immaterial, a spatial imaginary anchored to the material world not just through practice, but by emotion (Blunt and Dowling 2006; Marcus 2006; Rybczynski 1986). A home can invoke both belonging and alienation; it is an idea against which individual happiness is measured and individual identity is constructed (Bourdieu 1979; Duncan 1981; Pearson and Richards 1994; Rapoport 1969, 1982); the loss of a home can become a political catastrophe.

The variability of housing structures across the world and through time raises the question of the relation between built form and social action (see Oliver 1987 for a comprehensive survey), and whether one can equate consistent behaviour to regularity of form and function, or the converse (see Boozer 2015, for example, on the problematisation of variability in Roman Egyptian housing). Reasons for difference have been located in the realms of symbolism and the gendered use of space (e.g. Ardener 1981; Kent 1990; Jameson 1990, Pellow 2003; Weismann 1992), and house form is viewed as the materialisation of those requirements. Anthropologists have also addressed the ways in which the *contents* of houses are used to convey social meaning and rules about what may and may not be done in the home, and with what things (see, for example, the fundamental work of 1979); domestic objects are the means through which social meaning is reflected, enacted and negotiated (see, for example, Buchli 2013; Buchli and Lucas 2001; Daniels and Andrews 2010; Flanders 2003; Miller 1988, 2001, 2008).

In his exploration of the question of 'how does building belong to dwelling?' (1978: 347), Heidegger privileged the act of building over the act of inhabiting, a stance for which he was criticised by feminist writers for stressing an active 'male' act of construction over a passive 'female' act of cultivation, of home-making (e.g. Young 1997: 134–8). This rather mirrors archaeological field practice, for as Allison pointed out, the process of excavation effectively removes all contents from a house, making empty houses the primary source for the investigation of domestic behaviour (Allison 2004: 4).

Of course, the nature and distribution of objects do have a part to play in the identification of different rooms and spaces during excavation (Wallace-Hadrill 1994: 4; Wilke and Rathje 2010; Weiner 2010). There is a tendency for archaeologists to draw analogies from their own experience to identify toilets, beds and cupboards (see, for example, Childe on Skara Brae on Orkney: 1946: 25–31; Kemp 1989 on Amarna houses in Egypt; Evans 1900–5 on the palace of Knossos on Crete). Yet the specialisation of activities in rooms depends not only upon the number of rooms available relative to the number of people using them, but also upon social practice: the Japanese house, for example is designed for flexibility of use (Daniels and Andrews 2010), and the early modern bedroom was as much as place for socialising as sleeping. Allison's study of the distribution of the contents of thirty Pompeiian houses also highlights the flexibility and variability of room use, an approach to occupation contrary to what was expected from ancient visual and written sources (2004).

The disposition of domestic space is inextricably linked to the social construction of the home, which at is its most basic may be reduced to an individual's right of residence or right of entry. The concept of family is highly variable: nuclear families may consist of parents and children, or parents, grandparents and children; adult children may move from the family home to start their own families, or stay with their parents, in either patrilocal or matrilocal patterns. Husbands may take more than one wife, or, more rarely, wives more than one husband. Families may be defined by marriage or by blood, and overall by the activities that are deemed necessary for the group to function. Thus there are interweaving expectations: families are defined by action, and domestic architecture designed to accommodate that action (see Harell 1977, for an overview).

Family structures dictate the internal layout of buildings, and living areas, living quarters, even different structures may, in a perfect world, be assigned to different ages, sex, or sub-families. The Victorian ideal was to assign to children their own floor where they could be fed and educated and where they would sleep; certainly all who could afford it pushed the children's room to the top of the house, closer to servants than family (Flanders 2003: 2–62). The more divided a building is along sex lines, then greater likelihood that there will be provision for separate dining areas to which guests may be admitted, as in modern houses in eastern Libya, where the author was entertained in separate guest buildings that would abut the main house, but not share an entrance with it, and into which food and drink were carried from distant kitchens. Finally, houses may contain large, multi-family kin groups, with internal divisions prioritising family groups over function, as in long-house of the Saxon period. Families may also be spread over numerous buildings, perhaps within a compound.

If homes are ultimately defined by the presence of family, the viability of the family unit depends upon its economic efficacy. In the ancient world, the home was often the centre not just for food preparation, but for medium-term storage of goods, either basic foodstuffs or those conserved by pickling, bottling, salting, or sun- or smoke-drying. The home could also be the locus of essential industry: the production of, for example, cloth or clothing, pottery, stone tools being termed domestic in the literature by virtue of the scale of output, as much as quality and consistency. The

more complex the range of activities taking place within the economy of
the home, the more people involved, not necessarily related to the family:
servants, apprentices and employees, any of whom could have right of
residence, anywhere from the master's bedroom, to a separate servant's
quarters, to a different building altogether.

Thus the distinction between a house – a place of familial repose –
and household – an economic unit – is not necessarily a valid one prior
to the early modern period, and it is upon households that the processual/
structural archaeology from the 1960s onwards focused on. There were
two reasons for this. The first was an explicit recognition of a large degree
of arbitrariness in assigning functions to rooms that may in the past have
been multi-functional, as noted above. The second was a consequence of
the incorporation of science-based approaches to archaeology, which added
fine, previously invisible detail to the recovery of plant and animal remains
(see Weiner 2010). Pollen analysis allowed for a greater understanding of
past landscapes, and how they changed over time, and this itself became
part of a wider interest in the landscape as a social construct, rather than
a natural phenomenon. This being the case, the household stood at the
intersection between the individual and the environment, with the result
of the privileging of household and household economy within archaeology, rather than house and home (see Madella, Kovacs et al. 2013, for
typical approaches).

There was a second strand to archaeological investigation that treated
the house and its more immediate surroundings as a viable unit of study. In
the 1970s, semiotic approaches to archaeology led scholars to search for the
underlying grammars that tied disparate material classes together to form
a coherent whole. This was particularly successful in relation to the early
modern period, where rapid social changes necessitated an increase in the
material language of display. Henry Glassie's study of vernacular houses
in Virginia (1975) showed how Georgian notions of order and symmetry
extended outwards from houses to gardens, and inwards to the internal
layout of buildings, and their decor. Houses became vehicles for the study
of 'hierarchies of power', be they expressed as wealth, status, or gender.

Ultimately, semiotic and structural approaches to archaeology were
abandoned as archaeological interest shifted from trying to understand how

the world worked, to how it changed. The individual, rather than a passive recipient of shared cultural norms, was now to be understood as the active agent of social transition and particularly influential was the work of Pierre Bourdieu, a sociologist who looked to the home, or *habitus*, as the crucible in which children absorb the *doxa*, the taken-for granted beliefs and actions that are held unquestioningly. An important aspect of Bourdieu's work is in the argument that the *doxa* is constructed out of all aspects of life, both material and social into a total and intertwined environment (Bourdieu 1977). In *Distinction* (1984), Bourdieu explored taste as an all embracing concept, skewering the French middle classes in the predictability of their preferences in architecture, food, clothing, music – on their taste, in fact, but taste as relates to a wide range of material phenomena that make up the sensory environment and that relate to the material record.

However, archaeological interest was captured even more by a similar interest in the relationship between socio-economic environment and its reproduction and change. Giddens' structuration theory delineated the relationship between the structure and the agent. The former was defined, somewhat loosely, as the web of rules and resources available to the agent (an individual or group of individuals). For Giddens (1984), the structure is a body of routinised action that is created, rather than pre-exists, in the moment of action, a recursive relationship that is different at the moment of its creation depending upon the nature of the rules and resources being brought into play. Structuration captured the post-modern *zeitgeist*, and in archaeological terms either allied itself with science to focus upon micro-action in the domestic environment or, in spite of a theoretical reliance upon routines, became a justification for exploring the unusual and the atypical (see, for example, Dobres and Robb 2000; Meskell 1992, 2000).

There are, then, two diametrically opposed ways of examining the house archaeologically: one tightly focused on micro-activity within the home, the other widening the scope of enquiry to place the home within a network of economic and social relations. Both are valid and important ways of addressing the function of the house, but both present a catalogue of missed opportunities, for archaeologists have been brought no closer to bridging the gap between objects and emotion and between the fact of the

house and the idea of the home. This is partly due to the fact that archaeological practice effectively atomises domestic assemblages, distributing
them between object specialists who study them in terms of typology, and
focus upon their production and trade, rather than their effect as a group
upon human behaviour. What is needed, then, is a middle ground, where
a constellation of objects is studied within the context of a single house.

A constellation of objects is what archaeologists dig up; a constellation
of objects is precisely what we, as individuals, experience. The philosopher
Roger-Pol Droit somewhat wistfully recalled that, before embarking upon
a year long study of things, 'I used to perceive the object world and the
diversity of its contents as a single whole, more or less uninterrupted ...
and (above all) created for my own personal use' (Droit 2005: 184), and he
lamented the fact that by directing his gaze towards the particular, he lost
sight of the whole. Archaeology needs, ultimately, to find a way of fitting
contexts together; if our theoretical understanding is based upon the *habitus*
as a total socialising environment, then we should see the objects within
the home as a total assemblage. Certainly it is easier to work on something
rather than everything, but the problem remains of how to identify or
measure relative importance in the material world. The quality of materials or craftsmanship takes us so far into the realms of economic and social
value, but does not help us to address the problem of significance in the
everyday. Phenomenologists dealt with this by privileging objects relating
to the body and its movement through space, arguing that the body is the
medium through which the world is experienced (Merleau-Ponty 1962).
However, as Miller found in his study of a London street, while house
contents could present an overall organisational principle equivalent to a
social cosmology, consistency was located in individual dwellings; analysis
on the level of the street highlighted diversity rather than conformity; as
a result, he resisted the idea that certain classes of material could be held
as more significant than others in advance of study (Miller 2008: 290–4).
Moreover, as Halle pointed out (1998: 52–3), while all objects are theoreti-
cally symbols, that is to say they can be plausibly associated with meaning,
in fact only those deemed of special interest *by the researcher* are dignified
by the term, an inherently externalising, not to say circular process. Valid
though this may be for certain contexts, it is wide of the mark for the bulk

of the archaeological data, which constitutes a theatre of the mundane. As Miller argued 'mundane material culture, such as pottery ... achieves its cultural significance, ironically because its two major attributes are (a) its functionality and (b) its triviality ... Thus the significance of pottery is best appreciated in combination with many other elements of the material environment' (1988: 192). Hulin also found, in a study of Egyptian colonial culture in the second millennium Levant, that while some object types may carry more weight than others, their impact is heightened or lessened by their context, and their association with other objects of both similar or dissimilar types (2013). As Miller put it, 'it is the order of the relationship to objects and *between objects* [emphasis added by author] that creates people through socialisation' (2008: 287).

This association was understood and lampooned by Denis Diderot in his 1769 article *Regrets on parting with my old dressing gown*, in which the acquisition of a smart new gown highlighted the shabbiness of his surroundings and led to the ultimate replacement of almost every item within his study. McCracken (1988) coined the term the 'Diderot effect', seeing it as a warning of the effects of rising consumerism (for, crucially, the new and shiny objects in Diderot's study had the effect of making him less comfortable, literally less at ease, than he had been before). There is, then, in this essay, tongue in cheek though it may be, an implicit understanding of the way in which the room, the furniture, the objects and the man conspired to create – or in this case – uncreate a sense of home, and it should be noted that while the senses were engaged with the objects in Diderot's study, it was the emotional value he placed upon the objects that ultimately determined his sense of ease.

Architecture and behaviour

If archaeologists have yet to engage fully with the materialisation of the *habitus*, within architecture it is conversation thousands of years in the making. Writing in the mid-20s BC, and building upon Greek treatises up to 300 years older than that, Vitruvius Pollio devoted a whole chapter to what is essentially the relationship between plan, purpose and aesthetic qualities (Vitruvius *De Architectura* I.2). Of particular interest here is the notion of correctness, explicitly drawn from the Greek *thematismos*, or tradition, whereby different architecture orders are applicable to different functions: Jupiter the Thunderer in an open-air shrine, the austere Doric applied to the martial gods, such as Minerva, Mars, and Hercules, and the ornamental Corinthian being best suited to temples to the goddess Venus, or the nymphs (I.2.5). Vitruvius stressed the importance of stylistic consistency: 'if Doric entablatures are sculpted with dentils in the cornices, or triglyphs show up on top of cushion capitals and Ionic entablatures ... the result will be jarring' (I.2.6). This principle also extended to the building as a whole: magnificent interiors demanded equally harmonious and elegant entrances in order to be correct.

If for Vitruvius the function of a building dictated its style, this in turn demanded a visual consistency that also extended to decoration. Some of his recommendations are practical – the avoidance of difficult to clean convoluted plasterwork in smoky spaces, for example. However, he devotes a whole chapter in Book VII to the decoration of atria and peristyles, the location of figurative frescoes. Vitruvius was a firm believer in art following natural principles: the narration of myths, such as the wandering Ulysses was acceptable as long as it was realistic; the playfulness of the Pompeiian Third style, which include monsters, or 'tender shoots, sprouting in coils from roots, have little statues nestled in them for no reason, or shoots split in half, some holding little statues with human heads, some with the heads of beasts' (I.5.3) was not.

Vetruvian principles in architecture run like a river through western architecture, and were rejuvenated in 1570 by Andrea Palladio, who own treatise *I Quattro Libri dell'Architettura*, formed the guide for European building in the subsequent centuries. Of interest here is the implicit assumption that the form and decoration of a building can, in their harmonic principles, represent social order and stability.

However, by the nineteenth century, the idea that architecture could not only reflect social order, but create it, was taking root. Victorian industrialists with a philanthropic bent (many of them were Quakers) built not

just houses for their workers, but houses that were conspicuously better constructed and painted than housing normally available to the working classes
and situated within green spaces (Binns 2013). The idea, rigorously policed
on what became a self-selecting sample of success, was that clean, healthful
and sober environments produced, clean, healthy and sober individuals.

The principle that architecture can be used to shape emotional and
behavioural responses found its clear expression in the early twentieth
century, when numerous modernist movements struggled to bridge the
gap between rural nineteenth-century craft-life and twentieth-century
industrial mass-production. Acceptera! was the most explicitly realised
(Åhrén, Kreagh et al. 2008). Architects Gunnar Asplund, Wolter Gahn,
Sven Markelius, Eskil Sundahl, Uno Åhrén, and Gregor Paulsson presented
a manifesto for Swedish modernity which embraced not only architecture,
but interior design. Explicitly interested in anthropological views of the
family and mechanisms of social change, they saw style as resonant with
specific societies in space and time. The modern industrial world needed
a modern, mass produced style to both represent and shape it, a reflection
of widely held views in the USA and Europe best summed up by Loos'
influential article on 'Ornament and Crime' (1913). Loos argued that form
should follow function, and be simple. Ornament was an unnecessary
extra, which in itself lead objects to fall out of fashion, consigning otherwise useful objects to the dustbin (a principle without which archaeology
could not function). While objectionable in tone to modern ears, Loos
explicitly condemned elaboration in all forms, from shoe buckles to food;
again, the idea that houses and their contents relate to emotional and, here,
moral precepts, was pushed to the fore. In Germany, Gropius' *Bauhaus*
movement which initially was focused on interior design and the functional and technical quality of objects (Itten 1975). Acceptera! sought a
unifying functional style to domestic objects, an approach of which IKEA
is the direct heir. Similarly, in Finland, Artek, a Finnish furniture company founded in 1935 by an architect (Alvar Aalto), an interior designer
(Aino Aalto), an arts promoter (Maire Gullischen) and an art historian
(Nils-Gustav Hahl), again with the explicit aim of providing objects to
harmonise with the Aalto's buildings. Of course, the concept of architects
involving themselves in interior design was not new – Robert Adam or

Augustus Pugin spring to mind – but their work was to reflect a current, if idealised taste; the difference came in the belief in the transformative power of architecture and design. Steen Eiler Rasmussen (1959) and Juhani Pallasmaa (1996), influenced by phenomenologists, pulled the conversation back to the bodily experience of buildings, consciously drawing the haptic qualities of buildings – temperature, sound and light – into the centre of conversations on design.

It is clear, then, that archaeologist can learn much about the ways in which buildings and their contents work from the discipline of architecture. Architects take the conversation up to the point of dwelling, and bring together form, function and haptic experience. Archaeologists, even when contemplating the emptied space referred to earlier, can incorporate elemental affects into their understanding of domestic buildings (e.g. Moody 2009), although explicit studies are relatively rare. Even so, the architectural/interior design imagination is oriented towards the first inhabitants; archaeology recovers the last and is in effect overlaying any original vision with those of subsequent occupants.

Archaeology and behaviour

Returning to the total environments of Bourdieu (or perhaps Diderot), perhaps it is in style that archaeologists can seek to unify contexts: not the style of individual objects, but the total impact of multiple objects. Style attracted a good deal of attention in the 1970s and 1980s; it was seen as a means to track anything from local residence patterns (Frankel 1974) to the migration of whole groups of people (Dothan 1982), and also as a vehicle for social identity (Hodder 1982, Conkey and Hastorf 1990). Style was seen as a means of non-verbal communication, but Weissner's (1989) stress upon the way styles manifests as identification via comparison, is useful here. It brings into play the concept of individual choosing from a range of possibilities. A study of Cypriot imports into the Levant, for example (Hulin 2013) demonstrated that the decision to acquire a Cypriot pot would never have been a simple binary one (to have or have not), but would have been one that weighed Cypriot vessels against all other possible expenditures that could have performed the same function (such as local pottery, metal bowls, stone bowls) *and* other objects that did not, but which would have satisfied other areas of social or personal satisfaction (such as perfume, or jewellery). Thus the absence of a Cypriot bowl could equally be regarded as the presence of something else, a view which accords with Miller's observations (above) on the specificity and variability of household material cultures, all of which perform the same ultimate function, of reflecting and maintaining the emotional life of the inhabitants.

It is here that style and taste converge, but it is in anthropology and sociology that these issues have been addressed in relation to the home. As early as 1928, Chapin attempted a basic early index of social class based upon the inventory of living rooms. A more sophisticated study by Laumann and Hause (1970) found that living room styles expressed not only income but religious, social and political beliefs, findings that were mirrored by Dittmar (1992) and Halle (1998). However, the most wide-ranging and flexible study is found in Mary Douglas' *Thought Styles* (1996). Douglas explored, in a series of object focused essays, the relationship between attitudes to soft furnishings and attitudes to a variety of social phenomena, expressed along a continuum from conservative to liberal, and from socially enmeshed to socially dislocated (group-grid analysis). The essential point for archaeologists seeking to find an overarching framework for disparate material phenomena contained within one house is that the choice of any given thought style precludes the use of another. This is not to say that Douglas' scheme is a static one – people can and do change – but if as they do alter outlook and lifeways, so too their material world will change.

While these studies focus upon the social constitution of object worlds, the final link between the configuration of objects and the idea of home is to be found in psychology. Cooper Marcus, for example, views the house as a mirror of the self. More specifically, though, she regards the specific configuration of buildings to be less important to psychological connections (positive or negative) to the home than the movable objects within it (2006: 8).

How then to relate these positions to archeology? Clearly there is much work to be done to clarify the relationship between objects and architecture. Our movement through the world is shaped by objects, but we choose objects that facilitate that movement. A list of furniture from Deir el-Medina, in mid-second millennium Egypt, refers to 'couches for a man', a phrase that carries with it a whole host of conventions relating to the sexual divisions within the social sphere (McDowell 1999: 66). As object worlds become more complex, so do they become more restrictive: style trumps function (Hulin 2013). There is no objective reason why a plastic chair cannot be used at an Oxford college high table, but it never is: the architecture and style of the other chairs precludes it. In essence objects gang up on one another to reinforce a certain style in the eye of the beholder. The archaeology of houses and households lies in the delineation of architecture and a functional analysis of the distribution of objects within it. Building upon the architectural and anthropological studies outlined above, I would argue that the archeology of *home* lies in an appreciation of the functional and haptic qualities of both the house *and* its contents, and phenomenology of context.

Bibliography

Åhrén, U., Creagh, L., Kåberg, H., and Lane, B. M. (2008). *Modern Swedish Design: Three Founding Texts*. New York: Museum of Modern Art.
Allison, P. M. (2004). *Pompeiian Households. An analysis of the material culture*. Los Angeles, CA: Cotsen Institute.
Binns, S. (2013). *The Aesthetics of Utopia: Saltaire, Akroydon and Bedford Park*. Reading: Spire Books.
Blunt, A., and Dowling, R. (2006). *Home*. London: Routledge.
Boozer, A. L. (2015). 'The Tyranny of Typologies. Evidential reasoning in Romano-Egyptian domestic archaeology'. In R. Chapman and A. Wylie (eds), *Material Evidence. Learning from Archaeological Practice*. London: Routledge: pp. 92–109.
Bourdieu, P. (1971). 'The Berber House of the World Reversed'. In C. Lévi-Strauss, J. Pouillon and P. Miranda (eds), *Échanges et Communications: Mélanges offert*

à Claude Lévi-Strauss à l'Occasion de son 60 Anniversaire. Hague: Mouton: 151–61, 165–9.

Bourdieu, P. (1977). *Outline of a Theory of Practice*. Cambridge: Cambridge University Press.

Bourdieu, P. (1984). *Distinction: A Social Critique of the Judgment of Taste*. London: Routledge.

Buchli, V. (2013). *An Anthropology of Architecture*. London: Bloomsbury.

Buchli, V., and Lucas, G. (2001). *Archaeologies of the Contemporary Past*. London: Bloomsbury.

Chapin, F. (1928). 'A Quantitative Scale for rating the Home and Social Environment of Middle Class Families in an Urban Community'. *Journal of Educational Psychology*, 19(2): pp. 99–111.

Childe, V. G. (1946). *Scotland before the Scots*. London: Methuen and Co Ltd.

Conkey, M. W., and Hastorf, A. H. (1990). *The Uses of Style in Archaeology*. Cambridge: Cambridge University Press.

Daniels, I. M. and Andrews, S. (2010). *The Japanese House: Material Culture in the Modern Home*. Oxford: Berg.

Diderot, D. (1769). *Regrets on Parting with my Old Dressing Gown*. <https://www.marxists.org/reference/archive/diderot/1769/regrets.htm> accessed 20 January 2016.

Dittmar, H. (1992). *The Social Psychology of Material Possessions*. Hemel Hemstead: Harvester Wheatsheaf.

Dobres, M.-A., and Robb, J. E. (2000). *Agency in Archaeology*. London: Routledge.

Dothan, T. (1982). *The Philistines and their Material Culture*. New Haven, CT: Yale University Press.

Douglas, M. (1996). *Thought Styles: Critical Essays on Good Taste*. London: Sage.

Droit, R.-P. (2005). *How are Things? A Philosophical Experiment*, translated by Theo Caffe. London: Faber and Faber.

Duncan, J. S. (ed.) (1981). *Housing and Identity: Cross-cultural Perspectives*. London: Croom Helm.

Elias, N. (1939). *The History of Manners*. New York: Pantheon Books, English translation 1978.

Evans, Sir A. (1900–5). *Knossos: The Palace*. London: Macmillan.

Feldman, M. H. (2006). *Diplomacy by Design: Luxury Arts and an 'International Style' in the Ancient Near East, 1400–1200 BCE*. Chicago, IL: Chicago University Press.

Flanders, J. (2003). *The Victorian House*. London: Harper Perennial.

Frankel, D. (1974). *Middle Cypriot White Painted Pottery: An Analytical Study of the Decoration.* Göteborg: P. Åström.

Giddens, A. (1984). *The Constitution of Society: Outline of a Theory of Strutcturation.* Cambridge: Polity Press.

Glassie, H. (1975). *Folk Housing in Middle Virginia: A Structural Analysis of Historic Artefacts.* Knoxville, TN: University of Tennessee Press.

Halle, D. (1998). 'Material Artefacts, Symbolism, Sociologists and Archaeologists'. In C. Renfrew and C. Scarre (eds), *Cognition and Material Culture: The Archaeology of Symbolic Storage.* Cambridge: McDonald Institute for Archaeological Research: pp. 51–9.

Harrell, S. (1977). *Human Families.* Boulder, CO: Westview Press.

Heidegger, M. (1967). *Being and Time.* Oxford: Blackwell.

Heidegger, M. (1978). 'Building, Dwelling, Thinking'. In D. F. Krill (ed.), *Basic Writings: from Being and Time (1927) to The Task of Thinking (1964).* London: Routledge and Kegan Paul: pp. 343–64.

Hodder, I. (1982). *Symbols in Action: Ethnoarchaeological Studies of Material Culture.* Cambridge: Cambridge University Press.

Hulin, L. (2013). 'Conversations between Objects: Ambience and the Egyptian Ceramic World at Beth Shan'. In B. Bader and M. F. Ownby (eds), *Functional Aspects of Egyptian Ceramics within their Archaeological Context.* Leuven: Peeters: pp. 351–71.

Itten, J. (1975). *Design and Form: The Basic Course at the Bauhaus,* 2nd edn, translated by Fred Bradley. London: Thames and Hudson.

Jameson, M. (1990). 'Domestic Space in the Greek City-State'. In S. Kent (ed.), *Domestic Architecture and the Use of Space: An Interdisciplinary Cross-cultural Study.* Cambridge: Cambridge University Press: 92–113.

Kemp, B. J. (1989). *Ancient Egypt: Anatomy of a Civilization.* London: Routledge.

Kent, S. (ed.) (1990). *Domestic Architecture and the Use of Space: An Interdisciplinary Cross-cultural Study.* Cambridge: Cambridge University Press.

Laumann, E. and House, J. (1970). 'Living Room Styles and Social Attributes: the patterning of material artefacts in a modern urban commuity'. *Sociology and Social Research* 54: pp. 321–42.

Loos, A. (1913). 'Ornament und Verbrechen'. *Cahiers d'Aujourd'hui* 5: pp. 18–24.

McCracken, G. (1988). *Culture and Consumption: New Approaches to the Symbolic Character of Consumer Goods.* Bloomington, IN: Indiana University Press.

McDowell, A. (1999). *Village Life in Ancient Egypt: Laundry Lists and Love Songs.* Oxford: Oxford University Press.

Madella, M., and Zurro, D. (eds) (2007). *Plants, People and Places.* Oxford: Oxbow Books.

Madella, M., Kovács, G., Berzsényi, B., and Briz i Gordeno, I. (eds) (2013). *The Archaeology of Household*. Oxford: Oxbow Books.

Marcus, C. C. (2006). *House as a Mirror of the Self. Exploring the Deeper Meaning of Home*. Lake Worth, FL: Nicolas-Hayes.

Merleau-Ponty, M. (1962). *The Phenomenology of Perception*. London: Routledge and Kegan Paul.

Meskell, L. (1999). *Archaeologies of Social Life: Age, Sex, Class etcetera in Ancient Egypt*. Oxford: Blackwells.

Meskell, L. (2004). *Object Worlds in Ancient Egypt: Material Biographies Past and Present*. Oxford: Berg.

Miller, D. (1988). 'Appropriating the State on the Council Estate'. *Man* 23: pp. 353–72.

Miller, D. (2001). *Home Possessions: Material Culture behind Closed Doors*. Oxford: Berg.

Miller, D. (2008). *The Comfort of Things*. Cambridge: Polity Press.

Moody, J. (2009). 'Changes in Vernacular Architecture and Climate at the end of the Aegean Bronze Age'. In C. Bachhuber and R. G. Roberts (eds), *Forces of Transformation. The End of the Bronze Age in the Mediterranean*. Oxford: Oxbow Books: pp. 9–35.

Oliver, P. (1987). *Dwellings. The House across the World*. Oxford: Phaidon Press.

Pallasmaa, J. U. (1996). *The Eyes of the Skin: Architecture and the Senses*. London: Academy Editions.

Pearson, M. P., and Richards, C. (eds) (1994). *Architecture and Order: Approaches to Social Space*. London: Routledge.

Pellow, D. (2005). 'The Architecture of Female Seclusion in West Africa'. In S. M. Low and D. Lawrence-Zuániga (eds), *The Anthropology of Space and Place. Locating Culture*. Oxford: Blackwell: pp. 160–85.

Rasmussen, S. E. (1959). *Experiencing Architecture*. London: Chapman and Hall.

Rapoport, A. (1969). *House Form and Culture*. Englewood Cliffs, NJ: Prentice Hall.

Rapoport, A. (1982). *The Meaning of the Built Environment: A Nonverbal Communication Approach*. Beverley Hills, CA: Sage.

Rybczynski, W. (1986). *Home: A Short History of an Idea*. New York, Viking.

Wallace-Hadrill, A. (1994). *Houses and Society in Pompeii and Herculaneum*. Princeton, NJ: Princeton University Press.

Weiner, S. (2010). *Microarchaeology. Beyond the Visible Archaeological Record*. Cambridge: Cambridge University Press.

Weismann, L. K. (1992). *Discrimination by Design: A Feminist Critique of the Manmade Environment*. Urbana, IL: University of Illinois Press.

Weissner, P. (1989). 'Style and Changing Relations between the Individual and Soci-
     ety'. In I. Hodder (ed.), *The Meaning of Things. Material Culture and Symbolic
     Expression*. London: Unwin Hyman: pp. 57–63.

Wilke, R. R., and Rathje, W. L. (2010). 'Household archaeology'. *American Behavioral
     Scientist* 25: pp. 617–40.

Young, I. M. (1997). *Intersecting Voices: Dilemmas of Gender, Political Philosophy, and
     Policy*. Princeton, NJ: Princeton University Press: pp. 134–64.

JANE ANDERSON

2   Uncertain Futures, Obscure Pasts:
The Relationship between the Subject and
the Object in the Praxis of Archaeology and
Architectural Design

ABSTRACT

This chapter identifies the relationship between subject and object as being of significance
to the praxis of archaeology and architectural design. Insight into the complexity of this
relationship is important because it furthers our understanding of the relations between
humans, architecture and the wider world. Gell explains that objects can have agency
and influence us. This makes it possible for us to conceive of buildings as subjects. Buchli
describes the architectural object as existing in different material registers that can be tangible or intangible and that these differences enable us to use or be influenced by objects
to facilitate social relations. Lefebvre conceives of space as a practicing agent. The generation of spatial phenomena is therefore not wholly dependent on the will of individual
designers. These theories are tested through practice-based research conducted via two live
projects undertaken by the author with year one students of the Oxford Brookes School
of Architecture (OB1 LIVE). These projects were created in collaboration with the Story
Museum, Oxford and with Archeox, a community archaeology project in East Oxford.
A case study follows which looks at the written and built work of contemporary Japanese
architects and academics Atelier Bow Wow who use the ambiguity between subject and
object to sensitise us to the richness of the imaginative and design potential of our cultural
confusion between subject and object. Architects' and archaeologists' understanding of
the relationship between subject and object is made more difficult by the uncertainties
relating to the past, present and future context in which they work as well as cultural
ambiguities between the tangible, the intangible, the real and the imaginary. However,
consideration of inanimate objects as subjects and vice versa are essential conceptual shifts
needed to enable the creativity of something new and the re-creation of something lost.

At first glance, the disciplines of architecture and archaeology can be viewed
as diametrically opposed. On the surface it appears that the architect works
at the beginning to create a new building and the archaeologist works with
a building at the end of its life when it has become redundant. This chapter

identifies the relationship between subject and object as being of significance to the praxis of archaeology and architectural design. Insight into the complexity of this relationship is important because it furthers our understanding of the relations that form between humans, architecture and the wider world.

Literary, philosophical, anthropological, archaeological and architectural perspectives on subject and object are drawn upon to explain the complexities and contradictions of the relationship between subject and object. Gell explains that objects can have agency and influence us. This makes it possible for us to conceive of buildings as subjects despite the prevailing empirical sense that buildings are objects. Buchli describes the architectural object as existing in different material registers that can be tangible or intangible and that these differences enable us to use or be influenced by objects to facilitate social relations. Lefebvre conceives of space as a practising agent which enables architects and archaeologists to accept that the generation of spatial phenomena are not wholly dependent on the will of individual designers.

These theories are tested through practice-based research conducted via two live projects undertaken by the author with year one students of the Oxford Brookes School of Architecture (OB1 LIVE). These projects were created in collaboration with the Story Museum, Oxford and with Archeox, a community archaeology project in East Oxford. A case study follows which looks at the written and built work of contemporary Japanese architects and academics Atelier Bow Wow. The chapter describes their work as particularly helpful in revealing many of the ambiguities between subject and object that architects and archaeologists must contend with in their practice.

Architects' and archaeologists' understanding of the relationship between subject and object is made more difficult by the uncertainties relating to the past, present and future context in which they work as well as cultural ambiguities between the tangible, the intangible, the real and the imaginary. These ambiguities can manifest themselves in literal or metaphorical anthropomorphism between people and buildings. This ambiguity is used by Atelier Bow Wow to sensitise us to the richness of the imaginative and design potential of our cultural confusion between subject and object. The third-party involvement of an architect or archaeologist (as opposed to the intimate relationship between an inhabitant and their dwelling) gives them a unique insight into the complexity of the dynamic between subject and object. Atelier Bow Wow's intention is to reconnect inhabitants with their dwellings and yet still imbue them with the immaterial ideas that an architect's imagination can bring through the process of design. This can strengthen inhabitants' sense of place, heritage and culture. Atelier Bow Wow's work shows us that an architects' design process will be blinkered if they value creation to the exclusion of observation or documentation or if they always overlook the everyday for the extraordinary. Consideration of inanimate objects as subjects and vice versa are essential conceptual shifts needed to enable the creativity of something new and the re-creation of something lost.

Introduction

This study began as a result of practice-based research into two live projects undertaken by the author with year one students of the Oxford Brookes School of Architecture (OB1 LIVE) in collaboration with the Story Museum, Oxford and with Archeox, a community archaeology project in East Oxford. This chapter identifies the relationship between subject and object as being of significance to the praxis of archaeology and architectural design. It draws upon literary, philosophical, anthropological, archaeological and architectural perspectives on subject and object that further our understanding of the relations that form between humans, architecture and the wider world. The chapter makes the case for the work of contemporary Japanese architects and academics Atelier Bow Wow as being particularly helpful in revealing many of the ambiguities between subject and object that architects and archaeologists must contend with. Forming Atelier Bow Wow's written and built work into a case study we can see ways in which they have investigated and put into practice some of the theories discussed and developed their own methodologies that work sympathetically with the complexities of the competing claims of subject and object in order to give mutual benefit to the architect, the inhabitant and the city.

Architecture and archaeology

At first glance, the disciplines of architecture and archaeology can be viewed as diametrically opposed. On the surface it appears that the architect works at the beginning to create a new building and the archaeologist works with a building at the end of its life when it has become redundant. Of course, the importance of the building as a physical object must always be balanced by an equally important focus on its human occupants. It could be said that the archaeologist studies an absent subject and a surviving object while the architect works with a living subject and an absent object. The complexity of the relationship between the subject and the object is recognised as significant in the disciplines of archaeology, anthropology and material culture but is less commonly articulated in the field of architecture.

The identification of the subject and the object in architecture and archaeology is more complex and less diametrically opposed than it first appears. For example, the architect's living subject, their client, may be a developer and not the intended occupant of the building. In such situations the intended occupant probably won't be identified until after the architect's involvement in the project has ended. The building is normally designed to last beyond the occupation or lifetime of its initial inhabitants. Even when working with an owner-occupier, many engage an architect because they aspire to live a new and different life once they occupy their newly designed space. Some archaeologists work collaboratively in contemporary situations where the subjects are still in occupation and are engaged in the archaeological dig itself. Crea et al. (2014) worked with homeless people to excavate their inhabited sites in Bristol, such practices echo the participatory approaches that certain contemporary architects are adopting as part of their design process and that will be described below in the OB1 LIVE/Archeox project where participatory techniques were used in a collaborative architecture/archaeology project. In the OB1 LIVE/the Story Museum project, it will be seen that architects and archaeologists wrestle with similar ambiguities between subject and object when working with derelict buildings.

Not only is the absent subject an issue shared by architects and archaeologists, the absent object is also a central concern. As soon as a design project is articulated, a fragmentary object begins to exist in the minds of the client and architect. This object is initially understood through the physical existence of similar precedent examples and takes on an increasingly defined form through representational objects such as physical and digital drawings and models. Architects must try to predict the future from what they know of the past and present. Archaeologists must reconstruct the past from what they know of the past and present. Let us then reframe design as a predictive activity and archaeology as a deductive one, both disciplines working with similar uncertainties surrounding both subject and object as well as past, present and future.

A literary perspective on the relationship between subject and object

The Story Museum collaboration (2012–13) involved working with the museum on four connected projects. The first was to design storytelling spaces and form design strategies to enable them to occupy three linked derelict buildings as a museum for storytelling while preparing for a future renovation project on the site. The museum buildings are arranged around a courtyard in what was the medieval Jewish quarter of the city. The oldest buildings date back to the thirteenth century and have had several recorded uses including a pub and student lodgings for Merton College. In 1921 the site was acquired by the Postmaster General for use as a sorting office and telephone exchange. In 1934 a three-storey building was added that included larger telephone exchange spaces and postal strong rooms. Merton College bought the site back in 2003 and it remained unoccupied until the Story Museum acquired the lease in 2009 (Story Museum, 2014). The combination of the rich and evocative redundant spaces with their partially known back stories and the imaginative potential of creating a museum for storytelling proved a heady mixture and a fertile ground for us as architectural designers. The physical fabric of the building had been stripped back and repaired only to a point of structural stability and weather tightness but the place still had bunches of safe room keys on hooks, an ancient CCTV screen, notices on the wall and a staff canteen with kitchen cupboards full of pots, pans and crockery. The process of designing storytelling spaces in a place redolent of so many stories created a heightened awareness of the ambiguity and slippage between what was physical, factual, immaterial and fictional. These slippages occurred during conversations with the Story Museum, in observations of students engaged first in designing and then building their installations for the museum and in our reflections on the project (Anderson and Priest, 2013). One example of this occurred when students returned to the Story Museum after an absence of several months during which time they had been engaged in a second project to design speculative Story Towers for the museum. Upon re-entering the space, they inadvertently remarked 'It hasn't changed!' Logically they knew that their towers hadn't been built but they almost expected to see them there after spending so much time imagining the building with these towers added to its existing roof scape. Routinely and rarely questioning it, we all hold multiple possible perceived realities in our minds. These can be particularly divergent when we project our imaginations into another time or place, as architects and archaeologists do during the process of design and deduction.

In our reflections on the collaboration with the Story Museum we explored questions surrounding the ambiguity between fact and fiction, reality and imagination, the material and the immaterial in an architectural design project by looking through a literary lens and considering the relationship between the object and subject. Through a study of the work of architect, writer, artist and poet John Hejduk, we found a kindred spirit who declared the ambiguity between object and subject in his book about his architectural project, *The Collapse of Time*, stating that 'all are objects and all are subjects' (1987: 56). In English, our grammatical rules attempt to diminish this ambiguity. Grammatical rules are formed to clear up such confusion and rationalise a language. English makes a clear distinction between subject and object. The rules suggest to us that subjects are active and therefore probably animate, characterised as naming what the sentence is about while the object is passive and therefore possibly inanimate, receiving the action of the verb. Even when rationalised by grammatical rules, our language structure allows us to attribute agency to inanimate subjects. However, because of our cultural assumptions about the identity and hierarchy between a controlling subject and controlled object, any inversion of this assumption can sound absurd, comic, anthropomorphised or perhaps poetic to our ears. Hejduk's awareness of this relationship can be seen in an extract from his poem, *Sentences on a House*: 'A house roams at night when its occupants sleep' (1998: 120).

A philosophical perspective on the relationship between subject and object

René Descartes' Cartesian Dualism, in works such as the 1648 *The Description of the Human Body* and the 1649 *Passions of the Soul*, made a similar distinction to the grammatical one described above. He distinguished between the physical body and the non-physical mind with the mind being able to influence matter (Buchli 2013: 139). Although this concept has a beautiful clarity to it that is easily understood through our empirical experience of inhabiting the world as an individual, it does not reflect our experience when we consider it in relation to others, in relation to ideas and even in relation to matter. In his 1781 *Critique of Pure Reason*, Immanuel Kant retained this dualism (Lefebvre 1974/1994: 39) but altered the traditional relationship between subject and object by positing that we never have a direct experience of the physical or *noumenal* world because our experience is filtered through our senses and we therefore experience a *phenomenal* world. It was no longer enough for the subject to observe the object in order to make sense of the world. It became necessary for us to understand how the mind perceives the world, in particular space and time and cause and effect.

In *The World as Will and Representation*, first published in 1818, Arthur Schopenhauer shifts the focus away from trying to identify which end to start from in order to solve a dualistic subject–object problem. The subject doesn't cause the object and the object doesn't cause the subject. They are interdependent:

> the law of causation is itself only valid for representations ... thus, like the objects themselves, it exists only in relation to a subject, which is to say conditionally; this is why we can know it just as well when we proceed from the subject, i.e. *a priori*, as when we proceed from the object, i.e. *a posteriori*. (2010: 123)

Christopher Tilley describes the relationship between subject and object as being 'the central concern of material culture studies' (2011: 61). It is his depiction of the complexity of the relationship between subject and object that echo the findings from my own practice-based research and which therefore inform this chapter:

> Object and subject are indelibly conjoined in a dialectical relationship. They form part of each other while not collapsing into or being subsumed into the other. Subject and object are both the same, yet different. The ontological relationship between the two embodies this contradiction or ambiguity: same and different, constituted and constituting. Personal, social and cultural identity is embodied in our persons and objectified in our things. (2011: 61)

If we free ourselves from the empirical notion that objects can only be inanimate, passive material things and that subjects by contrast tend to be animate, active possessors of immaterial ideas, then we are open to observing and understanding the meaning behind their changing relationships as the materiality and identity of object and subject shifts. Inanimate objects are no longer passive. This shift in thought enables an 'understanding of architecture as an aspect of mind' (Buchli 2013: 2). For Pierre Bourdieu, 'Things also shape people through their effects in relation to the reproduction of habitus in relation to class' (Tilley 2011: 9). In anthropologist Alfred Gell's 1998 *Art and Agency* he describes how 'we have to look at how people act through objects by distributing parts of their personhood into things. These things have agency because they produce effects' on us (Hoskins 2011: 76). This clearly dismisses any empirical Cartesian assumptions about the hierarchy of mind over matter. From experience as an architectural designer, I would argue that once an object is exerting agency on us, it has become a subject. During the design process the architect is immersed in the future life of the building and that projected reality becomes the intended reality as shared with client, design team and others. The building is a subject. From this perspective and with the hindsight of Hejduk's fluid categorisation of buildings and inhabitants as shifting identity between object and subject, one can readily conceive of buildings as subjects and the inhabitants as their objects, influenced by them.

We have seen that objects influence us and therefore cannot be dismissed as passive. Our empirical assumption that objects have a physical materiality is also open to question. Anthropologist Victor Buchli describes different registers in which we can understand architectural form beyond the tangible: 'image, metaphor, performance, ruin, diagnostic, or symbol' (2013: 1). The difference in the materiality of these registers 'enables human relations' (Buchli 2013: 1) through and with objects. This material register, acknowledging that objects can be immaterial and that the subject can be social, increases the complexity and ambiguity between subject and object.

Buchli cites Carsten and Hugh-Jones' (1995) concept of the house as an 'illusory objectification' (2013: 72) where the house not only meets our physical need for shelter but also serves to resolve social tensions. For example, tension caused by the unification of two families through marriage may be resolved through establishment of a social convention that the wife must live with her in-laws. The form, organisation, meaning or materiality of houses may suggest, enable or perpetuate this convention. Buchli finds this particularly significant because society and the house achieve this through both the house's physical presence and its intangible social function. The house is not just a symbol of these social relations, it produces social relations through material and immaterial means. This makes it particularly difficult for us to disentangle the body and architecture and helps us to understand the power and persistence of architectural anthropomorphism discussed above in relation to Hejduk.

The effect of the architect or archaeologist in the dynamic between subject and object

Archaeological and anthropological studies of architecture understandably tend to focus on either ancient or vernacular buildings. While fascinating and revealing, this places an emphasis in the academic literature on buildings that were more likely to have been constructed by their prospective occupants and their communities. Such buildings were less likely to involve a distinct third party such as an architect or other similar figure who was given responsibility for the design of a building. This emphasis is increased further when studying domestic architecture, a typology that is often small scale or intimate and is therefore less likely to require specialised architectural involvement than public buildings. The live project collaboration between year one students at Oxford Brookes School of Architecture and Archeox, a local community archaeological group was notable for the insights that it brought regarding the significance of the presence of the architect or archaeologist in altering the subject object relationship.

Archeox (Archeox, n.d.) is a local community archaeological project based in East Oxford that was initiated by the University of Oxford's Department for Continuing Education. Year one students of Oxford Brookes School of Architecture (OB1 LIVE) collaborated with them in two connected projects. The first project involved the design and installation of a consultative exhibition at the Pitt Rivers Museum in October 2013. The exhibition required the design of interactive prototype displays for twenty-four small finds that Archeox had discovered at Bartelmas Chapel and Minchery Farm. Archeox project developer Dr Jane Harrison was our main contact and adviser helping us to understand the archaeological project and to develop an appropriate design brief. We shared an intention to engage the designers, community volunteer archaeologists and the public with the found objects, their materiality, their meaning and their proposed display in a museum context. Discussion with Dr Harrison brought forth certain parallels between the praxis of the architect and the archaeologist. Despite the apparent differences between the disciplines described at the beginning of this chapter, the importance to the individual of direct sensory engagement with objects and the personal significance of the moment of discovery was shared by architects and archaeologists. In addition, the role played by the experience-informed imagination of the individual practitioner is critical, albeit distinguished by its predictive use by architects and its deductive use by archaeologists.

The project began with the students being given the privilege of handling the finds that they were to design for. Their reaction to this tactile and material experience was electric and was pivotal to the project outcomes. The objects came to life in their hands, exemplified by a medieval crotal bell that rang as it was gently picked up by a group of students. Drawing on this experience, the display that this group subsequently designed and made for the bell suspended it from a sculpted hand and allowed the breeze to make it ring. Without this hands-on experience, a designer would find it much more difficult to absorb the meaning and behaviour of the object and to identify sympathetic ways to break away from a passive museum vitrine orthodoxy in their design proposals. Students had also been asked to make a film that showed their object and object display in use and told its story. Architects are traditionally associated with static representational media such as drawings and models. In their films, students combined Archeox's research with their own observations of the object in order to construct a story that processed both objective and subjective information. It was notable that these novice designers chose sophisticated mixed representational methods in order to animate their drawings and models and combine them with live action, stop frame, documentary and narrative techniques. Again, this unconventional and positive design outcome can be attributed to the emphasis on active engagement with the object that was embedded in the project. The consultative exhibition event in the Pitt Rivers Museum was in a sense a victim of the success of this hands-on strategy. Students were so keen to demonstrate their object displays and pass on their enthusiasm to visitors and Archeox participants that the event was very over-crowded, making hands-on engagement more difficult than it should have been. Nevertheless, typical visitor feedback to the question of what worked well about the exhibition was: 'the amazing imagination which has brought such small objects to life'.[1]

Reflecting on discussions during the project with Dr Harrison about the archaeologist's role and praxis; observation of the students' reaction and design response to the finds; and analysing the designs that resulted from the emphasis that we placed in the design brief on an interaction between object and exhibition visitor, all led to insights related to the significance of the architect or archaeologist as a third party when considering the relationship between subject and object. The presence of an architect or archaeologist creates a third party to an otherwise dualistic relationship between an object and a subject. They may also be detached from the occupant or user by cultural difference, by gender, by social position, by time, by space. Not only this, but the architect may be detached from the process of making and the archaeologist may not be the person who made the discovery. Drawing upon Buchli's description of tangible and intangible material registers enabling human relations, this third party detachment of the architect or archaeologist functions as an additional filter in the interaction between the physical material world and the intellectual social world. Although this detachment has the potential to create challenges for the archaeologist striving to arrive at novel yet reliable theories and for the architect striving towards innovative yet functional design proposals, their detachment from the conventional duality between subject and object gives them a unique insight into its complex dynamic.

The architect engages in the process of design with awareness that they will imbue the architectural objects that they design with ideas and that to do this they work with a material palette that includes the intangible parts of the material register such as symbol and metaphor. Hejduk pins this down expertly in his observation that 'art is the shell of thought' (1988: 340) demonstrating with clarity the elusive qualities of immateriality and agency that are possessed by objects. In deference to established subject–object hierarchies and social norms, people are the subject because they are

---

1   Sample of visitor feedback gathered by the author during the Archeox/OB1 LIVE, Found! exhibition at the Pitt Rivers Museum on 19 October 2013.

more important than buildings as objects, contemporary architects may feel obliged to describe their buildings as objects and their occupants as subjects. However their role as design agent affords them a curious and complex viewpoint on the inhabitants during the process of design.

Architects have duties towards not only their patron but all of the building's users and wider society. They must constantly shift their perspective on inhabitation from subject to subject and from subject to object as they design. For example, when considering the dimensional planning of a space or the ergonomics of a particular detail, the building's users may be considered as generic bodies more akin to objects than subjects. When considering the building user's experience they become subjects brought together as a series of likely types of user assembled from the architect's personal experience and specific research. When consulting formally and interacting informally with patrons, building users and the public during site visits, briefing events and project meetings, architects are able to engage with people as individual subjects. When considering the consequences of material choices that must be made, the architect is aware of the cultural and the physical implications. When considering the ideas that the architect will embed in the architectural object and the way that it will be occupied in the future, the building itself transcends its inanimate nature and becomes the living, breathing subject in the imagination of the architect. This may seem strange and perhaps a little detached from humanity and the everyday, but it is an essential part of the imaginative and creative process. If the material register can include the immaterial and if an object can have agency, it is not so difficult to consider inanimate objects as subjects. This is an essential conceptual shift needed in order to create something novel that doesn't yet exist (or recreate something that no longer exists). During the design process, the subject constantly shifts according to the fluidity of the context that the architect is engaging with. The architect needs to recognise and make these shifts consciously in order to grasp the complexity of the task of reconciling the architectural object with its human subjects in a way that is appropriate for the prevailing social expectations for that project.

Recognising the shifting and interdependent relationship between multiple objects and subjects within the evolving context of a design project is a complex task for the architect. Architects could learn much from archaeologists whose disciplinary need for repeatable and reliable deductions has led to the development of methodologies for recording the process of discovery that are far more meticulous than architects' often closely guarded or cryptic record of their own personal design process. This relative lack of transparency does inhibit discussion of the issue and obscures the methods that architects use to navigate the object-subject and contextual shifts described above. The following case study of the work and methodology of architects Atelier Bow Wow describes several methodologies that they have developed and disseminated that reveal the sophistication of their understanding of the design potential of the interdependence of subject and object. The reliability and originality of their methods as well as the general theories that they have identified about the development of Tokyo derived from studying the particularity of individual homes in a contemporary context should prove of interest to architects, archaeologists and anthropologists alike.

Case study: Atelier Bow Wow

Atelier Bow Wow was established in Tokyo in 1992 by architects and academics Yoshiharu Tsukamoto (1965–) and Momoyo Kajima (1969–). In addition to completing a diverse collection of inventive and influential private houses in Tokyo, they have written a series of books about them. This body of work is rare, if not unique, because the architects themselves have documented the entire research methodology and design process from inspiration to post-occupation for the whole collection of houses. The books begin with an analysis of the wider urban fabric, describe their response to this in terms of design strategy, show Atelier Bow Wow's predictions of how people will live in these houses, document the design process and outcomes for each house and conclude with a rare example of a post-occupation investigation by the architect of the inhabitation of the houses.

In discussing Atelier Bow Wow's unconventional methods and body of work, Tenurobu Fujimori describes his own experiences as part of an artistic group formed in 1986, their attempts to document Tokyo, particularly through redundant objects and the difficulty of applying this method to the creation of architecture:

> When we inaugurated the Roadway Observation Society, we discussed whether or not our observing and collecting would lead to creating things in the future. Concerning architecture, I felt this was entirely inconceivable. Collapse, confusion, and deviation from order are, after all, diametrically opposed to the true nature of architecture. (2010: 126)

Architecture, he explains, valorises creation above observation or collection. By directing their attention on Tokyo and by removing the expected architectural focus on creation, Atelier Bow Wow were able to identify the significance of the incidental in Tokyo's urban development.

Atelier Bow Wow's book, *Made in Tokyo*, was first published in 2001. In it they employ their observational and almost anthropological approach where they record Tokyo 'as though we were visiting a foreign city for the first time' (Kuroda, Tsukamoto and Kaijima 2010: 9). They were conscious of a thirty to forty-year cycle of almost complete rebuilding in Tokyo. 'The starting hypothesis for the survey is that in any city, the situation and value system of that city should be directly reflected through unique buildings' (Kuroda, Tsukamoto and Kaijima 2010: 10). By focusing on the formation of these buildings through their use rather than any aesthetic, typological or disciplinary categories, they identified the presence of strange programmatically hybrid buildings that they affectionately named *Da-me Architecture*, translated as no-good architecture. This approach chimes with Buchli's observation that 'it is often the generic and interchangeable nature of architectural forms in their apparently banal and unremarkable material qualities that actually enable novel kinds of habitations' (2013: 182). Of the seventy examples catalogued in *Made in Tokyo*, one typically curious domestic example is No. 46 'Apartment mountain temple' (Kuroda, Tsukamoto and Kaijima 2010: 132) which is a Buddhist temple located part way up a slope and accessed via the staircase and roof of an apartment block located at the bottom of the hill. They conclude that the reason why these buildings are important in gaining an understanding of Tokyo is because they were formed at a time when practical concerns were being prioritised over cultural ones. Therefore domestic and small scale cultural or commercial activity occupy the spaces in between the dominant infrastructure as part of a multi-scaled mixed ecology.

In *Pet Architecture Guide Book* (2001), Atelier Bow Wow explained that 'When we walk on the streets of Tokyo, we find amazingly small buildings between streets, along widened roads and spaces between tracks and roads' (Tsukamoto 2001: 9). They catalogue seventy-two found examples of this 'pet architecture'. They also proposed a further nine new pet architecture project proposals for these small found Tokyo spaces that were designed using the principles established by their analysis. Each pet is named, numbered, described, measured, and its location recorded. They are each catalogued by a single photograph, a drawn location plan and an axonometric drawing that includes the same photograph of a man and his dog to give a constant scale to each building. A particularly small domestic pet that they found is *No.10, Apartment* (Tsukamoto 2001: 32–3) which is a two-storey tenement of two apartments that is 4m wide, 2.1m deep and 5.5m high. It is located on a residual triangular piece of land between a residential road and the elevated Metropolitan expressway. Their conceptual strategy to anthropomorphise these buildings as pets deliberately deflects the expected response of society to dismiss these strange building objects on aesthetic grounds and to emphasise the close connection between the scale of these buildings and our own human scale. 'Since Pet Architecture has less consideration in its appearance, it shows a sense of wilfulness, unexpectedness and hand-made feeling in its structure, it cannot be done objectively but naturally' (Tsukamoto 2001: 8). *Pet Architecture Guide Book* is an analysis of how buildings form in response to their physical and cultural context and where the buildings are the anthropomorphised subject of that analysis.

By casting their gaze as widely as a city in order to understand patterns evident in the creation of individual dwellings, Atelier Bow Wow's atypical approach recalls Gell's (1988) concept of a house as 'a distributed object and distributed mind' (Buchli 2013: 6). *Pet Architecture Guide Book* observes and analyses pet architecture from the street. No interiors or plans are shown but the smallness of the buildings forms them and makes the nature of their occupation impossible to disguise. Tsukamoto observed that pet architecture connects 'two different subjectivities in architecture ...

Space lived by someone called the space of *representation* is always opposed to the *representation of space*, which is planned or designed by architects' (White 2007). Explaining that although he was unaware of Lefebvre when researching Pet Architecture, Tsukamoto then likens this reconnection of these two subjectivities to Lefebvre's theories in *The Production of Space* (1974) where 'the practicing agent is not a person, it is space itself' (Washida 2010: 250) and eliminating the distinction between designers and users. This desire to reduce the filter between designers and users connects to the practice-based conclusions described earlier in the chapter that arose from the OB1 LIVE collaborative projects where the architect or archaeologist as a third-party agent becomes significant in altering the dynamic between subject and object. Atelier Bow Wow's awareness of the potential disadvantages of this situation has led them to seek to reduce the distinction between designers and users in order to draw as deeply as possible upon the user's habits, experience and aspirations in order to create architecture.

Atelier Bow Wow put the design methodology that they evolved through their research into practice via the design of a large number of private houses, often in the curious urban situations and of the very small scale that they had identified. They were conscious that their wished-for natural production of space would be mediated by their unnatural presence as architects but their knowledge of these processes would inform their design response. They also recognised that there was no need for their architecture to share the incidental aesthetic of *Da-me Architecture*.

In *Graphic Anatomy* (2009) Atelier Bow Wow catalogued their body of residential work in low density urban areas and suburban/rural areas via objective orthographic line drawings. Twenty-four houses are shown in annotated sectional perspective and construction details in an attempt to show them as objectively as an anatomist would. Anticipated occupants, possessions and activities are also shown: 'contained within a single picture is the composition of rooms and components, the adjacent exterior environments, actions and locations, and the relationship between objects' (Tsukamoto and Kaijima 2009: 5). Towards the back of the book, project data is given for the original twenty-four houses plus an additional five. This includes a single black and white photograph of the exterior or a model, data on the project (team, dates, floor areas and construction method), 1: 200

plans and elevations and in most cases, a 1: 200 site plan. Of the twenty-four houses, the last seven were still being designed, were under construction or were unbuilt at the time of publication. The illustrations are an amalgam of different types of drawings that an architect would produce during the design process in order to communicate different types of information to colleagues, the client and the building contractor. Significantly, they appear to show the houses before construction, representing the house as the architect anticipates that it will be occupied and are valuable documents demonstrating the nature of design as a predictive activity as discussed earlier, albeit always informed by past experience. There is the possibility that visits to the houses that were completed prior to publication enabled some hindsight to inform the drawings of built houses, but they are certainly not a post-occupancy analysis.

Although the scale of these houses is more generous than the pets, the house's fabric and form is still designed to retain the tight mediating role between contextual fabric and activity and the human body and behaviour (Tsukamoto and Kaijima 2009: 119). Each house is very different and this diversity comes from the endless variation in the relationship between these two states. Atelier Bow Wow characterise this difference as occurring in the house's 'behaviour' (Tsukamoto and Kaijima 2009: 109) rather than its appearance.

Atelier Bow Wow's book *Behaviorology* (2010) describes thirty-one architectural projects and seventeen 'Micro Public Space' projects such as installations and furniture hybrids. Twenty-eight houses are included and the drawings of fourteen of the earliest were also documented in *Graphic Anatomy*. The built projects are recorded photographically with four to eight images for each house project accompanied by an introductory text and image captions that explain how the spaces relate to each other, to their context and to their inhabitants. These houses have been revisited post-construction in order to create the book and it is possible to compare the actual occupation of houses to their predicted occupation in *Graphic Anatomy*.

Gae House is particularly revealing. The house was completed in 2003 and was lived in by its original occupants when it was recorded for *Graphic Anatomy* and *Behaviorology*. It includes an unconventional horizontal first floor window that looks down on the street from the living space and is also used as a shelf for ornaments and found objects collected by the occupants. In one photograph (Tsukamoto and Kaijima 2010: 24), the photographer shows two little figurines sitting on the window in a position that makes them look as if they are stepping off the kerb of the street below. The house invites the inhabitants to engage with the street in unique, playful and potent ways. *Graphic Anatomy* didn't predict the window's use as a shelf for ornaments but always showed an awareness of the unusual connection between interior and exterior by drawing the exterior context as viewed through the glass in both sectional perspective and plan. Furniture and fittings right down to washing machine location and bicycle storage are all shown in their eventual locations. The large collection of books was evidently an important design consideration because they are clearly depicted in the drawings and dominate the space upon occupation. The critic who lives there is even drawn in the sectional perspective of his sunken Study space with his body and hands positioned in the same location relative to his desk, chair, laptop and paper within the space as he is shown in the photograph.

It could be argued that the photographer, Hiroyasu Sakaguchi A-Z for the majority of images in the book, may have been aware of the drawings in *Graphic Anatomy* and set up the photographs to reference them. As with most professional architectural photography, the photographs are almost certainly composed. However, Atelier Bow Wow's accuracy in predicting the nature of occupation can also be found in projects such as Mountain House (Tsukamoto and Kaijima 2009: 102–5, 144), which were still being designed when *Graphic Anatomy* went to press and could not have been drawn from life. Atypically for Atelier Bow Wow's houses it is located outside Japan in California, USA making it more difficult practically and conceptually for them to predict the uses of the space. However, *Graphic Anatomy* and *Behaviorology* show similar activities occurring in both the pre-construction drawings and the post-occupation photographs, in this case taken by Iwan Baan. Differences in the photographs compared to the drawings are trifling and include two extra chairs pulled up towards the stove and a hammock fixed to the structure of the beautiful and unusual first floor semi-external room (Tsukamoto and Kaijima 2010: 194–201).

One reason for the close correlation between prediction and occupation
is that these buildings are tightly designed around the occupants' activities and being of a modest size, the house defines very particular and often
unconventional spaces for activities to happen.

Making the houses a subject through anthropomorphism once more,
Atelier Bow Wow describe each house in its context thus: 'Each building
can be viewed as a sentient creature, endowed with its own unique intel-
ligence and a defining set of living characteristics' (Tsukamoto 2010: 9).
This particularity is derived from their concept of *behaviorology* which they
apply to three categories of entity: humans, natural elements and buildings within their urban or landscape context. This levelling of animate,
phenomenological and inanimate deliberately breaks down our empirical
Cartesian assumptions about subject and object as well as assumptions
about inanimate objects being incapable of exercising agency over us as
discussed earlier in relation to Gell. Atelier Bow Wow's design process
attempts to synthesise the different scales and temporal rhythms of humans,
natural elements and buildings in context and this mirrors Buchli's description of the house as a material and immaterial mediator between humans
and the world. Atelier Bow Wow believe that their approach is closer to
biology, sociology and anthropology than the more conventional privileging of individual expression established within the field of architecture
by modernist thought (Tsukamoto 2010: 8). From the perspective of the
architectural design discipline, their original methods and conclusions
derived from their careful and strategic observations of people, elements
and buildings would appear to share some common ground with the praxis
of an archaeologist or anthropologist:

> In places where certain attributes of a building repeat and accumulate, a streetscape
> order is produced ... Enduring repetition over time, both the unique elements and
> the overall compositions of built form could only survive through a process of
> continuous trial and error. (Tsukamoto 2010: 11)

Atelier Bow Wow's assertion that 'Behaviorology brings about an immediate shift in subjectivity, inviting many different elements together and
calling into question who or what may be the main protagonist of a space'
(Tsukamoto 2010: 15) shares an awareness of Lefebvre's ideas that are also

important to archaeologists and anthropologists in considering the ways that buildings shape us and we (inhabitants as well as third-party architects and archaeologists) shape them.

Conclusion

If we accept the significance of the relationship of subject and object in helping us to understand how architecture mediates between people, buildings and the wider world in material and immaterial ways, then it becomes easier to see this as a useful conceptual framework for architects, archaeologists and anthropologists. However, the subtle and shifting dynamic between subject and object, between people and buildings is difficult to uncover or demonstrate and is rarely articulated by inhabitants, probably because it goes against our empirical sense that animate people must be subjects and inanimate buildings must be objects. As described by Gell, objects can have agency and influence us. This makes it easier for us to conceive of buildings as subjects. Buchli describes the architectural object as existing in different material registers that can be tangible or intangible and that these differences enable us to use or be influenced by objects to facilitate social relations. Architects' and archaeologists' understanding of the relationship between subject and object is made more difficult by the uncertainties relating to the past, present and future context in which they work as well as cultural ambiguities between the tangible, the intangible, the real and the imaginary. These ambiguities can manifest themselves in literal or metaphorical anthropomorphism between people and buildings. This is not only evident in ancient and vernacular architecture but as demonstrated here, is used by contemporary architects such as Hejduk and Atelier Bow Wow to sensitise us to the richness of the imaginative and design potential of our cultural confusion between subject and object.

As demonstrated here, the involvement of an architect, archaeologist or anthropologist increases the complexity of the dynamic further. The location of their activities in time or space can act as a filter between the material world and the social world. Their third-party involvement can also distance the building from its inhabitants but it also gives them a unique insight into the complexity of the dynamic between subject and object. For architects, the relationship between subject and object shifts according to changes in context, participation and time as the design project transforms from the imaginary to the occupied. The Archeox project demonstrated that architects and archaeologists share an understanding of the importance in reducing the gap between the tactile and imaginative as illustrated by the significance placed upon physical engagement with objects and the moment of discovery. Atelier Bow Wow's awareness and understanding of the complexity of their third-party position and their Lefebvrian conception of space as a practising agent have led them to develop a design methodology they describe as being akin to the fields of biology, sociology and anthropology that seeks to reduce the distinction between designers and inhabitants. Their intention is to reconnect inhabitants with their dwellings and yet still imbue them with the immaterial ideas that an architect's imagination can bring through the process of design.

If it is clear that an understanding and consciousness of the subject and object dynamic is relevant to those disciplines with an interest in the interactions between the architectural, the human and the social, then it is helpful for them to understand the particular insights into this dynamic that they themselves bring. Architects have a strong sensitivity towards the way that the relationship between subject and object shifts over the course of the design process and are familiar with the very different and fluid perspectives of others as they engage with architecture by inhabiting, observing, discussing and imagining. This knowledge could be useful for archaeologists who 'find themselves actively producing the objects of such claims for heritage ... buildings move from being dwellings and functional and ritual objects to objects of heritage' (Buchli 2013: 60–1). The Story Museum project showed relevant themes related to heritage being explored by architects working with a derelict building. Archaeologists and anthropologists bring detached and methodological ways to describe and catalogue their observations. Atelier Bow Wow demonstrate that an architects' design process will be blinkered if they value creation to the exclusion of observation or documentation or if they always overlook the everyday for the extraordinary. Consideration of inanimate objects as subjects and vice versa are essential conceptual shifts needed to enable the creativity of something new and the recreation of something lost.

Acknowledgements

Many thanks to Tish Francis and Kim Pickin, the directors of the Story Museum, Jane Harrison, the project developer of Archeox and Helen Adams of The Pitt Rivers Museum for their insight and kind help during our OB1 LIVE collaborative live projects with them.

Bibliography

Anderson, J., and Priest, C. (2013). 'Fabrications for the Story Museum. What year one students and John Hejduk can teach us about reality and imagination in architectural design'. In *Writingplace*. TU Delft, The Netherlands, 25–7 November 2013. Abstract available online at <http://writingplace.org> accessed 23 December 2015.

Archeox website (2015) <https://www.archeox.net/project> accessed 16 December 2015.

Buchli, V. (2013). *Anthropology of Architecture*. London and New York: Bloomsbury Academic.

Crea, G., Dafnis, A., Hallam, J., Kiddey, R., and Schofield, J. (2014). 'Turbo Island, Bristol: Excavating a Contemporary Homeless Place'. *Post-Medieval Archaeology* 48(1) (February): pp. 133–50.

Fujimori, T. (2010). 'The Origins of Atelier Bow-Wow's Gaze'. In Y. Tsukamoto and M. Kaijima (eds), *Behaviorology*. Atelier Bow Wow. New York: Rizzoli International Publications Inc.: pp 122–9.

Hejduk, J. (1987). *The Collapse of Time and other Diary Constructions*. London: The Architectural Association.

Hejduk, J. (1988). *Education of an Architect*. New York: Rizzoli.

Hejduk, J. (1998). *Such Places as Memory. Poems 1953–1996*. Cambridge, MA: The MIT Press.

Hoskins, J. (2011). 'Agency, Biography and Objects'. In C. Tilley, W. Keane, S. Küchler, M. Rowlands and P. Spyer (eds), *Handbook of Material Culture*. London: Sage Publications Ltd.: ch.5.

Kuroda, J., Kaijima, M., and Tsukamoto, Y. (2010). *Made in Tokyo*. Tokyo: Kaijima Institute Publishing Co. Ltd.

Lefebvre, H. (1974). *The Production of Space*, translated by D. Nicholson-Smith, 1994. Oxford and Cambridge, MA: Blackwell Publishers.

Schopenhauer, A. (1818). *The World as Will and Representation*, edited and translated by J. Norman and A. Welchman, edited by C. Janaway (2010). Cambridge: Cambridge University Press.

Story Museum (2014). <http://www.storymuseum.org.uk/about-us/our-plans/building-history> accessed 15 December 2015.

Tilley, C. (2011). 'Objectification'. In C. Tilley, W. Keane, S. Küchler, M. Rowlands and P. Spyer (eds), *Handbook of Material Culture*. London: Sage Publications Ltd: ch.4.

Tilley, C. (2011). 'Theoretical Perspectives'. In C. Tilley, W. Keane, S. Küchler, M. Rowlands and P. Spyer (eds), *Handbook of Material Culture*. London: Sage Publications Ltd: pp. 7–12.

Tsukamoto, Y. (2001). *Pet Architecture Guide Book*. Tokyo: World Photo Press.

Tsukamoto, Y. (2010). 'Architectural Behaviorlogy' [*sic*]. In Y. Tsukamoto and M. Kaijima (eds), *Behaviorology*. Atelier Bow Wow. New York: Rizzoli International Publications Inc.: pp. 8–15.

Tsukamoto, Y., and Kaijima, M. (2009). *Graphic Anatomy*. Atelier Bow Wow. Tokyo: TOTO Publishing.

Tsukamoto, Y., and Kaijima, M. (2010). *Behaviorology*. Atelier Bow Wow. New York: Rizzoli International Publications Inc.

Washida, M. (2010). 'Atelier Bow-Wow as Artists: Changes in Art and the Potential of New Social Space'. In Y. Tsukamoto and M. Kaijima (eds), *Behaviorology: Atelier Bow Wow*. New York: Rizzoli International Publications Inc.: pp. 244–55.

White M. (2007). Atelier Bow-Wow: Tokyo Anatomy. *Archinect*. <http://archinect.com/features/article/56468/atelier-bow-wow-tokyo-anatomy> accessed 16 December 2015.

ANDREA PLACIDI

3   Furnitecture

ABSTRACT

Furnitecture: physical and spatial structures that perform the functions of both furniture and architecture, and serve as a link between them and their inhabitants. This chapter discusses the reciprocal relationship between architecture and its content, with reference to a meaningful environment for living. Furnitecture operates at an intermediary scale of design, smaller than a building but larger than most pieces of furniture. It has a critical mass capable of subverting and augmenting the perception of space, and thus becomes the connecting membrane that frames and defines the experience of home. Once it is established that furnitecture is the membrane, physical and immaterial, living and moving, attached to the architecture, then it becomes clear that it has existed in domestic settings for centuries. The concept furnitecture can be applied to all sorts of decorative choices made by people, even when unconscious of 'design'. Any home therefore can be considered a unique piece of furnitecture.

Furnitecture

In his book *Gnostic Architecture*, the American architect Eric Owen Moss discusses the complex relationship between inside and outside in architecture. In particular he proposes that there is a sort of spatial/experiential *glue* that connects the two, 'a cerebral underground [that] designates a criss-cross of emotions and ideas, piled over many years. The interconnections are so fine, so precarious, and so can't-be-numberedish, that it is not possible to break in. Start to disable the glue and it's gone: it's psychologically inviolable' (Moss 1999: 3.1). Similarly, any meaningful discussion on the home finds itself inevitably tangled up in a 'gluey bundle' made of possessions, meanings, habits, and design elements, from which it is difficult to dissect any specific part without forcibly excluding other interconnected components, memories, and domestic rituals. To explain the convoluted concurrence of inside spaces and the outside shape in a building, Owen Moss presented, as a demonstration of spatial continuity and reciprocal interconnection, a photograph of the small sculpture *Helmet Head No. 3* made by Henry Moore in 1960 (Figure 3.1).

Figure 3.1:   Henry Moore, *Helmet Head No. 3*, 1960 (LH 467). (Reproduced by permission of The Henry Moore Foundation.)

Owen Moss's fitting description of the sculpture can be applied to the outside/inside spatial relationship found in any home: '[In Moore's Helmet Head ...] there is the outside of the outside form, the inside of the outside form, and then a space in perpetual tensions. Then there is the outside of the inside form and, finally, the inside of the inside form. The sculpture serves as a psychological model for perpetual unravelling, in the sense that one could continue to go further and further in: more pieces, more spaces, more tension. Outside and inside are both coincidental and discontinuous. Fit and misfit' (Moss 1999: 3.15). The progressive process of inhabitation of a domestic dwelling over time follows a similar process of occupation of the available space, and creates a unique crystallisation in perpetual tension of possessions, adjustments, rituals and memories – a sort of significative membrane set between the internal articulation of the spaces and the skeleton of the building.

This chapter aims to bring to the fore these (mis)fitting domestic structures, proposing a reunifying category that allows for the discussion of disparate entities, physical entities as well as non-material atmospheric qualities, under the label furnitecture. The term furnitecture is relatively new to the discourse of design, and conventionally describes multi-functional structures that operate at an intermediary scale between furniture (small), and architecture (large). These structures have the ability to transform and augment habitable spaces, and influence and broaden living patterns into innovative environments. Most people probably expect that furnitectures are cutting-edge futuristic configurations only found in glossy magazines and boutique showrooms, and that furnitecture will never affect them or their home. But when one examines the concept, one discovers that it requires greater explanation, and has been around for centuries; that it should not be limited to the world of professional design, and may well appear in different permutations in everyone's home.

To this extent, the chapter provides a brief history of the term and concept, seeking both to explain the concept's timeless relevance to all dwellers. This is especially true if we consider the effects of membrane-like furnitectures to both material and immaterial spatial qualities. We should note that furnitecture is not, as most pieces of furniture, simply a physical entity with an objective presence. The concept of furnitecture as argued here extends to incorporate a plurality of devices that define the conditions of occupation as well as atmospheric qualities determined by light modulation, spatial articulation, and psychological responses. Defined as such, furnitecture provides a critical methodology to extrapolate and underline the intimate relation between people, their possessions, and the occupation of their homes, through an analysis of the connotative choices that shape every living environment.

Definition of the term 'Furnitecture'

A good definition of the versatility of furnitecture, written in 1990 by Stephen D. Ritchings (SDR Design), an architect/designer in the field is

> *fur*ni*tec*ture*: [...] 2. furniture which refers to, is related to, derives from, or is intended to accompany architecture. 3. furniture which mimics, imitates, or (God forbid) mocks architecture. 4. furniture made of architectural materials, or of recognisable substitutions thereof. 5. furniture which creates an architecture. 6. furniture which attempts to create an architecture. 7. architecture made of, or from, furniture. (<http://mobile.designaddict.com/furnitecture> posted by SDR Design in December 2004)

This definition suggests that there is a possible intermediary role between those who produce architecture (architects), and those who provide furniture (designers). As a design concept in critical publications and in exhibitions, the notion of furnitecture is well-attested from the second half of the twentieth century. The 1970s in particular were attuned to the concept. In a recent book dedicated to the argument, *Furnitecture: Furniture that Transforms Space* (Yudina 2015), the author's selection of examples begins in this period. In 1974 the American designer Ken Isaacs proposed in *How to Build your own Living Structures* (Isaacs 1974) a sustainable, modular, flexible, multi-functional structural system for human inhabitation which could reconfigure the entire volume of a room, since it was bigger than furniture but smaller than architecture. Isaacs's modular structure effectively constitutes a fore-bearer for the definition of furnitecture, as the resulting construction is neither furniture nor architecture, but a spatial membrane that connects/separates people within a lived environment (Figure 3.2).

Figure 3.2:   Ken Isaacs, *3-D Living Structure*, p. 34, 1974. (From the original publication
<http://popupcity.net/free-classic-how-to-build-your-own-living-structures-byken-
isaacs/>.) '3-D LIVING: Living Structures are a way for close people to be close in
a single space without getting in each other's hair – the level change really does it.'
Subdivision of internal spaces into individual domains, allowing different activities to
take place simultaneously.

Reinhold Zeigler, an American industrial designer, is given credit as the
first to explicitly use the term 'furnitecture' from 1979 onwards. He defined
his MATRIX habitats, which consisted of a modular grid beam system
inspired by Isaac's structures, as 'furnitecture – a cross between furniture
and architecture' (Jergenson, Jergenson and Keppel 2013: 45). Both Isaacs's
Living Structures and Zeigler's MATRIX habitats demonstrated the possibility for furnitectures to reconfigure and articulate the space of architecture by means of affordable continuous furnishing structures, creating
sub-spaces within the space inside a building.

Sharing similar concerns, an investigation of the potential of furniture
to upstage architecture (in the guise of micro-architecture) was presented
in an influential exhibition at MOMA in New York in 1972. The exhibition, *Italy: The New Domestic Landscape*, presented a review of Italian
designs with a critical consciousness in its catalogue and essays. What
emerged was that most Italian designers were determined to challenge
the functional platform of modern design established by the Modernists,
and to assert instead the 'ideological' role of design and its potential in

challenging people's habits to promote a radical and complex social renovation. Alongside a display of stylish objects of furniture, the exhibition
presented a series of *Environments*, spatial installations commissioned to
explore the possibility that habitable environments could exist as autonomous structures without necessarily a direct correlation with their host
building (Ambasz 1972). A similar intention was reproposed in 2008 by
Atelier OPA, a Japanese multidisciplinary design company that managed
to compact most of the functional fittings of a house and an office within a
series of portable containers, in essence enlarged travel 'trunks' that can be
reconstituted as a home/office in any host building. Called *Kenchikukagu*
[Architectural Furniture], these foldable rooms are in fact independent
small architecture, a sort of portable furnitectures.

    In the current century the discussion about furnitecture has moved in
two different directions and definitions. In an elegantly illustrated book by
Anna Yudina published in 2015 the emphasis is on the visual impact of the
subject and its design relevance, but with little attempt to provide an historical overview and a unifying definition of furnitecture. The design examples
presented in her selection vary from 'multifunctional furniture' (characterised
by storage/space organisers, hybridity of use, and flexible partitioning), to
more complex 'macro-furniture' that has the ability to create independent
spatial configurations. Those in the last category are relevant for this essay, as
they possess autonomous spatial qualities. Yudina divides them into plug-ins
structures (modular houses made from serial elements that expand the remit
of prefabrication), internal landscapes and inhabitable furniture (Figure 3.3).

Figure 3.3: Inhabitable furniture: CKR (Claesson Koivisto Rune for Dune New York),
Luna (Moon), 2005. (Reproduced by permission of CKR Claesson Koivisto
Rune Architects.)

Inspired by the lunar landscape, the soft structure encourages the evolution of static behavioural patterns with a plastic experiment in comfort and surface definition. The unifying element in her selections is that the pieces are all 'design products'; exciting objects that have been proposed in response to various needs and aesthetic values, but with little testing of actual functional performance. They seem more concerned with establishing new principles of design by means of conceptual extrapolations of conventional elements, than to interact effectively with the body and sensorial experiences of people.

More thought provoking, due to its greater anthropological scope, and thus ultimately more consequential because of its analysis of social implications, was the treatment of furnitecture in an exhibition *Living in Motion: Design and Architecture for Flexible Dwelling* (Vitra Design Museum, Weil am Rhein, 2002) curated by the historian of design Mathias Schwartz-Clauss. Schwartz-Clauss consulted with a series of experts about the sociological impact of hybrid scale design: Robert Kronenburg, architect and theoretician, Stephan Rammler, sociologist, Antje Flade, psychologist, Stephanie Bunn, anthropologist, and Annemarie Seiler-Baldinger, ethnologist. The exhibition was perhaps one of the first opportunities to reflect seriously on the implication of the term furnitecture on domestic inhabitation.

Shwartz-Clauss used 'furnitecture' explicitly as a unifying category to label what he described as 'perplexing hybrid forms, neither furniture nor architecture [...] in which dwelling and furnishing have been welded into a single, unified entity' (Schwartz-Clauss and von Vegesack, 2002: 12). His definition provided the common ground for the discussion of a series of disparate innovations from different cultural and geographical contexts applied to a range of inhabitable objects, not necessarily complicated to construct, nor expensive, which were presented in the catalogue. Examples of furnitectures were cited from nomadic cultures across the world; they included ingenious flexible solutions that testify to the human capacity to shape and modify existing objects (and spaces) to create specific environments and inhabitable living conditions, such as hammocks, inhabitable furniture, nomadic tents, caravans. They all offered shelter and a degree of intimacy, without necessarily being 'buildings', or designed in the traditional sense of furniture as independent objects.

The classifications in the exhibition's catalogue focused on qualities that are rarely linked to the static design categories applied normally to buildings or furniture. The chapters listed 'transportation, adaptation, combining, assembling and/or folding, and wearing/carrying [which extended to "clothing and accessories" that provide a sense of domestic comfort]' (2002: 13). These characteristics suggest an acceptance of transformation and change rather than permanent qualities imbued in the objects, and this marks a critical departure from Yudina's examples of design. Schwartz-Clauss's definition of furnitecture extended the design conventions to challenge the traditional antinomy between nomadic cultures and urbanised settlers: 'every nomadic lifestyle has its settled moments, just as every settled lifestyle has nomadic aspects' (Schwartz-Clauss and von Vegesack 2002: 17). According to Schwartz-Clauss, the distinction that our culture has made between nomads and settlers has resulted in the exclusion of huts, tents or igloos from our conception of architecture, just as we do not regard baskets, hammocks or pillows as furniture. Yet mobile, flexible and multifunctional domestic objects have a long tradition in western societies: they were characteristic of habitations in antiquity and medieval times, and were often rediscovered, particularly in the nineteenth and twentieth centuries.

The Vitra exhibition focused on sociological issues crucial to the concept of home, and this effected the definition of what might be a furnitecture. Importantly, in Europe it is only in the last three centuries that rooms have progressively acquired dedicated functions, and specific furniture has appeared. The home, rather than being a physical entity, could be intended '[...] more and more as a set of personal activities, habits and relationships than an established continuum of habitation in the same location. Communication technology has accelerated this trend [the detachment of homes from buildings]' (Schwartz-Clauss and von Vegesack 2002: 23). Accordingly, the curators emphasised that even a hammock might be considered a furnitecture since it was a human adaptation that permitted flexible living and created a temporary habitable environment. They deliberately steered the discussion away from the visual appearance of the *design* aspects of furnitecture, which are the basis of Yudina's study.

The work of both Clauss-Schwartz and Yudina have an evident contradiction that needs to be addressed particularly from the point of view of interior architecture, an emerging academic field that is concerned with the effects of architecture and design on people. Arguably Clauss-Schwartz's definition is over-inclusive and without boundaries, and Yudina has eschewed the problem of definition and is unwittingly exclusive; in her book furnitecture is presented as a 'provocative' object of design, made between 1970 and the present. To reconcile this contradistinction we should consider that even if architecture is the skeletal structure of a living space, it cannot be fully perceived at any one moment (as it is not possible to see the sides of a building at once, or indeed all the walls within a room), and thus requires movement and a mental extrapolation to be understood in its entirely. It has usually both an inside and an outside, but the issue is more complicated when the concept of a home is considered, as the initial quotation from Owen Moss (1991: 3.1) describing Moore's sculpture demonstrated. Furniture is instead conventionally made of movable independent objects within the space of the architecture. Those are freestanding structures (or built in storages) that lack the dichotomy of the interior versus the exterior. Notwithstanding aesthetic and cultural considerations, the scope of furniture is to serve specific functions, and the role of architecture is to facilitate these functions – yet the two are often designed separately, diminishing their spatial potential to coagulate into a coherent habitable environment. Furnitecture, operating between the two, performs as a spatial membrane that softens the transition between the skeletal architecture, and the versatile living that happens with in it. It is neither a void nor an isolated object. To better understand the concept, we should consider a remarkable piece of early furnitecture shown in Antonello da Messina's painting of St Jerome in his study (Figure 3.4).

Here a room without walls and ceiling appears contained in much larger space, where ergonomic and functional concerns have been carefully addressed. As an element of furniture, it operates on the inside of the architecture, *and*, as a spatial proposition, it provides the setting for a variety of functions. Furnitecture accordingly should be able to engage both with the skeletal architecture, and should be easily adaptable in use. The fact that furnitecture can occupy, and effectively replace, the space of architecture means that furnitecture has the potential to perform at intermediate scale, and to alter the conventional sequence of perceptions. The

Figure 3.4: Antonello da Messina, *St Jerome in His Study*, the National Gallery
London, 1475. (Reproduced by permission of the National Gallery Picture Library.)
Natural light articulates the space from opposite directions, isolating the study against
the darker background of the naves. The views onto the open landscape though the
windows create a dynamic contrast of visual and spatial forces.

visual backdrop is subverted, and meaningful elements, not the framing
skeleton, come to the fore of the experience. At the same time, other important sensorial information is either missing or amplified. The margins of the
space become a series of blurred edges, and therefore the interior qualities
within a furnitecture are often unpredictable and surprising. This partial
disorientation occurs when the traditional sequence of internal spaces is
altered, because it is not clear where the threshold between inside/outside
lies, or indeed what is the actual form of the building in relation to the

spatial experience. The multiplication of spatial effects can be disconcerting, but, if carefully orchestrated, creates positive responses, inserting a psychological response into architecture by animating structures that are normally performing only secondary roles.

The application of furnitecture

Furnitecture as discussed above is an elusive concept to define, and can be stretched to cover many architectural features. Furnitecture exists when actual space is 'formed', 'contained', or occupied within a building; in any other cases we are speaking only of 'super-furniture', objects of furniture with multiple functions. The continuity of the sensorial response triggered by furnitecture is enhanced, *despite* the discontinuity between inside and outside.

This was made evident in 2014 when the Royal Academy of Arts in London held an unconventional exhibition of architecture, or more precisely of the fundamental elements of architecture, *Sensing Space – Architecture Reimagined*. The show featured a series of installations designed by architects that attempted to recreate the qualities of their buildings without the skeletal frame of the building, by means of stand-alone sensorial/ spatial 'abstract' constructions. The exhibition did not display any models or drawings, or photographic images, but intended to convey experiential qualities by exposing the inner membrane of architecture. As the purpose of the exhibition was about extracting the essence of architecture, this in turn demonstrated the possibility for large-scale furnitecture structures to create spatial qualities independently, regardless of the physical presence of a building, or in spite of its actual physical configuration. This occurrence is not unusual in retail and commercial design (where spatial qualities are exploited to seduce costumers), but it is rare to discuss architecture without a reference to a building, in pure spatial terms.

Given the independent constitution of spatial membranes, the key to and importance of furnitecture in the context of an inhabited environment lies in its dynamic and flexible approach to the concept of home. It works on the premise that the house is not a static composed scenography, but an environment in a condition of constant evolution. When one understands this as the rationale for furnitecture, one realises the importance of flexibility (as opposed to static design) in the structure of home environments. A quick chronological survey of some Western Europe's significant historic periods shows this clearly. The concept of furnitecture has been part of carefully designed interiors in architecture since antiquity. The possibilities to animate a static interior with surface decoration are well known since ancient times, and the Romans particularly excelled in chromatic pictorial decorations with three-dimensional details in stucco that augmented the perceptive dimensions of space. Equally, flexible structures for inhabitation have been in use extensively in the past; examples of movable partitioning and multifunctional foldable furnitecture are well-documented, both in domestic environments and as part of travelling infrastructure. At Herculaneum, destroyed by the eruption of Vesuvius in AD 79, a remarkably well-preserved movable partition that allowed for the flexible division of public and private quarters was found in the *Casa del Tramezzo di Legno* (House with a Wooden Partition).

Flexible qualities of spatial articulation were further exploited in the Renaissance when coordinated domestic spaces for the wealthy families were manufactured by an array of specialised craftsmen. An interesting 'furnitecture-effect' was achieved with illusory perspectives in the inlaid wood panels in the Duke Federico da Montefeltro's private study in Urbino, made by Dutch artisans in 1476. The visual composition suggests a greater depth to the actual space, that expands and contracts in an array of shelving, sitting, and precious items, as a 'real' furnitecture would have achieved. An application of the same principles was used by (neo)classical architects who were able to create 'furnitecture' compositions by coordinating decorative patterns, architectural elements, and statuary. Robert Adam's meticulously coordinated interior at Syon house in 1760 for example features ancient, Renaissance, and neo-classical statuary at different scales of design, fitted into purpose-made settings, framed by elaborate stuccowork. This creates an orchestrated space in which the void and ambience are articulated by elements that are larger than furniture, but are not architecture. In Secessionist Vienna, there was a similar attitude towards the design of interiors: *Gesamtkunstwerk* [comprehensive artwork] resulted from the synthesis of various crafts, with classical motifs replaced by stylised elements that heralded a modern sensitivity towards restrained decorations, and primary geometric shapes.

Frank Lloyd Wright was one of the first modern architects to explore the spatial potential of furnitecture; in his work the sequence of internal spaces became a continuous spatial field that merged the inside with the outside, both in terms of views and the use of natural materials. 'Wright's work set the foundation for the revolution in domestic architecture that was to come. [The inspiration came from Japan where ...] the flowing space and unfettered integration with the site afforded by sliding walls and open plans, and the sensitivity to natural materials made a big impression on him. Space in the living areas flow uninterrupted, usually around the focus of a fireplace [...]' (R. Kronenburg in Schwartz-Clauss and von Vegesack 2002: 25). This created a good balance between the novelty of fluid modern space, and integrated furniture. One of the best examples of furnitecture was installed in the Kaufmann Residence (Fallingwater 1935), where the natural stones from the site were rearranged within concrete structures to provide the fittings for windowpanes, shelving, and soft furnishing. This allowed the house to blend perfectly into its surroundings, and for the continuity of the spatial field between inside and outside (augmented by extensive horizontal openings and the cantilevered balconies), making the dichotomy between the building skeleton and contained space redundant, a point well understood by Bruno Zevi, an Italian critic of architecture:

[Fallingwater] emerges from the landscape as a series of spaces without a specific 'form', because basic geometric shapes are no longer relevant, and there are no recognizable classical elements. Its voids have no enclosures, and there are no facades. There is no distinction between structure and load, because all the elements are involved in the resolution of the static diagram, which coincide with the spatial articulation. For the first time in the history of architecture, the composition of the voids coincides with the articulation of the volumes. (Zevi 1992: 219)

However, the modernist concept of 'absolute' space that followed in Europe in the 1920s placed an emphasis on the design of separate elements:

architecture and furniture became independent entities. This is almost the
opposite approach of furnitecture, and a stance that seems to separate itself
from the examples previously listed in which blurring of the boundaries
between architecture and furniture was appreciated. Le Corbusier's Villa
Savoye of 1931 is a good example of the disconnection between the modernist house and its overly designed separate pieces of furniture, notwithstanding the built-in chaise longue in the bathroom, and the fact that the
continuous ramp might be considered a form of 'kinetic' furnitecture. Yet
the price paid for the freedom of modernist design from decorative patterns was the disaggregation of the various elements of design, and with
the dominance of visual images in publications over the actual use of the
spacep; modern architectures increasingly became manifestos of intentions,
not real places. A noticeable alternative to radical modernism came from
a 'non-orthodox' architect, who designed and furnished a house that was
continuously inhabited by the original owners for over sixty years due to the
intelligent spatial solutions achieved by an integrated furnitecture. Gerrit
Rietveld, a cabinet-maker who only later became an architect (having been
influenced by the De Stijl Movement), designed and built the Schroder
House in Utrecht 1924 with a radical concept on the top floor. There he
replaced all fixed walls with sliding panels and bold patches of colours,
allowing for the spaces to be fully connected in the day, and subdivided
into 'rooms' at night, depending on the daily requirements. 'By being so
flexible, the Rietveld/Schroeder house seems to achieve more fully the
stated ambitions of the modern movement houses that ostensibly heralded
the free plan as the liberation of the living space, though in many cases it
really meant putting fixed walls into different configurations' (Schwartz-
Clauss and von Vegesack 2002: 31).

In more recent times, Japanese architect Shigeru Ban has shown a
similar attitude towards the empowerment of the inhabitants against the
rigidity of architecture. His homes make flexibility the core element in
their articulation by means of movable furnitecture. In the *Naked House*
in Saitama, Japan built in 2000, the rooms themselves become movable:
four wooden open frames of 3 × 3 × 3 meters mounted on wheels contain the basic functional furnishings within a simple continuous volume,
with all the servicing elements arranged along one side. The rooms can be

easily pushed to different places, creating cloisters of flexible continuous/discontinuous inhabitable space adjacent to windows, services, and even outside. Family members can live within a room or on top of it, be alone in a 'single' space, or meet together in an enlarged space consisting of several rooms that have been grouped together. 'The house is the result of my vision of enjoyable and flexible living, which evolved from the client's own vision toward a [modern dynamic of] family life interaction' (Shigeru Ban; <http://www.shigerubanarchitects.com/works/2000_naked-house>).

Since 1983, Steven Holl has similarly experimented with the flexible spatial concept of 'hinged space' in housing, where the walls are allowed to move by means of enlarged hinges. Hinged spaces are generated by walls that actively participate in the creation of interactive environments with the human beings who inhabit them. By pulling, pushing and physically manipulating the perimetrical spatial surfaces, people can rearrange the home to their liking, the available space becomes contingent upon the space they need (and not to the building shape). In the Fukuoka housing project in Japan, all apartments incorporate a degree of hinged walls, which can be considered a modern variation of tradition movable Japanese screens. The apartments are indeterminate and incomplete rather than rigid and fixed. The occupants' manipulation of space responds on their daily basis to patterns of sleeping, eating, work and leisure, but also to the external environment and the seasonal variation.

The hybrid examples of furnitectures as illustrated above with non-orthodox propositions instil a different understanding of the characteristics of 'design', as they suggest that a house is not a static composed scenography, but a dynamic environment in a condition of constant evolution. As we have discussed, in order to consider the theoretical potential of furnitecture, it is important to appreciate that furnitecture is not a 'futurist' concept to be developed, but it is part of our cultural heritage: the interweaving of interiors into the fabric of architecture was common practice until cultural ideology and technical advancements in material craft replaced it in modern times with 'stationary' independent furniture, as opposed to that which is integrated and/or movable. The reciprocal cooperation between the various artisans and craftsmen involved in the making of habitable space, which had survived until the last century, has regrettably been replaced today by professionals operating independently and remotely from the actual construction site and lived dynamics. At closer examination, however, flexibility is still intrinsic in any domestic space outside of the static appearances of design features. Even in conventional built houses many elements are designed to be physically moved: doors, windows, blinds, cupboards, and drawers at the very least:

> We are used to movable elements [in the house], so without being too radical we can imagine (as many designers have) what extrapolating this movement might achieve. Doors and windows could become opening and closing walls; roof skylight opening and closing roofs; cupboards and closet become moving rooms. [...] The boundaries are fluid between what is [perceived as] stationary and what is in motion, [...] with windows and doors as fluctuating zones between rooms or between inside and outside. (Schwartz-Clauss and von Vegesack 2002: 13)

With this is mind, it is clear that furnitecture does not have to be overly designed and expensive, to be present in everyone's homes. The following example demonstrates that an interior articulated by a deliberate assemblage of ordinary objects can become visually independent and surprisingly flexible. In 1997, the design practice LOT-EK (reads *low-tech*) transformed a typical New York City loft into a flexible, functional, and practical live/work space, guided by their passion for new and innovative uses of cast-off materials (Figure 3.5).

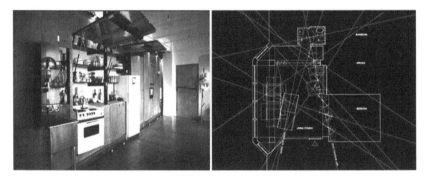

Figure 3.5: LOT-EK, *Miller-Jones Studio*, New York City, 1996.
(Reproduced by permission of LOT-EK.)

'The architects divided the space lengthwise with a 40 foot-long "containing" wall that serves as a cabinet for a variety of household facilities, such as kitchen, bathroom, and bedroom. Stove, oven and sink protrude partially when not in use like sculptures. The working table was made of disused fridges ...' (Smith and Ferrara 2003: 36). The position of the objects of furniture placed on the edge of the partition wall allowed for a partial access when closed, and reveals hidden functional spaces when the 'cupboard' doors are opened. The design strategy here was not concentrated on the qualities of the objects of furniture (in fact it uses deliberately found-objects) or the aesthetic qualities of the architectural detailing, but on the reciprocal positioning of the element of the house (a furnitecture approach) in relation to the variable use of the space – in this case a design office during the day, and a living environment in the evenings.

Even though every house has some degree of flexibility, it requires significant effort, inconvenience and expenditure to release it by altering, converting or extending. The failure of overly designed rigid modernist buildings to provide a meaningful setting for people's activities demonstrates that buildings that suit us best should have a significant degree of adaptability, flexibility and capacity for change. However, even in the cases of an *inflexible building*, its occupation and progressive alteration by decoration and/or furnishing can be described as a flexible process, and whatever the original purpose of the space, a building can be utilised in different manners. The resulting spatial 'membranes' created by each process of inhabitation (whether consciously, but clearly deliberately to some extent) alters/modifies the relationship between the skeleton and the content of architecture, suggesting the ubiquity of furnitecture as a nominal concept to describe the condition of inhabitation.

Conclusion

In this chapter, we have proposed the application of the term furnitecture to any items that serve as a spatial and atmospheric structure articulating the skeletal interior of architecture. When one understands that furnitecture

is the membrane, physical and immaterial, living and moving, articulating
the architecture, then one is made aware that it has existed in domestic
settings for centuries. Also the word can then technically, and surprisingly
for many, be applied to all sorts of decorative choices made by people who
are unconscious of 'design' idiosyncrasies. Any house therefore can be
considered a unique piece of furnitecture.

Clauss-Schwartz in the Vitra exhibition, which deliberately canvassed
opinions of social scientists, was conscious of this, but was less concerned
with distinctions between furnitecture and objects of furniture, than he
was with the definition of flexible homes. We have emphasised that furnitecture is not simply about design concerns, and should not be mistaken for
a design category. The origin of interior design was the act of amalgama-
tion of different crafts toward a given goal, not the 'mismatch' of random
separate objects that is dictated today by a market focused on producing
independent pieces of furniture. Furnitectures respond to a primordial
human desire to inhabit and mark more permanently the inhabited environment; to articulate and to personalise the space in which human day-to-
day rituals take place. Merleau-Ponty, in his 1948 essay on the perception
of space, argues that the classical Newtonian conception of space, which
relies on the assumption of absolute space within which physical objects
have immobile location, was misleading:

> [Domestic] space is composed by a variety of different regions and dimensions, which
> can no longer be thought of as interchangeable and which effect certain changes in
> the bodies which moves around within them. Instead of a world in which the dis-
> tinction between identity and change is clearly defined, with each being attributed
> to a different principle, we have a world in which objects cannot be considered self-
> identical, one in which it seems as though form and content are mixed, the boundary
> between them blurred. (Merleau-Ponty 2008: 38)

With this in mind, the concept of furnitecture allows for a deliberate connection between the internal world of furnishing and the external realm
of architecture and building. It focuses on the individual as the source of
the design strategy. The continuity of perception is more relevant that the
apparent distinction between inside/outside, and the separation between
architecture and the pieces of furniture. This suggests that in a home '[...]

architecture is fundamentally a people-system, not a thing-system; and that (incidentally) architecture without architects is impossible, [...] but that architecture without building may be quite possible, since use-situations can exist without buildings for them ...', as proposed by Nathan Silver in his essay 'Architecture without Buildings' (Silver 1969: 279). The ramifications of this 'reverse' approach to design, where forms are not intended as visual entities (the buildings) but as patterns of use (the form of occupation), suggests not the disappearance of buildings, as the title of Silver's essay would imply, but challenges the obsession of architects with them.

Instead of a design process that starts with raw materials and ends with a form that enables functions, Silver argued that patterns of use already exist and should constitute the main focus of the design; the building should only be an instrument to enhance the future inhabitation process. 'What we have been accustomed to thinking is form in architecture may be partly content, and what we have assumed was content may sometimes suffice for form' (Silver 1969: 281). We should consider the consequences of this *architecture without buildings* from a perceptive point of view referring again to Maurice Merleau-Ponty's from his essay 'Eye and Mind' (Merleau-Ponty 1964). Because the body extends itself and affects consciousness, perception becomes the means through which consciousness is established as an integral part of the world of individuals. Applied to architecture, phenomenological analysis proposes that any rational objective understanding of buildings is an illusion (even if we possess a complete knowledge of the design blueprint), and that the role of subjective experience is the key through which people truly experience lived space. The modernist implication that architectural space could exist as a separate entity (indeterminable by direct perception) is successfully challenged. Merleau-Ponty argued 'I do not see [space] according to its exterior envelope; I live in it from the inside; I am immersed in it. After all, the world is all around me, not in front of me [...]' (Merleau-Ponty 1964: 178). When architects and designers approach the design of a building, the issue should not be how to rationalise space but rather how to make space accessible to people in the implementation of their activities. The interior should be formed by extending spatial qualities around people's actions by means of furnitecture, which reconciles the distinction between people and their environment.

Bibliography

Ambasz, E. (ed.) (1972). *Italy: The New Domestic Landscape* (exhibition catalogue). New York: Museum of Modern Art.

Isaacs, K. (1974). *How to Build your own Living Structures*. New York: Harmony Books.

Jergenson, P., Jergenson, R., and Keppel, W. (2008). *How to Build with Grid Beam – a fast, easy and affordable system for constructing almost anything*. Gabriola Island, BC: New Society Publishers.

Johnson, A. (2015). *Improbable Libraries*. London: Thames and Hudson.

Lam, A., and Thomas, A. (2007). *Convertible Houses*. Salt Lake City, UT: Gibbs Smith.

Merleau-Ponty, M. (1948/2008). *The World of Perception*. London: Routledge.

Merleau-Ponty, M. (1964). *The Primacy of Perception, and other essays on phenomenological psychology, the philosophy of art, history, and politics*. Chicago, IL: Northwestern University Press.

Moss, E. O. (1999). *Gnostic Architecture*. New York: Monacelli Press.

Schwartz-Clauss, M., and von Vegesack, A. (eds) (2002). *Living in Motion: Design and Architecture for Flexible Dwelling* (Exhibition and Catalogue). Weil am Rhein: Vitra Design Museum.

Scoates, C. (ed.) (2003). *LOT-EK Mobile Dwelling Unit* (Exhibition UCSB). New York: D. A. P. (Distributed Art Publishers).

Silver, N. (1969). 'Architecture without Buildings'. In C. Jencks and G. Baird (eds), *Meaning in Architecture*. New York: G. Braziller.

Smith, C., and Ferrara, A. (2003). *XTREME INTERIORS*. Munich: Prestel.

Yudina, A. (2015). *Furnitecture: Furniture that Transforms Space*. London: Thames and Hudson.

Zevi, B. (1992). *Il Linguaggio Moderno dell'Architectura – guida al codice anticlassico* (5th edn with critical notes). Turin: Piccola Biblioteca Enaudi.

PART II

Practising Habitation

WENDY MORRISON

4   You Are Where You Eat: Worldview and the
Public/Private Preparation and Consumption
of Food

ABSTRACT
Based upon the study of rural domestic assemblages from the Late Iron Age and Early
Roman period of southern Britain, this chapter explores the connection between the use of
space for food preparation, consumption, and disposal and the worldview of the individuals
involved. Innovations in the later Iron Age, influenced by increased exposure to continental
foodstuffs, containers, and preparation techniques were widely accepted in some homes and
largely rejected in others. This must be more nuanced than a simple economic interpretation:
who could and could not afford to buy exotic things? Equally, there must be a more complex
narrative than the simple assimilation/resistance model – rejection does not always mean
resistance. Using Douglas' matrix of cultural possibilities, we can begin to relate domestic
assemblages and domestic organisation of space to the individuals who surrounded themselves with them and make some suggestions about what drove their consumer choices. Can
we tease out an understanding of how past peoples saw and related to the world around
them from the archaeological remains of domestic cooking and eating spaces?

Introduction

Imagine an archaeologist 2,000 years in the future, with few written records
to explain twentieth-century Britain. He examines two settlement sites –
one has structural remains of a rural stone domestic dwelling with several
phases of continuous occupation. Its remains indicate a significant period
of disrepair prior to end of use. An adjacent building suggests the keeping
of horses for transport. The second settlement, contemporary to the final
phase of the first, indicates the use of more advanced building techniques

and materials. Evidence for transport is shown by the rusted remains of
a sophisticated motorised vehicle, which epigraphy suggests was named
'Cortina'. What is our archaeologist to make of these sites? The dilapidated
building with primitive transport must be a low status farmstead whilst the
settlement with the sophisticated artefact implies a higher economic and
social status. Rather, with the benefit of living in these times, we can recognise that the country house with stables is far more 'high status' than the
estate housing. The exercise indicates the possibility of getting it wrong if
one relies solely on a perspective rooted in economic dichotomies, particularly when they are generated from a modern sense of value and meaning.

Perhaps high/low status is as meaningless as some other binary pairs
(e.g. natives/Romans), in understanding how people respond to their world,
yet in spite of Pope's statement that 'the continued use of the public/private
dichotomy is lamentable' (2007: 225 fn33), and of Hodder's admonition to
be critical of 'the universality of our own assumptions' (1986: 45), I believe
that there is still room for development in the use of binary opposition.

It seems that nearly every generation of archaeologists produces a
new theoretical framework, drawn from a related social science, that tears
down what went before, a linear march of 'theoretical evolution', working
toward a grand all-inclusive theory which will offer up the answer to 'the
Ultimate Question of Life, the Universe, and Everything' (Adams 1979).
Sadly, this has created a Sargasso Sea of social science theory, where the
discarded detritus of past thoughts lie abandoned. In many cases, as I have
argued elsewhere (Morrison forthcoming), the baby has been thrown out
with the bathwater. In the determination to pluck something 'new' from
other disciplines and apply it to archaeology, valuable 'old' ideas have been
cast aside or largely ignored even if they are connected only tangentially to
a discarded framework. It is in this context that I will introduce structuralist anthropologist Mary Douglas's Cultural Theory or 'grid/group' theory;
this tool has the potential to help us see how ancient peoples saw the world
around them, and by extension, how they saw themselves.

Although identity in general has led to much spilt ink in archaeological
circles, the identity of the Late Iron Age/Early Roman (LIA/ER) inhabitants of Britain in particular has been under much scrutiny and theorisa-
tion. Archaeologically, however, the concept of identity is a thorny one;

contemplating the identities of people long dead based on the materials that survived the intervening centuries or millennia is ever fraught with difficulty. Some have gone as far as to suggest that this branch of investigation is itself a dead end: 'Identity is beyond the reach of archaeology' (Brather 2002: 174). Yet Roymans' definition of identity as an impermanent result of 'developing collective self-images, attitudes, and conduct' (2004: 2) hints strongly that glimpsing ancient worldview may be a way into ancient identities. One important aspect of 'attitude and conduct' relates to the demarcation of space in public and private realms.

Public and private space

The forms of structure which people create are a reflection of multiple factors: the tangible, such as the availability of suitable materials, and the intangible, such a taste, choice, and social conventions. People constructing buildings and enclosures are 'informed by cultural knowledge and they act within cultural constraints' (Wilk 1990: 35). How far can we understand these cultural constraints by examining the remains of structure in LIA/ER Britain, at a time when traditional single-room roundhouses were being transitioned into rectilinear, multichambered structures? Let us first consider the possible ramifications of changing architectural styles.

The Hindi word for room *kamra* originates from the Portuguese *camara*. Prior to the introduction of loan words into the Hindi language there was no immediate mechanism for expressing a permanent, integral partitioning of a domestic structure. Buildings such as the Mughal forts and even provincial domestic dwellings in rural areas today make use of only one solid wall structure, the external walls. Interior divisions are either non-extant in smaller residences, or when privacy *is* called for, partitioned by use of hanging carpets, blankets or moveable screens. Thus the public and private domains of the dwelling are highly mutable and this hints at the ability to experience a multiplicity of public and private identities within a fixed setting.

One might extrapolate this example to the LIA roundhouse, in which often very little is known about internal division and yet one can infer from the assemblages of materials often found on floor surfaces that there was some sort of sub-division of use of space. This has been explored archaeologically through both cosmological and sociological lenses (Hingley 1989; 1991; Pearson and Richards 1994; Gilesand Parker Pearson 1999). Later, when Roman building traditions are more firmly embraced this flexibility in internal division and use of space and identity is lost and becomes quite literally cast in stone. Thus the location of rooms and the access allowed to separate permanent rooms becomes the chief way of maintaining the public/private dichotomy within the familial and domestic setting.

It would be wrong to assume that there was a totally linear evolution in the architectural design of domestic structures in Britain;[1] evidence from some locations around the island suggest that the tradition of circular construction, both in timber and in stone, lasted unchanged in some places well into the third and perhaps fourth centuries. In general, however, these are exceptions to the rule, but it is precisely these variations in practice that attract interest and present the opportunity for Cultural Theory to be used.

Going back to the Hindi linguistic example, there is, prior to the domestication of foreign loan words in the relatively recent period, no word for *privacy*, *private*, or *to make private*. Proximal words *gopnīyatā* and *nijī* exist but they carry within them negative connotations, suggesting sneakiness, deceit, or malevolence in the desire to keep something hidden, rather than any innocent or integral desire to have privacy. These dyads – public and private, hidden and exposed, sneaky and honest – deserve exploration. Simply assuming prehistoric communities viewed privacy as we do today, or even as their Classical world contemporaries did, will not suffice. Rippengal (1996: 69–70) suggests that a major reason for the difference between the Iron Age structures and the Roman-influenced ones is the differing worldview held by the two. He describes the division as falling

---

1   Mattingly (2006: 368–9) suggested that the number of later roundhouses were likely underestimated, based on unexcavated cropmarks of rural sites. It may be that round remained a more common architectural template well into the second century and beyond.

between nature and culture and that the very construction of the house becomes a symbol of the natural world against 'modern' innovation.

Thus in this frame, the Iron Age roundhouse demonstrates what in the current vernacular is described as 'architectural honesty'; that is, it conceals nothing about its components. The roundhouse is organic in shape, built in materials that come from life and have themselves a 'lifespan'. These round-houses were impermanent structures, 'rapidly and inevitably subject to all the natural processes of decay and degeneration' (Rippengal 1996: 69); to this I would also add regeneration. The rebuilding of roundhouses on or adjacent to the sites of identical precursors may suggest a birth-death-rebirth cycle for some structures (Harding 2009: 278–9; Webley 2007).

Contrast this with the construction of the rectilinear, Roman-inspired buildings. Timber is disguised under layers of plaster and paint, stone is used for many faces and supports. Roofs are clad not in natural reed thatch-ing but in baked terracotta or stone tiles. Interior walls are put up, hiding routine activities and natural earth floors are replaced with rammed chalk or mortar. Even indoor heating comes not from an open, honest central hearth fire, but instead rises unseen from hidden underground chambers through flues (Rippengal 1994: 94–5).

Clarke (1998: 35) decries these observations as romantic and accuses Rippengal of resurrecting the noble savage myth by relating 'honesty' to the open and organic nature of the Iron Age home. I cannot speak for Rippengal's intentions when remarking on these dichotomies, but for me, they present a very clear opposition in worldview which works well with the social structures suggested by grid/group typology. That they may be romantically phrased may not make them any less true.

Understanding worldview

At this point, the concept of worldview should be defined, as it will feature prominently in subsequent discussion. A worldview – or *eine Weltanschauung* as Kant put it – (Naugle 2002: 59), is a concept enveloping one's beliefs and impressions which allow one to make sense of the world around us and to figure out how to act accordingly in it. The definition has been expanded upon over time, and now is generally understood to be 'an all-encompassing philosophy of life, composed of a personal or a social ideology' (ibid. 64).[2] The Oxford English Dictionary defines worldview as a 'set of fundamental beliefs, values, etc., determining or constituting a comprehensive outlook on the world; a perspective on life'. This can be understood as a concept of the world held by either an individual or a group and it is in the spirit of this definition that the term will be used in the following chapters.

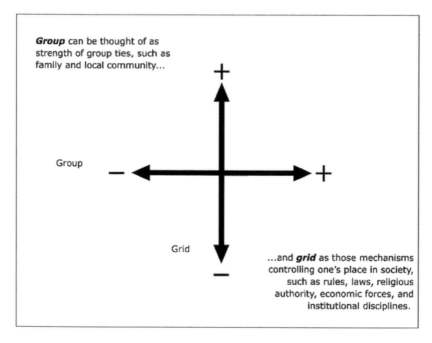

Figure 4.1: The Grid Group Relationship. (Image: author.)

2   For comprehensive review of the uses of Weltanschauung and 'worldview' in phi-losophy, sociology and theology, see Naugle 2002; Naugle's purpose, however, is to advance an argument for appropriating the terms for use in the Christian Evangelical movement.

In trying to compare the conditions for the existence of different kinds of worldviews, Douglas (1970; 1982b; 1999; 2003) developed a matrix model, called grid/group (Figure 4.1). The grid axis of the matrix inversely corresponds to the degree of autonomy an individual has over the selection of their role(s) in society – the 'dimension of individuation' (Douglas 1982a: 190). For example, gender or age may restrict an individual to a limited set of social roles. A high-grid position indicates that there social roles are rigidly fixed; a low-grid position designates a society where individuals have more freedom to choose their social roles. As the grid decreases, one can expect boundaries to become increasingly weak, and subject to arbitration among increasingly competitive individuals (McLeod 1982: 138).

The group dimension is connected with an individual's commitment to their community, what Douglas describes as the degree of social incorporation (ibid.). Individuals in the high-group position are tightly bonded by loyalty to others in the group (and the notion of the group itself); low-group individuals are more 'free agents' and 'there may be little cohesion between the actors and a limited sense of interdependence' (Linsley and Shrives 2009: 501).

Ultimately, the grid/group matrix forms four distinct cultural groups, or worldviews: individualists, egalitarians, hierarchists and fatalists (Figure 4.2). In its simplest terms, grid/group offers possible answers to the questions 'Who am I?' and 'What can I do?' (Tansey and O'Riordan 1999: 78). Given that identity has been described as a multi-dimensional classification, or mapping, of the world and one's place in it – 'who's who, and what's what' (Jenkins 2008: 5) – it becomes obvious that the grid/group matrix can offer some insight. Below I will describe their characteristics in brief, although only two types are pertinent for the case study in this chapter.

E – Egalitarian (weak grid, strong group)

> Ideally this group has little or no internal differentiation. All members have equal say over the decisions taken by the group.[3] With no strong voice, internal conflicts are rarely resolved with ease. Self-regulation in the group exists by threat of expulsion – no

---

3 However, it is understood 'that so-called egalitarian societies are rife with inequalities' (Sassaman 2010: 171).

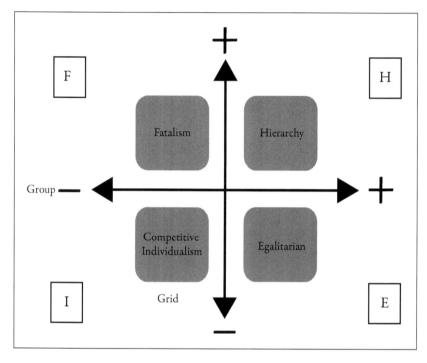

Figure 4.2: Grid Group 'Worldviews'. (Image: author.)

one has the authority to make laws or mandates. Due to the seriousness of the only mechanism for discipline, disagreements are often internalised and hidden, leading to factionalism and splitting. Group boundaries and membership are strongly defined. (e.g. a commune)

H – Hierarchy (strong grid, strong group)

This group is defined by strong group boundaries and a rigid system of rules and social controls. Everyone knows his place within the social order and there is loyalty to the group regardless of station within it. Tiered authority allows for a variety of disciplinary options, allowing for easy resolution of internal conflict. (e.g. an Edwardian household)

I – Individualist (weak grid, weak group)

Individuals in this type of community have very weak bonds holding them as a collective and loyalties can shift rapidly. The rule of the day is opportunism, with each individual succeeding or failing by their own merit. Controls are also weak, although there may be several individuals at any time vying for overall influence of the remainder. (e.g. a 'Big Man' society)

F – Fatalist (strong grid, weak group)

Fatalists fall outside of any true group identity but unlike Individualists, they are controlled from outside their sphere of influence. There are strong restrictions on behaviour and there may be very little personal choice permitted in their lives. (e.g. a prison population)

Technically, the zero-point – the nodal confluence of the diagram – is the realm of the individual who neither exerts control over others, nor is controlled himself. He exists without group affiliation and without any imposition of rules. This space is occupied by the Hermit/Recluse. However, this category is usually exempted from applications of Cultural Theory either because of the rarity of the condition or because it is too difficult to comprehend the worldview of total social withdrawal.[4]

Douglas postulated that communities inhabiting each quadrant of the matrix had reached a consensus (subject to change) 'about the best kind of society to live in' and 'about the good life and right behaviour' (1982b: 7). Can we see this 'consensus' (and for consensus, read 'choice') in the detritus left behind in the archaeological record? Figure 4.3 shows how archaeological observations may suggest the quadrant with which a community most closely aligns.

In a sense, high grid/low grid and strong grid/weak grid are every bit as much binary pairs as inner/outer and savage/civilised; the utility of Cultural Theory is that by placing these two binary pairs in a matrix, far more variation and room for nuance is permitted. Holistic assemblages from individual sites can be used in order to create polythetic classifications of sites. Polythetic classification 'identifies classes by a combination of characteristics, not requiring any one if the defining features to be present in all members of a class' (Douglas 1982a: 200–1). Only a majority of possible

---

4   But see Thompson et al. (1990: 29–33) and Mitleton-Kelly (2004: 14–23) for a less fleeting sociological treatment of the Hermit.

representatives need be present in each case, which softens the edges of the
dichotomy. One thing to keep in mind – in no sense was Cultural Theory
ever meant to be the definitive answer to all questions about social structure. Humans, separately or collectively, are far too complex to be stuffed
into a box; at any given time, Douglas writes, 'all four types [of cultural
bias/worldview are] competing with one another' (1999: 96). With this
caution, we can begin to think about interpreting site assemblages through
the lens of the matrix. For the following case study, we will primarily be
looking at domestic cooking/eating assemblages.

An example from Roman Britain

There are many reasons for examining the preparation of food and drink,
and the consumption visible through ceramics, and to a lesser extent,[5]
the glass vessel assemblage, in order to think about the worldviews of
their users. Consumption can be a symbolic action, with goods becoming
either more or less desirable based upon the role they play in a 'semiotic
landscape' (Gell 1986: 110). The LIA/ER transition is a time when many
new methods and materials were widely being introduced for the average
consumer, and these goods will have had great impact on the choices made
in daily dining practices. The worldview of the consumer must come into
play when interpreting the success or failure of a new object to thrive in
a new environment.

In the attempt to understand the social dynamics connected to consumption, the best place to look is household behaviour (Blanton 1994: 197).
The introduction of new ceramic forms, as well as new cooking and dining

---

5   A lesser extent, not because of lesser utility but rather that vessel glass for this period
     so rarely survives in any meaningful quantities or condition in the archaeological
     record.

practices has the potential for disrupting societal structure (Pred 1986). One consideration is the location of where the ceramic material was being used and where the cooking was carried out. Cooking at the front of the house, near an entrance increases the potential for the activity to be observed by outsiders as suggested by the evidence from in the Low Countries and Germany, whereas in Denmark indications are that the cooking was conducted at the more private rear of the structure (Webley 2002: 298). If visibility were desired, this might have repercussions for how open one might be to changes in architectural design, unless some accommodation for cooking in plain sight could be made. Ethnographic examples exist for the great importance of knowing who made the food, such as among the Brahmins of India (Karve 1962: 22). Public or private prejudices are expressed through cooking, eating, and drinking: drinks may be for strangers, meals may be more intimate (Douglas 1972a: 65). To share a drink can occur anywhere; to partake in a prepared meal suggests the intrusion of those outside the home into the intimacy of the living space.

The site of Claydon Pike, in rural Gloucestershire, England, presents a settlement with a long occupation from the middle Iron Age through to the post-Roman period. In the examination of the LIA and ER settlement phases, one sees a major shift from circular architecture to rectilinear, a change that seems to have occurred around the latter half of the first century AD. An aisled building (B1 – Figure 4.5) measuring nearly 19m in length, was erected directly over the site most likely to have served as a domestic focus in the LIA. Indeed, one may speculate from the relatively loose chronology that the aisled buildings may have been co-existent with the scanty evidence for domestic structures hinted at by Gully 506, and Gully 1645 (in black, Figure 4.4). Its associated finds suggest an interior of some sophistication, with a fragment of painted wall plaster and some window glass recovered. As neither a floor surface nor any internal structure to indicate divisions remained, only concentrations of material can suggest the internal layout. The northern end of the building had a greater concentration of animal bones suggesting specialised use of that area.

	Egalitarian	Individualist	Hierarchist	Fatalist
Boundaries	Boundaries are significant and may often be reconfigured	Boundaries are few and sporadic; if present, they fluctuate frequently	Physical boundaries may exist; social boundaries are more effective	Boundaries are significant and may change capriciously
Ritual activity	Cosmology reflects scapegoating/witchcraft; purity and cleansing are required	Cosmology reflects a pragmatic view; rituals may be spontaneous and idiosyncratic	Cosmology reflects structure; routinised traditions and sacrifices	Cosmology reflects a 'millennial/end-of-the-world' bias; ritual activity may not occur
Personal display – body	Bodily differentiation of the individual is limited; few items of personal adornment	Bodily differentiation of the individual may occur; other avenues of display may take precedence or replace personal adornment.	Bodily differentiation of the individual through adornment is common; sumptuary rules may regulate ornamentation	Bodily differentiation of the individual through adornment is rare; symbolic systems are unelaborate
Personal display – feasting/dining	Decoration on tableware is uncommon; imports and exotic ingredients rare	Openness to exotic foodstuffs and materials to enhance competitive displays; tableware may be decorated	Decoration is common; imported materials may be present or imitated where they integrate with routinised symbolic display	Decoration is rare; access to imports or exotic foodstuffs is highly limited
Storage of resources	Surpluses are not obvious; all resources held in common	Surpluses are acquired by individuals for competitive feasting and/or gifting	Group orientated goals allow for surpluses to be acquired and held by authority	Storage of surplus not observed;

Zonation of space	Enclosures are not subdivided; no evidence of specialisation	Space is not normally divided, however may be divided to provide competitive arenas; specialisation is frequent	Space is frequently divided; zonation regulates activities	Enclosures are subdivided; specialism is not observed
Treatment of 'exotic' material	May be used in ritual 'cleansing' deposition	May be used to enhance competitive gifting networks	May be used to supplement/complement existing symbols of rank within the collective	May not be offered due to exclusion; may be rejected based on voluntary withdrawal
View of the natural world (after Thompson et al. 1990)	Nature[6] is ephemeral and has negative effects to be countered	Nature is benign and has positive effects to be taken advantage of	Nature is perverse/tolerant and has positive effects if placated	Nature is capricious and has negative regardless of behaviour
Attitudes to risk	Oppose risks that will inflict irreversible dangers on the group	Entrepreneurial; will risk new ventures to achieve success	Will risk new encounters if advised by experts/authorities	Ignores risk; neither seeks out opportunity nor avoids risk

Figure 4.3: Alignment to Grid Group Options. The italics indicate archaeological visibility. (Table: author.)

6   Thompson and others use the term *nature*, although it is acknowledged that this concept may have modern Western and romantic overtones. *Cosmos* might be a term to define 'that which is beyond direct human control and predictability', but I choose to retain *nature*.

As most of the pottery comprised flagons, cups, bowls, dishes, and mortaria, perhaps it can be surmised that this was a dining area. Structure B2, an apparent westerly extension to B1, was related to pit 2526, which contained equally large amounts of animal bone as well as a ceramic assemblage more in keeping with cooking – jars were by far the more dominant with flagons, dishes and cups in smaller numbers. Given this evidence, the food preparation area can be seen to have been kept distinctly separate from the dining. Dining may be viewed as a public activity; with the cooking removed from prying eyes, the methods of food preparation then enter the realm of the private.

With regards to the local 'native' fabrics, there appears to be a clear preference for either the early 'Belgic' fabrics or their locally produced Roman-influenced equivalents. It would seem that when the LIA fabrics drifted out of production, they were replaced at Claydon Pike by reduced coarseware, of which nearby North Wiltshire and Savernake origins were favoured, hinting at a preference for local production over imports (Booth 2007: 132).

Likewise, the preferred forms of containers remained largely unchanged across the LIA/ER transition (Figure 4.6), with the only noticeable shift being a slight increase in dishes, commensurate with a slight decrease in jars. In either case, the dominance of locally produced wares during the first century suggests *openness* to new materials and dining practices, but *preference* for the traditional.

The northern area of the site depicted in Figure 4.4 (which saw the least intense domestic settlement and may have served more as a functional space for animal paddocking and metalwork) had a higher concentration of LIA preferred fabrics, where the more intensely occupied southern half showed a dominance of the fabrics that continued to be popular in the ER period (Meadows 2001: 222). Noting that the north produced more amphorae and fewer personal adornment objects than the south, which seemed to show preference for adornment and mortaria, Meadows suggested personal preference between different households, although also allowing that the apparent differentiation might be representative of change over time.

Either way, she believed that the evidence showed a presence of 'Roman-like' objects on the site prior to the ER reorganisation of the site

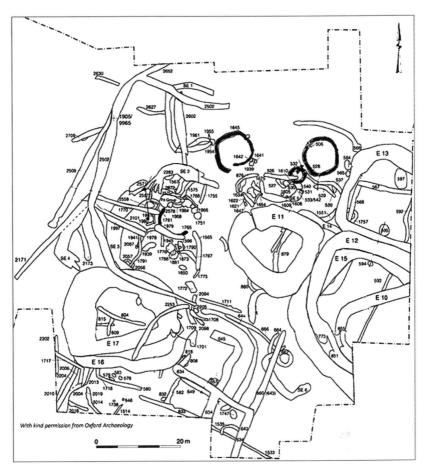

Figure 4.4: Iron Age phases of occupation. The darkened rings indicate probable domestic structures. (Reproduced by permission of Oxford Archaeology.)

(ibid. 226). This may have been two different LIA households, living in equality, only with different preferences for what things to eat or use. An alternative explanation may be that the southern area represented a place of communal aggregation whilst the northern area was the actual dwelling and working spaces of individuals. This tradition may have continued even after the adoption of new building techniques, as the ceramic evidence in

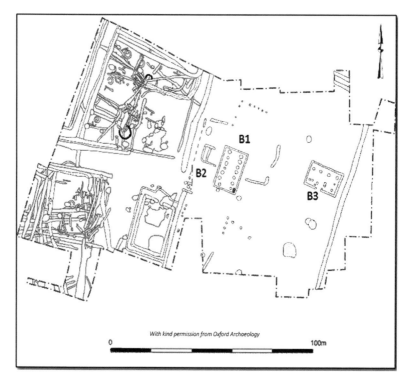

Figure 4.5: Early Roman phases of occupation. (Reproduced by permission
of Oxford Archaeology.)

building B1 indicates feasting and food preparation whilst the other areas
are dominated by jars (ibid. 212).

The actual sherd count for Samian ware, an apparently highly prized
ornate tableware, recovered from the earlier phase is surprisingly low (Miles
et al. 2007: 79) yet of the sherds recovered, less than 6 per cent were from
decorated vessels. This has been interpreted as either as a choice driven by
a form of religious austerity or 'a reflection of the relative poverty of this
rural site' (Webster 2007: CD-ROM section 3.2.3). Given other evidence
(too numerous to detail for the purposes of this chapter) that Claydon
Pike was in fact a thriving and wealthy community, this seems to be a false

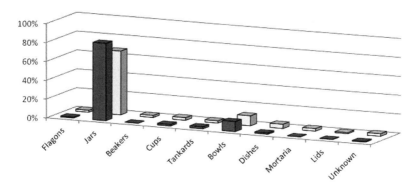

Figure 4.6: Comparison of forms from LIA (dark) and ER
(light) phases. (Image: author.)

line of speculation. Certainly the choice of plain bowl is markedly different from many similar contemporary sites in the region, but this is likely
saying more about the choices of the inhabitants than about their lack of
purchasing power.

In her analysis of the food containers, Meadows observed that the
Roman-style vessels in use at Claydon Pike were not so much related to
serving as they were to 'the flavouring of food' (2001: 248). With mortaria more frequently recovered than cups and beakers, it seems likely that
preparing food with new ingredients was perhaps more important than
serving and eating that food from new tableware. Although Meadows
argued that food prepared with elaboration was a marker for wealth, it
may not be necessary to think of the addition of olive oil and wine to the
local gastronomy as a technical elaboration. Indeed, what may be visible
at Claydon Pike may be the LIA version of a modern Westerner eating
Chinese takeaway with a fork and knife – the ingredients may be imported,
but the tableware comfortably familiar.

If we look at the evidence, through the 'cultural bias' matrix, we could
perhaps have two majorly divergent views of Claydon Pike:

- a strict hierarchy with the LIA peasants living in the northern part of the central site and the owner in the southern part, where domestic evidence suggests
  a more variety of materials (Rippengal 1996: 203; Meadows 2001: 233). By the

early Roman period, the southern dwelling(s) are replaced by rectangular buildings where the affluent residents drink wine from beakers and eat foods with
Roman flavours while their inferiors drink beer from tankards in more humble
and traditional structures.

- a broadly egalitarian community where display is secondary to the prosperity
  of the farm. A lack of storage pits or four post structures may suggest imported
  grain held in a common store, a function of building B3 by the early Roman
  phase. Building B1 and its LIA predecessor may have been communal areas
  where members of the community gathered for feasting and deliberation, perhaps even from neighbouring farmsteads. Wealth of the site is attested to by the
  pre-conquest access to imported foodstuffs, but tableware is distinctively local
  in form and fabric.

Although by the late third and fourth centuries, Claydon Pike is clearly
hierarchical, with a 'proper' small villa and lesser 'cottage-type' buildings
as well as a demarcated cemetery (Miles et al. 2007: 169–84), the above
summaries illustrate that from the LIA to the mid-second century the
picture of social structure is less clear. The overall assemblages indicate
a conservative rural society, a definition in keeping with either scenario.
Can we determine which might be more correct? This is where Cultural
Theory can help shed light.

That the settlement falls to the right of the group line in the matrix
is clear; carefully delineated boundaries can be the first signs of outlining
a group identity. The settlement not only used enclosures and ditches to
mark out 'us' from 'not us' but a gated entryway to the settlement was also
constructed. It is unlikely from the evidence that this gateway and the
related fencing was in any way intended to provide defence from a physical threat; rather it helped to identify who belonged and who didn't in a
manner suggesting defence from cosmological threat.

If we concede that this site falls to the right in the group category, where
might it reside on the grid axis? Douglas wrote that 'grid is visible in the
physical signs of discriminated rank, such as food or clothing' (1982a: 192).
At Claydon Pike in the LIA/ER period there is little evidence for this
type of discrimination. Low grid communities exhibit little in the way of
organisation. Apart from the organisation imposed by the geology (forcing settlement to remain in the gravel islands rising out of the marsh) and
the provision of boundaries, organisation of space seems without rigid

regulation. There is no apparent designated location for middening of waste or for treatment of the dead in this period (Meadows 2001: 223). Access to all aspects of life in the settlement seems to have been free of limitation based upon any sumptuary basis.

Habitation occurring in the 'domestic zone' in the LIA was replaced by B1; if we can speculate that B1 was contemporary with roundhouses at 565 and 1645 (black rings in Figure 4.4), then looking at the rest of the evidence from animal bone and the food containers begins to create a picture. Perhaps that area marked a location for communal eating in the LIA, of the kind described Diodorus Siculus (V.28), and was still performing that function in the ER period, albeit under a new Romano-British style roof. The aisled hall now becomes the aggregation point for the people who live and work on the farm, and perhaps even neighbouring farms as well. Dining may have taken place in the northern part of the building, based on the concentration of finds; not long after the aisled hall is built, an extension to the building is required, in the form of a specialised kitchen area (B2). The aisled building may not be so much the high status home of the owner, as the 'village hall' serving all the residents of the farming community and on occasion, entertaining visitors from further afield who provided the farm with business. The public consumption of Roman-style foods eaten may be seen to have its counterpoint in the 'traditional' use of materials and methods conducted out of site privately in the kitchen wing. Douglas observed that 'ostentatious hospitality is a feature of a low-grid ethnography' (1982a: 197) and if such hospitality was occurring, yet within a largely unaltered traditional framework, then it would seem that Claydon Pike in the LIA/Early Roman period could be placed within the lower right hand corner of the grid-group matrix – designation Type 'E'.

Discussion

Economic theories can tell us how the people of Britain got the materials that they wanted; Cultural Theory can help explain why they may have wanted them. Asking this question allows us to contemplate the worldview of the people being studied. The archaeologist can utilise the relationship between choice and ways of life (Giddens' *lifeworlds*: Scott 2007: 83) by inverting the 'means-end reasoning chain' (Thompson et al. 1990: 57); that is, rather than deducing preferences from ways of life, we can begin to speculate about ways of life based upon preferences. Giddens (1984: 12–13) and Merton before him (1936) maintained that unintended consequences play a key role in social organisation; in forming social structures, individuals make any number of commitments, both by design and in unanticipated ways. Yet whilst 'preferences emerge as unintended consequences of attempting to organise social life in a particular way' (Thompson et al. 1990: 57), this should not be seen as a way of relegating choice-making to the realm of the unconscious. If preference formation is unintended, acting upon those preferences or deliberately changing them is not. If preferences can be patterned from the structure of the social organisation, then the inverse relationship should be explored. However, if predetermined (even unintended) preferences seem to eliminate the free will of the agent, one should not forget that the act of *choosing* is still very much embodied in the individual; one is free to capitulate to ones preferences or to redefine or disguise oneself by changing those preferences.

In truth, the binary pair is sometimes *not* particularly useful, most notably in the now-abandoned savage/civilised model of 'Romanized' Britain. Yet another pair is used in nearly every discussion of LIA and Roman archaeological sites – high status/low status. The label 'high status' still carries with it all the colonial baggage of Romanization, suggesting a betterment of life and happiness that could only be achieved with the accumulation of Roman things. We can, from our modern Western-world perspective, appreciate that high status equates to having indoor heating and decorated Samian dishes. Yet what if this perspective is not the same as the worldview held by those living in Britain in the first centuries BC and AD?

If we can deduce social structure from choices, this has real potential archaeologically, where often all that remains are the fragments of material choices. After discovering *what* people have chosen, we can use Cultural Theory to explore *why* they may have chosen it.

Bibliography

Adams, D. (1979). *The Hitchhiker's Guide to the Galaxy*. London: Pan Books.

Blanton, R. E. (1994). *Houses and Households: A Comparative Study*. New York: Plenum Press.

Booth, P. (2007). 'The Pottery'. In D. Miles, S. Palmer, A. Smith and G. P. Jones (eds), *Iron Age And Roman Settlement In The Upper Thames Valley: Excavations at Claydon Pike and other sites within the Cotswold Water Park*. Oxford: Oxbow Books: pp. 186–9.

Brather, S. (2002). 'Ethnic Identities as Constructions of Archaeology: The Case of the Alamanni'. In A. Gillett (ed.), *On Barbarian Identity: Critical Approaches to Ethnicity in The Early Middle Ages*. Turnhout: Brepols: pp. 149–75.

Clarke, S. (1998). 'Social Change and Architectural Diversity In Roman Period Britain'. In C. Forcey, J. Hawthorne and R. Witcher (eds), *Proceedings of the Seventh Annual Theoretical Roman Archaeology Conference*. Oxford: Oxbow Books: pp. 28–41.

Douglas, M. (ed.) (1970). *Witchcraft, Confessions, and Accusations*. London: Routledge.

Douglas, M. (1972a). 'Deciphering a Meal'. *Daedalus* 101(1): pp. 61–81.

Douglas, M. (1972b). 'Symbolic Orders in the Use of Domestic Space'. In P. J. Ucko, R. Tringham and G. W. Dimbleby (eds), *Man, Settlement and Urbanism*. London: Duckworth: pp. 513–21.

Douglas, M. (1982a). *In the Active Voice*. London: Routledge and Kegan Paul.

Douglas, M. (ed.) (1982b). *Essays in the Sociology of Perception*. London: Routledge and Kegan Paul.

Douglas, M. (1999). 'Four Cultures: The Evolution of a Parsimonious Model'. *Geojournal* 47: pp. 411–15.

Douglas, M. (ed.) (2003b). *Essays in the Sociology of Perception*. London: Routledge.

Gell, A. (1986). 'Newcomers to the World of Goods: The Muria Gonds'. In A. Appadurai (ed.), *The Social Life of Things: Commodities in Cultural Perspective*. Cambridge: University Press: pp. 110–37.

Giddens, A. (1984). *The Constitution of Society: Outline of the Theory of Structuration*. Berkley, CA: University of California Press.

Giles, M., and Parker Pearson, M. (1999). 'Learning to Live in the Iron Age: Dwelling and Praxis'. In B. Bevan (ed.), *Northern Exposure: Interpretative Devolution and the Iron Ages in Britain*. Leicester: University Press: pp. 217–31.

Harding, D. W. (2009). *The Iron Age Round-House*. Oxford: University Press.

Hingley, R. (1989). *Rural Settlement in Roman Britain*. London: Seaby.

Hingley, R. (1991). 'The Romano-British Countryside: The Significance of Rural Set-
    tlement Forms'. In R. F. J. Jones (ed.), *Roman Britain: Recent Trends*. Sheffield:
    J. R. Collis Publications: pp. 75–80.

Hodder, I. (1986). *Reading the Past*. Cambridge: University Press.

Jenkins, R. (2014). *Social Identity*. London: Routledge.

Karve, I. (1962). 'On The Road: A Maharashtrian Pilgrimage'. *The Journal of Asian
    Studies* 22(1): pp. 13–29.

Linsley, P. M., and Shrives, P. J. (2009). 'Mary Douglas, Risk and Accounting Failures'.
    Critical Perspectives on Accounting 20(4): pp. 492–508.

Mcleod, K. (1982). 'The Political Culture of Warring States China'. In M. Douglas
    (ed.), *Essays in the Sociology of Perception*. London: Routledge and Kegan Paul:
    pp. 132–61.

Mattingly, D. (2006). *An Imperial Possession: Britain In The Roman Empire,
    54 BC–AD 40*. London: Allen Lane.

Meadows, K. I. (2001). *The Social Context of Eating and Drinking at Native Settlements
    in Early Roman Britain*. Unpublished PhD Thesis: Sheffield.

Merton, R. K. (1936). 'The Unanticipated Consequences of Purposive Social Action'.
    American Sociological Review 1(6): pp. 894–904.

Miles, D., Palmer, S., Smith, A., and Jones, G. P. (2007). *Iron Age and Roman Settle-
    ment in the Upper Thames Valley: Excavations at Claydon Pike and other Sites
    within the Cotswold Water Park*. Oxford: Oxbow Books.

Mitleton-Kelly, E. (2004). 'The Information Systems Professional as a Hermit: Of
    Plural Rationalities, Information Rejection and Complexity'. *Innovation: The
    European Journal of Social Science Research* 17 (4): pp. 289–323.

Morrison, W. A. (Forthcoming). 'Babies and Bathwater: Why "New" Archaeology
    is not always the Best Solution to Old Problems'.

Naugle, D. K. (2002). *Worldview: The History of a Concept*. Cambridge: W. B.
    Eerdmans.

Pearson, M. P., and Richards, C. (1994). 'Ordering the World: Perceptions of Archi-
    tecture, Space, and Time'. In M. P. Pearson and C. Richards (eds), *Architecture
    and Order: Approaches to Social Space*. London: Routledge: pp. 1–37.

Pope, R. (2007). 'Ritual and the Roundhouse: A Critique of Recent Ideas on the Use
    of Domestic Space in Later British Prehistory'. In C. C. Haselgrove and R. E.
    Pope (eds), *The Earlier Iron Age In Britain And The Near Continent*. Oxford:
    Oxbow Books: pp. 204–28.

Pred, A. R. (1986). *Place, Practice and Structure: Social and Spatial Transformation in
    Southern Sweden, 1750–1850*. Cambridge: Polity Press.

Rippengal, R. (1994). 'Villas as a Key to Social Structure? Some Comments on Recent
    Approaches to the Romano-British Villa, and Some Suggestions towards an

Alternative'. In E. Scott (ed.), *Theoretical Roman Archaeology: First Conference Proceedings*. Avebury: Aldershot: pp. 79–101.

Rippengal, R. (1996). *Romanization, Society and Material Culture: An Archaeological Study of the Significance of Romanization in the Context of Roman Britain*. Unpublished PhD Thesis: Cambridge.

Roymans, N. (2004). *Ethnic Identity and Imperial Power: The Batavians in the Early Roman Empire*. Vol. 10. Amsterdam: University Press.

Sassaman, K. E. (2010). 'Structure and Practice in the Archaic Southeast'. In Robert W. Preucel and Stephen A. Mrozowski (eds), *Contemporary Archaeology in Theory: The New Pragmatism*. Oxford: Wiley-Blackwell: pp. 170–90.

Scott, J. (2007). 'Giddens and Cultural Analysis: Absent Word and Central Concept'. In T. Edwards (ed.), *Cultural Theory: Classical and Contemporary Positions*. London: Sage: pp. 83–105.

Siculus, D. (1989). *Library of History*, translated by C. H. Oldfather, Vol. 5. Cambridge, MA: Loeb Classical Library.

Tansey, J., and O'Riordan, T. (1999). 'Cultural Theory and Risk: A Review'. *Health, Risk and Society* 1(1): pp. 71–90.

Thompson, M., Ellis, R., and Wildavsky, A. (1990). *Cultural Theory*. Boulder, CO: Westview Press.

Webley, L. (2002). *A Social Archaeology of the Iron Age Household: Domestic Space in Western Denmark, 500BC–AD200*. Unpublished PhD Thesis: Cambridge.

Webster, P. V. (2007). 'Samian Ware'. In Miles et al. CD-Rom Section 3.2.3.

Wilk, R. R. (1990). 'The Built Environment and Consumer Decisions'. In S. Kent (ed.), *Domestic Architecture and Use of Space: An Interdisciplinary Cross-Cultural Study*. Cambridge: Cambridge University Press: pp. 34–42.

MATTHEW JENKINS AND CHARLOTTE NEWMAN

5   London in Pieces: A Biography of a Lost Urban Streetscape

ABSTRACT

London's West End in the eighteenth century is frequently regarded as the epitome of urban improvement and Georgianisation. This chapter combines material culture and documentary sources to present a series of building biographies for Tilney Street that imaginatively recreate the physical urban landscapes that modern development has over-ridden. Tilney Street highlights the nuanced nature of Georgian domestic living where, even in the elite location of Mayfair, wealth, social position and up-to-date fashions do not align. This methodology generates biographies about communities and individuals who owned, occupied and visited these buildings at the dawn of modernity. These close-grained biographies explore and critique wider ideas of urban social practices.

The eighteenth century marked a change in material culture constituted by consumer goods, houses, and landscapes. These cultural products were linked to new ways of living, and are interpreted as both expressing and encouraging ideas of order, symmetry and segregation. Academic analysis of eighteenth-century streets and houses is heavily influenced by two major ideas – the 'urban renaissance' and Georgianisation or the Georgian Order thesis. While describing a broadly similar process, the varied terms reflect disciplinary differences, with historians writing about urban improvement and archaeologists writing about Georgianisation (Borsay 1989; Johnson 2010; Deetz 1996). However, both historians and archaeologists frequently focus on the big picture and how these processes play out on a regional or national scale. This paper highlights the value of in-depth, small-scale analyses that enable the investigation of how and if these larger narratives work at ground level (Ginzburg 1993; Lepore 2001). It focuses on one London street: Tilney Street. Populated by fashionable members of polite society, this was a complex landscape, located outside the Grosvenor Estate and the main fashionable hub of Mayfair. The material evidence of the houses is equally complex in terms of their size and level of decoration. Tilney Street highlights the varied nature of both Georgian domestic living and urban improvement.

Through adopting interdisciplinary methodologies, this paper seeks new ways to explore London streetscapes and domestic spaces. The analysis of both urban improvement and the use of domestic interiors in the eighteenth century is largely the province of historians and social geographers (e.g. Stobart et al. 2007; Ogborn 1998; Vickery 2009), with architectural historians and archaeologists rarely contributing to the debate. As a result, these ideas are principally explored without close examination of the material evidence. Welcome recent research includes important contributions by Peter Guillery on the small houses of London and Rachel Stewart on how the town house was implicated in the performance of wider social relations (Guillery 2004; Stewart 2009).

Through collating strands of material culture, most notably English Heritage's Architectural Study Collection (ASC), this paper demonstrates how material culture set within an archaeological theoretical framework can offer a unique opportunity to explore eighteenth- and nineteenth-century housing and illuminate our understanding of architecture, fashions and society in London. The ASC is made up of over 6,000 objects that tell a story of London's historic buildings. Initially started by London County Council's architects' department, collecting began in the early twentieth century at a time of increasing interest in built heritage (Thurley 2013). Consisting of a vast array of fascinating architectural objects, the collection's particular strength is in tracing the development of London homes of the middling classes from the eighteen and nineteenth centuries. Geographically the collection is spread across London to include a huge range of building styles and types, from grand country houses in Hackney to terraces in Mayfair.

Over the past ten years, archaeologists in the UK and USA have developed methods using biography to offer alternative interpretations to historic buildings and associated material culture (Deetz 1998; Lucas 2006; Mytum 2010). In a summary of these approaches, Lucas has highlighted two strands of archaeological biographies (Lucas 2006, 41). The first approach focuses on individual and households biographies, which examines both the minutiae of a particular household and the larger themes drawn from that analysis. The second approach originates in artefact studies that concentrate on the life history of material culture and how the meanings of objects change and are renegotiated over time (Gosden and Marshall 1999). Building biographies allow the researcher to connect buildings with people and to interpret how both house and owner influenced each. Archaeologists have successfully used biographies to inform larger social processes, including how wealth, status and gender relate to material culture. Archaeological biographies enable new connections to be made through the interplay of architectural, archaeological and documentary evidence.

Drawing inspiration from recent scholarship, this paper's approach combines material culture and related documentary records to recreate a London streetscape. This entails the detailed analysis of houses to map the minute changes made to their fabric, form and function, which can be used to shed light on their changing uses and meanings over time. When combined with the study of wills, deeds, maps, newspapers, and photographs, it can be used to generate a series of stories and experiences of the communities and individuals who owned, occupied and visited these buildings in the developing modern era.

By adopting a methodology that focuses on the integration of different data sets, this research aims to create a series of building biographies for Tilney Street that contribute a new perspective to the study of built London and its residents. Creating a close-grained narrative for the communities and individuals who owned, occupied and visited these buildings, this approach is employed to challenge the over-arching narratives that dominate the humanities' understanding of early modern cities and explore and critique wider ideas of urban social practices.

A London streetscape: Discovering Tilney Street

Tilney Street, initially Tinley Row, forms part of a complex pattern of development in Mayfair. It lies outside the Grosvenor Estate, with Grosvenor Square approximately 400 yards (388m) away up South Audley Street

(Figure 5.1). Created between 1749 and 1750, Tilney Street first appears in the rate books in 1751 (SOL Nos 1–4 Tilney Street). The ad hoc nature of development immediately around Tilney Street meant houses were constructed in a piecemeal fashion at odds with Georgian regularity. The plots are relatively shallow, varied in shape and size, and plots 1–3 could not feature a garden. Although constructed in the mid-eighteenth century in the 'Georgian' style, these houses were later greatly remodelled.

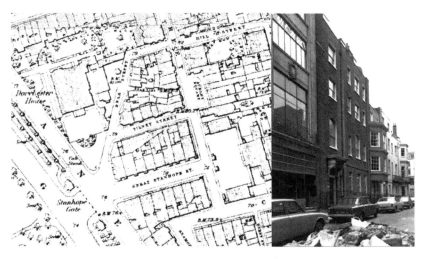

Figure 5.1: Left: 1878 OS map centred on Tilney Street (© and database right Crown Copyright and Landmark Information Group Ltd (All rights reserved 2016) Licence numbers 000394 and TP0024); Right: street view of Tilney Street facing west, illustrating Nos 1–3 (London Metropolitan Archives, City of London).

Tilney Street is a significant streetscape. In 1981, Nos 1–3 Tilney Street were added to the statutory list of buildings of special architectural or historical interest. Despite this listing, by 1986 the houses had been vacant for twelve years due to structural defects (SOL Nos 1–4 Tilney Street). In 1987, refurbishments took place and items were salvaged from Nos 1–4. In total, ninety-three objects, mostly fixtures and fittings, were removed to the ASC. The Historic England archive also contains detailed interior photographs for several other properties. In 1986, shortly after refurbishment works, 2, 3 and 4 Tilney Street collapsed, preventing any additional salvage work (ibid.). However, when combing these objects and photographs with documentary and cartographic evidence it is possible to virtually reconstruct these vanished houses and create biographies of the buildings and their inhabitants. Crucially, this research and reconstruction enables an examination of Tilney Street within the context of Mayfair, offering a lens to investigate important wider themes including urban improvement and domestic living.

A social context: Tilney Street and Mayfair

The West End is often viewed as the epitome of improved eighteenth-century urban space. Mayfair allowed for a clean slate with a landscape unhindered by older houses and street formations (Stillman 1988: 215). Grosvenor Square led the way with a new form of urban living, with the Old Bailey Online (<http://www.oldbaileyonline.org/static/London-life18th.jsp>) emphasising the 'consistent, stuccoed facades, and regulated, privatised green spaces' (anon, nd). London and particularly the West End are perceived as models for urban improvement and developments in the provinces. Peter Borsay suggests classical architecture created a uniform aesthetic. When combined with regular, wide and straight roads, this had the effect of 'ordering and "civilising"' the urban landscape (Borsay 1989: 74). Sarah Tarlow (2007: 93) notes that in the second half of the eighteenth century, England's principal cities created new streets almost universally embraced the classical style. This 'ordering' of the street is seen as beginning in London (Tarlow 2007: 105; Girouard 1990: 158). While Borsay argues that cultural ideas could flow into London as well as out of it, he acknowledges the great influence of the capital and specifically singles out London's 'fashionable West End' as the original point for the square, the centrepiece of this new form of urban landscape (Borsay 1989: 75).

It should be noted that many of these accounts do not take London as a focus and studies of improvement are focused on national and regional studies rather than detailed consideration of the capital (e.g. Borsay 1989; Stobart et al. 2007). Through-provoking recent work has also started to explore the diversity in the appearance of streets and neighbourhoods and the possibilities for transgression (Stobart et al. 2007: 97; Tarlow 2007: 120; Ogborn 1998: 91). Sweet has also analysed the complex relationship between politeness and urban renewal (Sweet 2002). However, an emphasis on order and regulation is still the dominant scholarly model when considering urban improvement, an order and regulation that is challenged when the physical evidence is considered in detail. This model downplays the variety of inhabitants and buildings within this new classical landscape, even in Mayfair, the apogee of improvement. The social elite were concentrated in the area around Grosvenor Square, radiating east along Brook Street and Grosvenor Street and west along their Upper equivalents (Sheppard 1977: 83–6). However, the SoL suggests the area contained a wide variety of inhabitants, including both gentry and tradesmen, who themselves encompassed a range of social statuses (ibid.). The SOL goes on to comment that the perception that 'this part of Mayfair was the almost exclusive province of the well-to-do and the well-connected is in some respects highly misleading' (ibid. 86). This aspect of the SOL's work is often passed over when urban improvement is considered by scholars.

Although Tilney Street is firmly in Mayfair, its location is somewhat liminal. There were gentry in South Audley Street, but the fashionable inhabitants were in the minority compared to tradesmen. Guillery notes the areas mixed character, stating that in the 1740s the areas south of the estate 'remained sparsely built, inchoate and marginal' (Guillery 2004: 74). Amanda Vickery's use of the term 'genteel' is useful in this context, a term that encompasses lesser landed gentry, established tradesmen and professionals (Vickery 1998: 13). There might be distinctions between them in terms of professions and possession of land, but they often had personal, professional and civic connections even as they shared ideas of taste and material culture (Stobart 2011: 107).

While broadly classical, houses along many of the major streets differed considerably in size and architectural embellishment (Sheppard 1977: 103–9). In the second half of the eighteenth century, uniformity was challenged with fashionable alterations to facades and house plans (ibid. 119–27).

Peter Guillery (2004, 74) emphasises this in his study of London's small houses. Both north of Grosvenor Square and west of Bond Street were very small irregular buildings housing artisans and lower middling shopkeepers. The awkward presence of Francis Tregagle's house on Dean Street, meant that when South Audley Street was extended and Tilney Street created, regular, ordered houses were not possible (SOL Nos 1–4 Tilney Street). The irregularity of the houses is also apparent from the street with No. 4 being 27ft wide, No. 3 being 33ft 6in and No. 2 being a very narrow c. 17ft 3in. The order and regularity indicative of urban improvement were noticeably lacking from Tilney Street. In contrast, Chesterfield House stood on the other side of the road on South Audley Street (Sheppard 1980: 290). It was built from 1748 to 1749 by Sir Isaac Ware (Port 1995: 34) for Philip Dormer Stanhope, the fourth Earl of Chesterfield, who served as a prominent politician and diplomat (ODNB Cannon 2012). In 1845 the *Quarterly Review* described it as 'the magnificent mansion which the Earl erected in Audley Street' in which was 'his spacious and beautiful library, looking on the finest private garden in London' (anon, 1845).

Ladies, earls and spinsters: A story of Tilney Street and its form, function and use

1 Tilney Street

By the late 1980s, the exterior of No. 1 Tilney Street had a stucco finish masking external alternations, but nineteenth-century interior features survived. The ground floor retained a staircase, panelling and dentilled cornices and the first floor featured more elaborate nineteenth-century decoration. At some stage between 1830 and 1835 the rates increased from £120 to £135 (SOL Nos 1–4 Tilney Street). It is possible that during this time a smaller house on the return of Tilney Street was incorporated into No. 1. From No. 1 Tilney Street the collection the ASC holds thirty associated objects, the second highest concentration from the street. Photographs detailing the first-floor interiors also survive. These objects and photographs illustrate decorative schemes, but specific objects groups offer an insight into the use of wall coverings and security measures (Figure 5.2).

Figure 5.2: A: cornice from No. 1 Tilney Street (© English Heritage);
B: first-floor view of No. 3 Tilney Street (London Metropolitan Archives,
City of London); C: cornice from No. 1 Tilney Street (© English Heritage);
D: flock wallpaper removed from No. 1 Tilney Street (© English Heritage).

By the end of the nineteenth century, photographs and ASC objects suggest that the interior had primarily two concurrent styles of decoration. Photographic evidence illustrates a lavish composition of wooden panelling and decorative plaster work with a loose floral design. A sporadic collection of objects were also collected from the first floor. Dating to the 1830s or 1840s, a plaster cornice moulding featuring husks and fruit survives from the first-floor rear room. A dado rail was also recovered from a similar period. Featuring decorative oak leaves and bells, this decorative dado was recovered from the first-floor front room suggesting that a similar decorative theme was maintained throughout the first floor. A section of picture rail was also recovered and most likely removed from the hallway. The rail is particularly elaborate featuring a thick roll top with additional mould details. The density of this picture rail enabled it to hold larger, ornate pictures.

In 1795, Arthur Stanhope took up residence in Tilney Street and the first-floor rooms were most likely designed during his residency. It is possible Stanhope was inspired by the Louis XV style after visiting the French styled interiors of Chesterfield House (SOL Nos 1–4 Tilney Street). The interiors of No. 1 were not unfamiliar Stanhope as he was guardian to his nephew the sixth Earl of Chesterfield (ibid.). Stanhope also had prominent social connections and used Tilney Street to host them. For instance, in 1834 the *Morning Post* (4 March 1834) noted 'The Ho. Arthur Stanhope will give a Grand Diner on Monday next to the Duke of Gloucester, Duke of Wellington, and other illustrious personages, at his house in Tilney-street, Park-lane'. Stanhope and his wife entertained members of the British royal family such as the Duke of Gloucester on several occasions (*Sussex Advertiser* 25 Nov 1833) as well European royalty including 'The Landgravine of Hesse Homberg and the Princess Augusta [who] honoured Mrs Arthur Stanhope with a visit' (*Morning Post*, 27 March 1835). Evidently the rooms of No. 1 Tilney Street were considered appropriate and proper spaces in which to entertain elite society.

The second phase of decoration dates to the second half of the nineteenth century. This scheme was featured in the ground-floor front room and was loosely inspired by seventeenth-century decorative schemes. Particular attention was paid to the ceiling, which assumed a vague Jacobean style. The Jacobean theme is further evident in a surviving thin oak internal door also from the ground floor front room. The side that faced into the room is elaborately decorated, featuring panels forming a linenfold effect. Although now painted white, the door was probably varnished at first to enhance the oak effect. By the mid-nineteenth century, the Stanhopes had left Tilney Street, but their successors were also of note including Colonel Henry Cartwright from 1865 to 1870 and Reginald Brett MP from 1885 to 1894. Evidently these residents required an interior to match their status and that of the guests they would have entertained at No. 1 Tilney Street.

No. 1 is the only house to have associated surviving wallpapers (Figure 5.2D). These papers provide a valuable insight into the occupant's choice of decoration and taste. The first paper is a lavish double flock paper with a distinguished large-scale pattern most likely recovered from a formal room in the house. Dating to the first half of the nineteenth century, the dark bottle-green flock features large abstract floral elements with leaves and scroll work. From the eighteenth century, flock papers were regarded as a high-quality product, associated with luxury and the aristocracy (Hoskins 1994). The double flock effect of this paper added to the luxurious appearance of the house. The second surviving fragment of wallpaper is a laminate featuring four different papers. The simplistic, floral style of these papers suggests they were most likely used in a private female space or a dressing room. The similarities in all four designs further suggests the occupants' clear decision and consistency regarding taste, but with the desire to keep their space fresh and light.

The collection for No. 1 includes an eighteenth-century door and window, which provide an insight into security. Dating to the second quarter of the eighteenth century, the nail-studded door features original iron strap hinges, a handle and a wall bolt attachment. Removed from the basement at the front of the house, it is unsurprising that this door would feature fixtures to improve its security. Through time additional fixtures have been added to improve the doors effectiveness, for example three different bolts and a late nineteenth-century latch have been added at varying stages. The addition of twentieth-century security fittings underlines technical improvements, but that none of the previous methods were removed indicates that new fittings were to improve on existing methods rather than replace them. The phasing of door fixtures implies the owners wished to increase security through time. Such actions may signify a more security conscious society or reflect anti-social issues in the neighbourhood.

No. 1 Tinley Street, provides insights into the decision-making of interior decoration and security. It also, importantly, illuminates the social make-up of the street. For in terms of occupants, Tilney Street was not as marginal as its position and awkwardly constructed housing would suggest. Stanhope was a prominent member of polite society and was also not the only member of the social elite living on Tilney Street. Mrs Fitzherbert, the lawful wife of the Prince of Wales, lived at No. 6 from 1805 until her death in 1837 (ODNB Levy 2012). Mrs Fitzherbert regularly gave prominent balls and routes and a newspaper article from 1806 comments:

> The Route given by Mrs Fitzherbert on Wednesday evening, at her house in Tilney-street, was by far the most splendidly arranged and numerously attended, of any fashionable Gala this season ... Not less than 2000 persons of the first fashion were present. (*Bury and Norwich Post*, 2 April 1806)

4 Tilney Street

A photograph of No. 4 survives from before the collapse showing the building refronted in the art deco style, giving no indication of the original façade (LMA 75/7798). Although no photographs exist for the interior, the ASC contains a high concentration of objects from the house, thirty-nine in total.

The surviving cornices point to three episodes of interior decoration. The initial ornamentation that occurred during the construction of the house from 1749 to 1750, then the first-floor front room was redecorated at the end of the century and then the first-floor back room was restyled at the beginning of the nineteenth century. The dating of the first-floor cornices is based on stylistic grounds. Given their proximity in dates, the cornices could have been constructed at the same time, however the probability is that they were two separate episodes. What is certain is the decision of the various occupiers to redecorate the first floor but leave the ground floor untouched. This decision is consistent with previous work analysing eighteenth-century interiors (Cruickshank and Burton 1990; Jenkins 2013). This work demonstrates the emphasis that was placed by contemporaries on the first floor as the primary venue for entertainment, particularly in narrow-fronted terrace houses. These have only one room facing the street and extend backwards in narrow plot. The dining room was often situated on the ground floor and, while it would be richly decorated, the style of decoration was often old-fashioned (Cruickshank and Burton 1990: 70). The drawing room, which was often situated in the first-floor front room would, in contrast, be 'the height of fashion' (ibid.). Work carried out on

York during the eighteenth century supports this model, with the first
floor containing the finest decoration, followed by the ground floor and
the second floor a distant third with the bare minimum of elaboration
(Jenkins 2013, 50). In practice, this meant that in No. 4 Tilney Street, the
bold projecting cornices enriched with modillions and egg-and-dart that
were fashionable in the middle of the eighteenth century, were still appropriate for the dining room and could be used without the need for updating.

The earliest occupants of No. 4 were Lady Buchan followed by the Earl
of Rosebury (SOL, Nos 1–4 Tilney Street). It was during the occupation of
a Miss Vansittart between 1876 and 1805 that the redecoration of the front
room occurred and her will sheds light on her wealth and status. Susanna
Vansittart was a spinster and she left six thousand pounds of bequests independent of the residue of the estate, in addition to bequeathing jewels to her
sister and two nieces (NA PCC, PROB 11/1338/45). Vansittart was therefore moderately wealthy. She was able to afford the restyling of the front
room and was concerned enough with entertaining to warrant the expense.

The second episode of remodelling probably occurred during the occupation of Thomas Myers who lived there between 1805 and c.1830 (SOL Nos
1–4 Tilney Street). Myers was an MP and, although he was wealthy, when he
died his property was mortgaged to the value of £38,500. He instructed that
this should be cleared through the sale of his property and the balance given
to his children, indicating the high value of his estates (HoP Thorne 1986).

The evidence from No. 4 supports previous research that has explored
the importance of the first-floor front room for entertaining and its relationship to the rest of the house. It also provides insights into the status
of Tilney Street within Mayfair and helps to illuminate how this fits
in with the wide theme of urban living. The surviving decoration for
No. 4 Tilney Street is fine but not exceptional, but like the residents of
No. 1 Tilney Street, this did not prevent the Earl of Rosebury or the MP
Henry Myers from living there.

3 Tilney Street

No. 3 is a more substantial, wider property than No. 4, with a street front-
age of 33ft, but the present structure bears little resemblance to the original

building. The ASC holds one surviving fragment however the building can still be investigated. Photographs were taken before the collapse and include many of the principal interior rooms (Figures 5.2B and 5.3A).

Figure 5.3: A: ground-floor view of No. 3 Tilney Street (London Metropolitan Archives, City of London); B: first-floor dining room of No. 5 Tilney Street (London Metropolitan Archives, City of London); C: hallway from No. 2 Tilney Street (London Metropolitan Archives, City of London); D: drawing room of No. 5 Tilney Street (London Metropolitan Archives, City of London).

The exterior photograph shows a narrow-fronted town house of four storeys with attics (LMA 76/7800). No. 3 lacks some of the fine decoration of later houses in Mayfair and Bloomsbury, but it does have signs of elaboration. It is four bays wide, with the western bay (lighting the stairwell) divided from the rest of the house by a projecting brick pilaster. The windows are elegantly proportioned in accordance with Palladian principals, whereby the height of the windows could vary from three quarters high as wide to twice as high, the latter signalling the prominent rooms for entertaining (Cruickshank and Burton 1990: 139). The ground-floor windows are taller than those on the first floor, which is unusual for a house of the mid-eighteenth century and comparable with No. 3 Chesterfield Street in Mayfair (ibid. 144). The importance of the first floor was increasingly emphasised in the exterior façade of Georgian buildings, with the windows on this floor becoming progressively elongated in the second half of the eighteenth century. Although lacking individual emphasis, the windows above ground level retain typical Palladian proportions. The different elements of the fenestration gave the house an old-fashioned appearance when first built.

There are two interesting aspects of the internal decoration. The first is the use of replicated cornices on both the first and ground floors. As noted previously, cornices usually varied considerably from floor to floor and indeed from room to room. They were used to distinguish and signpost different rooms and the use of space. There are some differences between the ground and first floors which would have ameliorated this and helped to signal the transition to a different space, such as the different dado rails and in particular the fact that the first-floor rooms would have had wallpaper above the dado rails, allowing for greater distinctiveness. Yet the use of identical cornices sets No. 3 apart from the other properties on Tilney Street and indeed goes against the common practice in Georgian interior design (Cruickshank and Burton 1990: 70; Jenkins 2013: 50).

The second noteworthy aspect of the decoration is that the primary decorative features date to the original construction of the house in the middle of the eighteenth century. In the subsequent years, very little was done to update the decoration and to take account of changes in fashion. This is surprising given the evidence from other properties in Tilney Street, which sees investment in accommodating newer fashions applied to particular rooms, especially those that were most frequently used for entertaining such as first-floor drawing rooms. It is notable that the other houses on Tilney Street saw a range of investment during the nineteenth century and this is certainly true of Mayfair as a whole (Sheppard 1977:

119). Even the much narrower property of No. 2, which was ostensibly not as high status as No. 3, saw a variety of alterations and improvements during the nineteenth century, particularly in the latter half.

From 1776 until 1805, the householder was a Miss Clayton (SOL Nos 1–4 Tilney Street). Martha Clayton was a spinster who had formerly lived on Brook Street before moving to Tilney Street (NA PCC PROB 11/1377/241). Her will shows considerable personal wealth, leaving £19,000 in stock and annuities, as well as Exchequer annuities that yielded £84 per annum. The subsequent occupants were even more illustrious, being Lord and Lady Chichester, with Lady Chichester continuing to live at Tilney Street after the death of her husband until her own death in 1813 (NA PCC PROB 11/1545/193). In her will Lady Chichester leaves bequests amounting to just over £11,000. While this does not represent great wealth to a person of aristocratic status, the bulk of the estate went to her eldest son Thomas on the death of her husband the Earl of Chichester in 1805 and she in turn leaves the residue of her estate to her son the current earl. The next occupant was John Vernon Esq, a bachelor who was a lawyer at Lincoln's Inn. The individual legacies are not extensive, amounting to approximately £4,000 but he also leaves a mansion house with an estate in Buckhurst Hill, Berkshire and a bequest of £300 a year (NA PCC PROB 11/1700/271).

The few changes made to the first floor of No. 3 were carried out in the early nineteenth century and this corresponds with both the occupations of Lady Chichester and John Vernon. They were both wealthy and could have afforded more extensive updates and changes to both the exterior elevation and the interior decoration. Yet both chose not to do this. The same disjunction continues through the rest of the nineteenth century, with a continued absence of any substantial modifications coupled with aristocratic occupants, including Viscount Emlyn, Dowager Countess Cawdor and Lady Wharncliffe (SOL Nos 1–4 Tilney Street).

No. 3 highlights the nuanced nature of Georgian domestic living and how, even in the elite location of Mayfair, wealth, social position and up-to-date fashionable interiors do not always perfectly align. Elite members of society could and did refrain from following fashion trends in favour of eclectic tastes to personalise their domestic space. Practice thus differed from precept and the application of Georgianisation was more arbitrary than received wisdom suggests. Tilney Street as a whole seems to have attracted an older demographic and this may partly account for the conservatism of the domestic fixtures and fittings, both in terms of the taste of the occupants and the decreased likelihood of regular entertaining.

5 Tilney Street

Like No. 3, No. 5 (Figures 5.3B and 5.3D) stands out as one of the larger houses on the corner of the street, with a width of just under 37ft. Yet in terms of interior decoration it is similar to Nos 1 and 4, with considerable updating in the late eighteenth and early nineteenth centuries with the decoration used to signify distinctions and divisions between rooms. The façade of the house is rendered and has horizontal rustication on the ground floor with canted bay windows on the western elevation and pedimented windows at first-floor level.

Comparisons in interior décor between Nos 1, 4 and 5 suggests that when these houses were originally constructed they employed similar décor and taste. This indicates that many of the houses on this row of were built by the same speculative builder. However, the inclusion of identical internal decoration is unusual as often just the building shell was sold to the first occupier and it was their responsibility to fit out the interior (Cruickshank and Burton 1990: 117). The entrance hall is unusual in running parallel to the street rather than at right angles, with the ground-floor rooms opening off this to the west. It has an open-string staircase running the full length of the house. The ground floor has a mixture of decorative features dating to different periods. The dining room retained its original decoration, while the staircase hall and parlour were both updated from the original. These interior changes date to the later eighteenth and early nineteenth centuries, possibly the result of two distinct episodes of decoration or one single change.

The first-floor rooms are similar to the parlour, retaining the original panelling, but including later decorative features such as Regency fireplaces. The rooms also feature extra elaboration, including the addition of later eighteenth-century Adam-style plasterwork to the panelling, the architraves and the ceiling. The two back rooms have been connected by a wide opening with Adam-style decoration on the architrave, which is of a distinctly heavier style that the rest of the plasterwork and is likely a later edition. This style of opening is also seen in No. 3 and is a common feature or alteration of the early nineteenth century. There are a number of possible reasons for the popularity of this feature. This was the period that saw the peak of the fashion for routs (Cruickshank and Burton 1990: 46) and the prevalence of these openings may be linked to need to accommodate larger numbers of friends and acquaintances at social gatherings. Alternatively, it may be that the practice of situating the principal bedroom on the first floor started to decline, particularly in narrow-fronted town houses that could only accommodate two rooms to a floor. This is a subtle but still distinct episode in the story of domestic privacy that has been not been discussed in depth before. The drawing room, also situated on the first floor, was no longer considered adequate to host larger gatherings and that ancillary rooms were now necessary. These had always existed but were typically smaller rooms used to host more intimate gatherings (Greig 2006: 116; Jenkins 2013: 237). These smaller rooms were now being amalgamated to create larger spaces and their previous dual function as either boudoirs or bedrooms was set aside. The blurred lines between public and private space that previously existed on the first floors of Georgian town houses starts to disappear and bedrooms are more firmly relegated to the second floor.

The strongest candidates for carrying out the changes are the Englefield family. Lady Englefield lived at No. 5 from c.1780 until c.1790, following the death of her husband the sixth Baronet (SOL Nos 1–4 Tilney Street). Her eldest son, the seventh Baronet, Sir Henry Englefield took over the house and lived there until his death in 1822. The bulk of the alterations to No. 5 coincide with the Englefields' residency, although some of the later changes could have been carried out by the subsequent occupant Lord Yarmouth who lived there until 1835. Yarmouth was an MP and a strong supporter and confidant of the Prince of Wales, the future George IV (ODNB Hochstrasser 2008). Yarmouth had succeeded to the marquessate in 1822, around the time he took up residence in No. 5, supplying him with considerable wealth including over £85,000 per annum (ibid.). The insertion of the opening between the back rooms on the first floor is a likely alteration by Yarmouth. This is a distinctive feature of the early nineteenth century and the elaboration (although in a similar Adamesque style to that in the rest of the house) is much heavier than the light beading employed elsewhere.

In the later eighteenth and early nineteenth centuries, No. 5 was substantially updated. The occupiers chose rooms to improve that reflected the pattern of targeting the spaces used for entertaining, either for more informal, daytime gatherings in the parlour, or the more formal focus of the drawing room. The difference in decoration between floors, highlights the importance placed on the first floor as the most exclusive space for entertaining in the house. Once again, the peripheral location of Tilney Street and the mixed character of housing along the rest of the street did not stop extremely wealthy occupants such as Lord Yarmouth and Sir Henry Englefield from living there.

2 Tilney Street

No. 2 Tilney Street (Figure 5.3C) is markedly different from its neighbours. Almost crowded by Nos 1 and 3, No. 2 is a three-bay, four-storey building, which is dominated by a two-storey canted bay featuring three windows and crowning cornices. The projection is supported from the ground by two columns capped with Corinthian capitals. No. 2 has the least surviving sources but its varied nature does enable us to comment on the building in the context of the street.

The interiors of No. 2 are similar to some of those in No. 1, but not as elaborate. Like No. 1, the first-floor front room features a dado and decorated panels with scroll detailing. The room's focal point is a revived Louis VI style marble fireplace surmounted by a large compo mirror set within the panel scheme. Although decorated, this scheme does not compare to No. 1's more lavish scheme on its first floor. Dating to the late eighteenth century, the staircase turned balusters and newel posts in a plain Ionic style. Stained to look like mahogany and more decorative than functional, a surviving piece of banister sections comes from a dog-leg staircase.

On the ground floor, photographic evidence details a broken cornice suggesting that in the early nineteenth century, visitors entered into the front room. With no evidence of an original hallway and, with the especially plain cornice, guests did not experience the same level of grandeur they did at other Tilney Street houses (Figure 5.3C). It is difficult to trace any documentary references to the occupants of No. 2, so it is difficult to determine the motivations behind the interior choices. During the nineteenth century, the occupants were primarily women or retired MPs. These residents may not have valued material concerns or entertained eminent guests in the same way as those at No. 1 or No. 4. The Hon. Reginald Brett, for example, moved into No. 2 from No. 1 around 1894. The appeal of No. 2 may have been its comparable smallness and understated nature, which gave it a homely, informal and private atmosphere compared to the rest of the street. He may have wished to reduce his socialising while writing his first essays as a historian, especially the 'The Yoke of Empire, Sketches of the Queen's Prime Ministers' published in 1896.

The narrowness of No. 2 emphasises that the order and regulation that is often considered a hallmark of urban improvement by scholars was not always manifested in practice, even in elite residence districts. These shortcomings were not just visible to the householders but readily discernable from the street to contemporary passersby. However, viewing the lack of space and the interior design as shortcomings could in itself be a mistake. These were simply choices, made by residences who could have afforded larger and more fashionable properties but chose No. 2 for a variety of reasons.

Conclusion

Building biographies offer the opportunity to consider a variety of social interactions, processes and perceptions, from those relating to the micro-scale of Tilney Street to those with wider implications for Georgian urban life. The use of biographies highlights the potential of small-scale studies to critique and add nuance to wider national and regional models of urban landscapes and domestic living during the period. Ideal conceptions of improved urban landscapes and plans of proposed schemes are all important evidence of eighteenth-century attitudes and aspirations (Ogborn 1998: 91), but so too is the actual configuration of the streets the inhabitants walked through every day. Tilney Street is in Mayfair, which is traditionally viewed as a focal point of urban improvement. However, once the street is looked at in detail, both the physical and documentary evidence create a much more complex picture.

Even in the West End, the landscape and homes of the occupants were rife with contradiction, eschewing easy demarcation according to wealth, occupation or status. The façade of a building might provide some clues as to the status of an inhabitant, but this would not be the whole story and in some cases is misleading. There was a complex mixture of individual status, size of property, precise location and decorative details.

The methodology outlined in this article allows for the imaginative reconstruction of destroyed urban environments. To some extent this is nothing new and is a staple part of the academic toolkit of historians and historical geographers. However, it is the ability to reconstruct the physical environment in detail that is important. The detail allows the physicality of space to be explored. For a long time, the scholarship of existing buildings highlights the significance of the positioning of rooms and movement and access through the house, for example 'how architectural space has been consciously sub-divided and allocated in the past' (Fairclough 1992, 348) and how it helps to reflect and structure social performance (Giles 2000, 19). Placing social practices in actual physical spaces allows for the exploration of how they were performed on an everyday level and the possibilities and constraints of the space. This article provides a methodology of how the same techniques can be applied to destroyed urban buildings. The ideals and aspirations of urban improvement by eighteenth-century contemporaries are important but so too is how these processes worked at ground level. In a similar fashion, domestic interiors were nuanced spaces and simply because you were of a high social status and could afford the latest taste in interior designs did not mean that you wanted them in your home.

Abbreviations

ASC – Architectural Study Collection
EHA – English Heritage Archive, London
HoP – History of Parliament
NA – National Archives
ODNB – Oxford Dictionary of National Biography
PCC – Prerogative Court of Canterbury
SOL – Survey of London

Bibliography

Primary sources

NA PCC PROB 11/1377/241 – Will of Martha Clayton
NA PCC PROB 11/1338/45 – Will of Susanna Vansittart
NA PCC PROB 11/1545/193 – Will of Lady Chichester
NA PCC PROB 11/1700/271 – Will of John Vernon Esq

Published secondary sources

Anon (1845). 'Art. VI – The Letters of Philip Dormer Stanhope, Earl of Chesterfield', including letters now published from the original MSS. Edited with notes by Lord Mahon, 4 vols, 8vo. *Quarterly Review* 76: p. 484.

Anon. The Old Bailey Online. 'London and its Hinterlands: London 1715–1760'. <http://www.oldbaileyonline.org/static/London-life18th.jsp> accessed 19 April 2015.

Borsay, P. (1989). *The English Urban Renaissance: Culture and Society in the Provincial Town, 1660–1770*. Oxford: Clarendon Press.

Borsay, P. (1994). 'The London Connection: Cultural Diffusion and the Eighteenth-Century Provincial Town'. *The London Journal* 19(1): pp. 21–35.

Cannon, J. (2012). 'Stanhope, Philip Dormer, fourth Earl of Chesterfield (1694–1773)'. *Oxford Dictionary of National Biography*, online edn, September 2012 <http://

www.oxforddnb.com.ezproxy.york.ac.uk/view/article/26255> accessed 19 April
2015.

Cruickshank, D., and Burton, N. (1990). *Life in the Georgian City*. London: Viking.

Deetz, J. (1996). *In Small Things Forgotten: An Archaeology of Early American Life*.
New York: Anchor Books.

Deetz, J. (1998) 'Discussion: Archaeologists as storytellers'. *Historical Archaeology*
32: pp. 94–6.

Fairclough, G. (1992). 'Meaningful Constructions – spatial and functional analysis
of medieval buildings'. *Antiquity* 66: pp. 348–66.

Giles, K. (2000). 'An Archaeology of Social Identity: Guildhalls in York c.1350–1630'.
British Archaeological Reports British Series 315. Oxford: Archaeopress.

Ginzburg, C. (1993). 'Microhistory: two or three things that I know about it'. *Critical
Inquiry* 20(1): pp. 10–35.

Girouard, M. (1990). *The English Town: A History of Urban Life*. New Haven, CT,
London: Yale University Press.

Gosden, C., and Marshall, Y. (1999). 'The Cultural Biography of Objects'. *World
Archaeology* 31(2): pp. 169–78.

Greig, H. (2006). 'Eighteenth-century English Interiors in image and Text'. In J. Aynsley and C. Grant (eds), *Imagined Interiors: Representing the Domestic Interior
since the Renaissance*. London: V and A Publications: pp. 102–27.

Guillery, P. (2004). *The Small House in Eighteenth-Century London: A Social and
Architectural History*. New Haven, CT: Yale University Press.

Hochstrasser, T. J. (2008). 'Conway, Francis Ingram-Seymour, second marquess of
Hertford (1743–1822)'. *Oxford Dictionary of National Biography*, online edn, May
2008 <http://www.oxforddnb.com.ezproxy.york.ac.uk/view/article/25167>
accessed 19 April 2015.

Hoskins, L. (ed.) (1994). *The Papered Wall: The history, patterns and techniques of
wallpaper*. London: Thames and Hudson.

Johnson, M. (2010). *English Houses 1300–1800: Vernacular Architecture, Social Life*.
Harlow: Longman.

Lepore, J. (2001). 'Historians who love too much: reflections on microhistory and
biography'. *Journal of American History* 88(1): pp. 129–44.

Levy, M. J. (2012). 'Fitzherbert, Maria Anne (1756–1837)'. *Oxford Dictionary of National
Biography*, online edn, September 2012 <http://www.oxforddnb.com.ezproxy.
york.ac.uk/view/article/9603> accessed 19 April 2015.

Lucas, G. (2006). 'Historical Archaeology and Time'. In D. Hicks and M. C. Beaudry (eds). *The Cambridge Companion to Historical Archaeology*. Cambridge:
Cambridge University Press: pp. 34–47.

Mytum, H. (2010). 'Ways of Writing in Post-Medieval and Historical Archaeology:
introducing biography'. *Post-Medieval Archaeology* 44: pp. 237–54.

Nurse, B. (2008). 'Englefield, Sir Henry Charles, seventh Baronet (c.1752–1822)'. *Oxford Dictionary of National Biography*, online edn, January 2008 <http://www.oxforddnb.com.ezproxy.york.ac.uk/view/article/8812> accessed 19 April 2015.

Ogborn, M. (1998). *Spaces of Modernity: London's Geographies 1680–1780*. London: Guildford Press.

Port, M. H. (1995). 'West End Palaces: The Aristocratic Town House in London, 1730–1830'. *London Journal* 20(1): pp. 17–46.

Sheppard, F. H. W. (ed.) (1977). 'The Grosvenor Estate in Mayfair, Part I: General History'. In *Survey of London*, Vol. 39. London: London County Council.

Sheppard, F. H. W. (ed.) (1980). 'The Grosvenor Estate in Mayfair, Part II: The Buildings'. *Survey of London*, Vol 40. London: London County Council.

Stewart, R. (2009). *The Town House in Georgian London*. New Haven, CT, and London: Yale University Press.

Stillman, D. (1988). *English Neo-Classical Architecture Volume One*. London: A. Zwemmer.

Stobart, J. (2011). 'Who were the Urban Gentry? Social Elites in an English Provincial Town, c.1680–1760'. *Continuity and Change* 26 (1): pp. 89–112.

Stobart, J., Hann, A., and Morgan, V. (2007). *Spaces of Consumption: Leisure and Shopping in the English Town, c.1680–1830*. London: Routledge.

Sweet, R. (2002). 'Topographies of Politeness'. *Transactions of the Royal Historical Society* 12: pp. 355–74.

Tarlow, S. (2007). *The Archaeology of Improvement in Britain, 1750–1850*. Cambridge: Cambridge University Press.

Thorne, R. G. (1986). 'Myers, Thomas (1764–1835)', The History of Parliament: The House of Commons 1790–1820, ed. R. Thorne. <http://www.historyofparliamentonline.org/volume/1790–1820/member/myers-thomas-1764–1835> accessed 19 April 2015.

Vickery, A. (1998). *The Gentleman's Daughter: Women's Lives in Georgian England*. New Haven, CT: Yale University Press.

Vickery, A. (2009). *Behind Closed Doors: At Home in Georgian England*. New Haven, CT: Yale University Press.

Unpublished secondary sources

Jenkins, M. (2013). 'The View from the Street: Housing and Shopping in York during the Long Eighteenth Century'. University of York PhD thesis.

Survey of London Nos 1–4 Tilney Street. English Heritage Archive, London.

ANTONY BUXTON

6   Feasts and Triumphs: The Structural Dynamic of Elite Social Status in the English Country House

ABSTRACT

This chapter seeks to explore the manner in which social status is expressed through the structuring of space, in the distinction between the external context and the habitation, in the differentiation of constructed space (with reference to Lefebvre and Bourdieu) and in movement between differentiated spaces within the dwelling (Merleau-Ponty). The English 'country house' offers a rich comparative case study over four centuries, and demonstrates the manner in which the physical structuring of the elite social dynamic reflects both domestic group relationships within the habitation and the values of the wider society. Whilst the country house could be seen as an attempted perpetuation of existing expressions of status, changes in that external culture – arguably ultimately generated by control and productive exploitation of assets and concomitant changes in social relationships and hierarchies of power – are reflected in modification to the structuring and consequent social dynamic of the country house. The country house and its spatial-social dynamic can therefore be seen as demonstrations of responses to the changing conditions of modernity.

Writing in a chapter entitled 'On Building' in the earlier part of the seventeenth century in his volume *Essays or Counsels, Civil and Moral* (1627: 195), the English statesman, jurist and essayist Sir Francis Bacon argued: 'I say you cannot have a perfect palace except you have two several sides; a side for the banquet ... and a side for the household; the one for feasts and triumphs, and the other for dwelling'. The elite house should thus provide for a clear distinction between high status ceremony and day to day living, in which the writer recognises that spatial organisation plays an essential role. This chapter aims to explore the way in which domesticity – manifested by dwelling structures and domestic actions and relationships – is physically constructed to create an expression of and enactment of elevated social status in the elite English 'country house'.

Human habitation is the context for many of the activities which comprise human existence and experience. We might argue that the essential elements of the home are the provision of shelter and physical security, a context for subsistence often in association with others in a group, and the formation of a core unit to provide not only biological but also cultural reproduction (Fortes 1958: 8). These diverse elements and the manner in which they combine to create what we might term a 'domestic culture' are elegantly modelled by Pierre Bourdieu (1977, 1990) in his theory of practice and concept of *habitus*. 'Practice' is the term given to the totality of domestic activities significantly differentiated by the configuration of domestic space, regulating the manner of social engagement and associated values and sentiments. The conformity of the domestic group to this 'structuring structure' and its transmission from generation to generation is referred to as *habitus*. Broadly speaking in Bourdieu's observation there is a tendency in *habitus* towards tradition, but innovation in *habitus* can occur – modifying the social culture – in ways we will explore below.

In what way do the requirements of an elite dwelling differ from those of a lower social status? Bourdieu was examining a domestic culture – that of the Kabyle agriculturalists in North Africa – largely based on subsistence. He notes the operation of agency between members of the household and the expression of hierarchies of age, gender and activities. Indeed, we may observe that a significant element of domesticity is *dom*ination both within and beyond the domestic unit, of both the natural and social environments; the etymological element '*dom*' deriving from an Indo European term for mastery (Benveniste 1973: 249–51). The notion of the elite *house* however presumes an elevated status within the wider community. This may be based on the householder's birth or age, on ritual position, or may also be derived from superior material wealth, which can be invested in the dwelling to express status and the provide a context for its enactment. The English country house can be viewed as a particular form of habitation, dedicated not only to shelter and subsistence, but also to the articulation of the elevated social status of the head of the household. The anthropologist Claude Lévi-Strauss identified a shift from primacy of kinship links to that of the household in medieval Europe; within 'house society' the habitation becoming the representation of group identity and continuity (Lévi-Strauss 1987: 151). The English 'country house' became a particularly successful model for the elite house. Important criteria of genteel status were a life free of labour and conspicuous display; as William Harrison opined in 1587, he who 'can live without manual labour, and thereto is able and will bear the port, charge and countenance ... [will be]... reputed for a gentleman ever after' (113–14). Set in a tamed and productive nature – the countryside – and distanced from the urban source of much wealth creation, the country house embodied status through disposable wealth, grandiose and yet not generally overly ostentatious; a large, elegant, architectural statement, richly furnished, and a repository of decoration and art. It demonstrated the wealth of the builder and provided a possibility of the perpetuation of his or her reputation and lineage. But it also provided an important locus of social theatre to articulate, cultivate and maintain that status, based on external political and economic conditions. The elite household has traditionally consisted of the three broad social elements: the householder and his or her family, the household servants, and external guests or peer group deemed important for the maintenance of status. This chapter will argue that space has been configured both horizontally and vertically to regulate movement and access to places and people through the dwelling and therefore social discourse between these social elements. Such a focus has been the subject of comprehensive and forensic studies of access by Hillier and Hanson (1984), Johnson (1999), West (1999) and Hanson (2003) amongst others. Employing a broad chronological survey of pertinent examples this chapter will argue that the structuring of space, and movement through space – stimulating sensory and affective responses – result in the articulation of elite status in the English country house, in a manner dictated not only by the internal domestic social dynamic but strongly influenced by external and more generalised notions of social status in the wider economic, political and social sphere. The examples chosen will demonstrate modifications of such social structuring from the fifteenth to the nineteenth centuries to reflect changing notions and expressions of elite status beyond the house – status acquired and maintained as feudal estate, position acquired at court, the operation of polite association, and the expression of moral and commercial probity – and the country house can thus be viewed not simply as an institution resistant to change, but one which in many ways successfully adapted to the forces of modernity.

Social status can be communicated in a variety of ways, from remote representation (imagery) to dress and ceremony. But physical proximity and personal recognition and approval by look, gesture or address are frequently considered to be indicators of acceptance and approval, and reciprocally confirmation of social pre-eminence by attendants. Certain activities and their physical context – in particular shared consumption of drink and food, and conversation – can also reinforce this social dynamic social. The spatial dimension of social intercourse therefore carries powerful status connotations. Context too is crucial, as for example the delineation of spaces within which degrees of movement are permitted. The social *inclusion* provided by association and the distance indicated by *exclusion* become effective ways in which built structures can regulate potential social engagement and articulate the social hierarchy. Buildings can indicate both inclusivity for those within and exclusion for those without, and the transition from exterior to interior a proof of inclusion. Internal spatial division through built structure can further articulate relative distinctions in status within the household. Lefebvre argues that space becomes a potent signifier of status only by the creation of opposition: 'Some would doubtless argue that the ultimate foundation of social space is prohibition ... the gulf between [the members of a society], their bodies and consiousnesses, and the difficulties of social intercourse ... in an "environment" made up of a series of zones defined by interdictions and bans' (Lefebvre 1991: 35). Merleau-Ponty (1965: 100) argues that 'spatiality' is not one of position but of *situation*. Movement can be both conceived (abstract) and enacted (concrete), and both the possibility and enactment of movement are central to engagement with and experience of the world (Merleau-Ponty (1965: 111). The location of activities in differentiated place, and movement of the individual and group from location to location – both horizontally and vertically – within the built structure therefore becomes potentially socially definitive. In the words of Hillier and Hanson (1984: ix): 'architecture ... provides the material preconditions for the patterns of movement, encounter and avoidance which are the material realisation – as well as sometimes the generator – of social relations' (Barron, West 1991). Potentially structural elements such as walls create social barriers, doorways create thresholds of social transition and stairways the possibility of social elevation. If space can shape social relationships, then movement is an essential element in that dynamic.

The operation of social space presents a complex combination of human thought, action and experience. The architectural construction is epistemological in so far as it was – and is – subject to a clear articulation of principals of ideal form and physical social ordering, either explicitly or by inference (Whyte 2006). It has also been recognised that the definition of space as 'place', by structure or other form of semiotic differentiation is experiential, operating at a sensory and affective level – 'a practico-sensory totality' – which may be reinforced by sets of non verbal signals such as art, decoration and furnishings (Lefebvre 1991: 62). In identifying social space as potentially both biologically and socially reproductive Lefebvre (1991: 32) also argues that it is inextricably linked with economic production. Potentially, the relationship of the individual and group to social space then informs and defines their 'place' in both the physical and social world.

Space – or distinct 'places' within the dwelling narrating elements of the social discourse – operate both as practice and as habitus. As noted above this 'structuring structure' can persuasively direct actions and articulate values. In Amos Rapoport's terminology, *activity systems* complement and occur in *systems of settings*. His analysis of the domestic domain comprises fixed features (buildings), semi-fixed features (furnishings) and latent features (people and meanings). Structures, being relatively immutable tend to maintain the pre-existing habitus, whilst the contextualisation (or meanings) of place through furnishings and decoration can be more easily modified (Rapoport 1990: 9–16). At the time of building, then, the configuration of space might be expected to represent the intended orchestration of social discourse, in a manner which is deemed to articulate status. But existing houses were subjected to changing notions of social engagement, and consequentially spatial reconfiguration though structural alterations. Indeed, changing modes of engagement always evolve out of antecedents: 'Wherever a society undergoes a transformation, the materials used in the process derive from another, historically (or developmentally) anterior social practice' (Lefebvre 1991: 190). Since an important purpose of the country house was to provide continuity of the biological group succeeding generations could well inherit the spatial practice of their forbears, in the modification of which the country house becomes a complex amalgam of successive expressions of status.

Late medieval 'estate' and early modern emergent comfort: Horizontal internal hierarchy

The English country house ultimately derives its *raison d'être* from the medieval elite house, establishing a strong connection between the status of the knight – honourable, courageous and superior to manual labour – and the holding of land. Under the feudal system all land deriving ultimately from the king in return for the oath of loyalty and the promise of military service by the lord and his retinue, and in an economy very largely agricultural, the land and those who worked it represented wealth and status. Lévi-Strauss identified a shift from primacy of kinship links to that of the household in medieval Europe; the 'house society' the structural representation of group identity and continuity (Lévi-Strauss 1987: 151). The social heart of the medieval house was the hall, the scene for the redistribution of the produce of the land in symbolic commensality uniting the whole household as a community, but also differentiating spatially between those of more elevated status – the lord, his family and guests at the 'upper' end on a raised dais – and those at the 'lower' end proximate to the entrance passageway and the service area of kitchen, buttery and pantry. Prior to the introduction of the side hearth the hall was customarily heated with a central hearth vented through the roof; a communality of comfort. The desirability of this commensal expression of this internal community is found in Bishop Grosseteste's advice to his niece, the Countess of Lincoln: 'Make your household to sit in the hall, as much as you may ... and sit you ever in the middle of the high board, that your visage and cheer may be showed to all men ... for that will be to your profit and worship' (Quoted in Girouard 1978: 30). The purpose of the ceremony attending medieval commensality was the enactment – through spatial distribution and also through actions, such as the personal attendance on the lord at table – of the important medieval notion of estate by which society was rigidly ordered (Huizinga 1924: 47). Adjacent to the upper end of the hall was the parlour, a place for private retreat or audience for the head of the house, and usually on an upper floor the chamber (or solar) for the private accommodation of the family. Already the desire of householder for greater privacy was noted by William Langland in his late fourteenth-century work *Piers Ploughman*: 'All well-to-do people now make it a rule to eat by themselves in a private parlour to avoid the company of the poor; or else they quit the main hall, whih was built for people to eat in together, and use a separate room with its own fireplace' (Langland 1992: 97). Further accommodation might be provided by lodging ranged around a court – the parallel development to the walled 'motte' enclosure surrounding the inner defensive 'bailey' tower in the medieval castle – a space which acted as a more diffuse place of concourse and activity of the household and guests, extending also to the differentiated status of an outer and inner court (Johnson 2002). At Haddon Hall in Derbyshire such accommodation has been added inside a perimeter defensive wall, but at Compton Wynyates in Warwickshire (Figure 6.1) the house has been conceived as accommodation around a courtyard, one side of which features the hall, parlour and chamber, extending the feudal unit with personal lodgings which suggest an emerging desire for comfort – both physical and affective. The primary access by the gateway suggests a domestic introversion. We could characterise this form of spatial organisation essentially as a *horizontal* form of internal hierarchy, circumscribed by external walls, and progressing from court to hall; the hierarchically inclusive household.

The house of the sixteenth-century humanist courtier: Elevated discrimination

The establishment by the Tudors of a strong centralised authority meant that the 'court' now was significantly that of the royal household, where favours could be sought and position enhanced (Bush 1984: 105–9; Loades

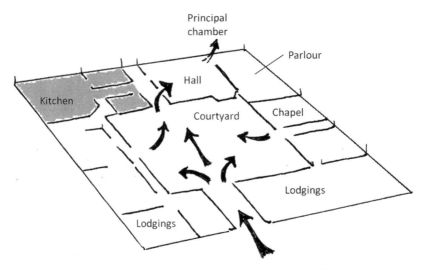

Figure 6.1: Socio-spatial dynamic: Compton Wynyates late fifteenth – early sixteenth century. Service provision in grey. (Image: author.)

1989: 18.21). The courtyard became increasingly an internalised and diminished element of the country house as at Sir William Cecil's Burghley House (c.1560). Nevertheless, Sir Christopher Hatton's Kirby Hall (1570–5) featured an external walled entrance *court d'honneur* in the French manner, still expressed over a century later in Blenheim Palace (1705–c. 22), whilst the internal and side court there had become a kitchen service yard. However, the chief development in the later sixteenth- and early seventeenth-century country house was the compaction of the country house into an integrated and outward-facing structure, characterised by extensive employment of glazed windows. This optical emphasis – the site chosen for perspective both onto and from the house – represents the shift from an inturning orientation into the household to a greater engagement with the external world. The contemporary philosophical shift towards a humanist emphasis on order and reason – qualities desirable in the courtier – was expressed in the adoption of more symmetrical facades, enhanced by references to Roman architectural decoration – in particular the ascending Roman orders – and this focus on intellectual virtue was reflected in a more distinct social differentiation within. New elite social space created on upper floors around the chamber expressed increasing social discrimination; the hall remained a place of entry and servant commensality – and a partial reference to traces of Medieval estate – whilst the family and guests socialised in a chamber now graced by the title 'great' or 'best', accessed by a grand staircase, the ascent of which became a significant part of the enactment of differentiation of status. In particular, this new arrangement was devised to cement alliances with the *external* peer group, rather than, as previously, the extended household. This discrimination is epitomised by the complaint around 1580 of a Mr Marlivate to Sir Thomas Kytson of Hengrave Hall in Suffolk at being obliged to dine at the 'square board in the hall' with the steward instead of being entertained at 'the Lord's board in the great chamber' (Gage 1822: 22, quoted in Girouard 1978: 88). An item of furnishing, the 'court' cupboard also articulated the social agency of the best chamber in which it was customarily found. Consisting of a number of open shelves for the display of high-value cups and eating vessels which demonstrated the status and largesse of the host, the contemporary meaning of the term 'court' indicated the enactment of the rituals of the court in this space; in the words of the contemporary Thomas Wilson (1553: iii. f. 92v) 'When we see one gaye and galaunte, we vse to saye, he courtes it' (Buxton 2015: 152–4). The notion of 'court' had thus migrated from relative inclusivity to increased discrimination within the household.

A sequence of rooms led off the best chamber; a withdrawing chamber for the company when the best chamber was being reconfigured (say from dining to dancing), the personal bedchamber of the head of household and beyond a closet for storage but also serving as a most private space. In tandem with this sequence a long gallery also made its appearance, acting as another space for social discourse, combined with the perspective of the surrounding estate. In time the gallery would also become the repository of prized art objects, including portraiture recording the powerful associations of the family, and their continuity through the generations. The late Tudor country house had therefore been transformed from a spatial dynamic of a relatively inclusive horizontal hierarchy to one of vertical social discrimination. Employing this form of distribution the powerful Tudor aristocrat, Elizabeth, Countess of Shrewsbury built Hardwick

New Hall in Derbyshire (1590–7) (Figure 6.2) probably making use of the expertise of Robert Smythson, a gentleman precursor to the professional architect, informed both in the creation of an interior expressing the new social dynamic, and in attendant architectural features making clear reference to the antique roots of the this humanist philosophical reorientation. Interior decoration and furnishings were also employed to reinforce both the ideology and social dynamic of this new social space, and contemporary furnishings – tapestries and embroidery created by the lady of the house and her staff, made liberal references to classical allegory; for example, Ulysses' Penelope and her virtues of loyalty and patience, and in a 'Sea Dog' table fidelity and patience, code for courtly virtues derived from emblem books.[1]

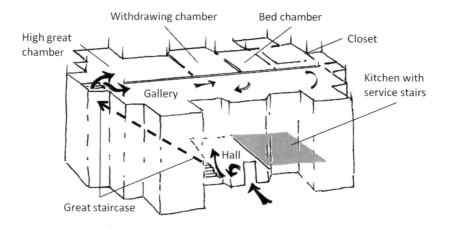

Figure 6.2: Socio-spatial dynamic: Hardwick New Hall 1590–7.
Service provision in grey. (Image: author.)

Not only were new houses created in this form, older ones were adapted. Broughton Castle in Oxfordshire saw a large scale transformation in the second half of the sixteenth century by Richard Fiennes, sixth Baron Saye

---

1   Andreas Alciat, *Liber Emblemata*, Augsburg 1531: Plate XCVII. 'The reputation of
     woman, not her beauty, should be widely known'.

and Sele from a medieval 'hall house' to one of Tudor social discrimination. The medieval hall was floored over to create a suite of chambers above, giving on to a long gallery. Where the kitchen was originally situated a new wing contained a great chamber above and large dining parlour below, accessed by a new grand staircase. Suitably the exterior was also refashioned to impose a degree of humanist symmetrical order. The late sixteenth-century Tudor country house can therefore be seen as one in which *internal* social differentiation was articulated by the creation of elevated and more discriminating social space, reflecting the personal aspirational nature of humanist philosophy and the greater emphasis on alliances with the social peer group.

Late seventeenth- and early eighteenth-century aristocratic discernment: Horizontal and vertical social filtering

The sequence of social rooms on the upper floor evolved into a more highly structured form of spatial agency in the seventeenth century; the apartment. Credited to the remodelling of her father's Paris *hôtel* by the Madame de Rambouillet early in the century, the result was form of domestic accommodation combined with a context for highly regulated social engagement, adopted in elite houses across Europe. Seeking to establish a greater control over her social engagement – in particular a preference for company which engaged in refined conversation and manners, or *civilité* – she removed her bed from its place in the principal chamber to a more intimate *chambre á alcove*, and remodelled her *cabinet* (the French term for the closet) into a *loge de Ziephir*, a suitable setting for conversations with her cultured friends or *précieux* (Thornton 1978: 14–15). The distinction in space – further articulated by furnishings or *ameublement* expressing suitable sentiments – thus expressed social selection, given a visual significance through the alignment of the doors to the succeeding rooms – the *enfilade*. Concurrently the house was planned in such a way that the necessary servant attendance was as unobtrusive as possible, accessed by back passages and stairways, and domestic services frequently placed in a semi-basement. (No longer considered significantly part of the extended household, servants were now very much deemed a socially inferior, functional part of the household). In new houses such as Belton House in Lincolnshire built Sir John and Lady Brownlow (1684–6, architect possibly William Winde) social rooms could now be placed adjacent to the raised entrance hall, accessible by external stone steps. This arrangement also lent itself to the creation of symmetry *within* the house, by pairing apartments around the central axis of hall – as impressive entrance – and saloon – the context for less discriminatory acts of commensality and entertainment of the peer group. Effectively a formalisation of the sixteenth-century elevated social portion of the house, a mode of further social *discrimination* within the household and social *selection* amongst peers, the apartment was widely imitated across Europe and became the ideal model for the important concept of 'distribution' (Thornton 1978: 18). This emphasis on structural order and harmony could be seen as an expression of the discerning quality or '*virtu*' of genteel rank; in the words of the Earl of Shaftesbury in his *Characteristics of Men, Manners, Opinions, Times* (2004 (1711): 273): 'Nothing is surely more strongly imprinted in our Minds, or more closely interwoven in our Souls, than the Idea of Sense of Order and Proportion'. Typically, the distinct spaces in the apartment might be of relatively small dimensions – suggesting exclusivity – but exaggerated in height – suggesting elevated status. This model of the 'the house of parade' dominated the later seventeenth and early eighteenth centuries. Ham House in Surrey (Figure 6.3), on the River Thames above London was a remodelled house from earlier in the century. The original builder, the Elizabethan courtier Sir Thomas Vavasour, created the house c. 1610 with a great hall – which remains – and his successor William Murray, first Earl of Dysart created a suite of state rooms on the first floor accessed by a grand staircase (National Trust 1995: 60, 61; see Figure 6.3). Murray's eldest daughter made a second marriage to the Duke of Lauderdale, and in the 1670s the couple embarked on an enlargement of Ham House, constructing symmetrical apartments along the south front, on the ground floor for the Duke and Duchess and above for Queen Catherine of Braganza (National Trust 1995: 65–7). Although access was by the Jacobean hall, peer collective commensality took place in the saloon from which a strictly linear access progressed to the increasingly private parts of the apartments, culminating in the Duchess's orientally styled closet for the discerning consumption of tea and conversation.

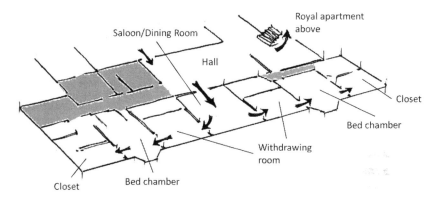

Figure 6.3: Socio-spatial dynamic: Ham House early and late seventeenth century. Service provision in grey. (Image: author.)

Other houses were significantly rebuilt to this model. Boughton House in Northamptonshire was rebuilt (c. 1685) by the Francophile and court favourite, Ralph Montagu (later first Duke of Montagu). The fortune of his step daughter Elizabeth Percy enabled her husband, Charles Seymour, sixth Duke of Somerset also to substantially rebuild Petworth (1688–96) in West Sussex in this French taste. The ground floor apartments, employed by the Duke and Duchess for social reception and accommodation were symmetrically arranged around a Marble Hall, the upper royal apartments accessed by a grand staircase decorated with murals by the French artist Laguerre (National Trust 1997: 68–71). Notably all of these house owners were significantly involved in the royal court on its restoration after the Civil War and Interregnum. And the sense of entitlement was enhanced by decorative furnishings which drew their inspiration from the court of the absolutist French monarch, Louis XIV. Having fled his native country due to religious persecution the French Huguenot artist Daniel Marot provided for both Boughton and Petworth furnishings in the manner of Versailles.

Mid-eighteenth-century social peer association: Horizontal circulation

Following the death of the last Stuart monarch, Anne in 1714, and the accession of the Hanoverian line there was a considerable diminution in the importance of the court as a theatre of elite status. The national context of power and influence was shifting to Parliament, and its intense interest in the cultivation of wealth through commerce, both at home and abroad. (Some of the most esteemed decorative items of the later seventeenth century had been porcelain and lacquer ware traded from the Far East). This was however a form of oligarchy; the parliamentary electorate restricted to those with significant property, and the members of parliament frequently country gentlemen. The cultivation of peer alliances amongst gentry and wealthy merchants therefore became the important exercise in the establishment and maintenance of elite status, in which the country house played a central role. The domination of the apartment in the design and social construction of the house was gradually diminished by the introduction of rooms of association. (In the external fashionable world, most notably during the London season and at provincial centres such as the resort of Bath assembly rooms and assemblies acted as the focus of social life (Girouard 1990: 77).) Houghton Hall (Figure 6.4), the power house in Norfolk of the Robert Walpole (first Earl of Orford), the Whig 'prime' minister who dominated British politics from this ascent to power around 1721 to his political demise in 1742 (Oxford Dictionary of National Biography), was apparently built with the profits of his political position and played a crucial role in regular political gatherings of Whig Parliamentary allies. The house incorporates apartments but also makes provision for rooms of association through circulation. The decoration of Whig elite houses fell largely to William Kent, noted for his lavish use of marble and gilding. At Houghton he employed classical allegorical themes such as that of Venus (love) and Neptune (the sea) in the salon, with ostentatiously carved and partly gilded furniture, aptly of mahogany timber from the West Indies, the source of growing wealth through plantations cultivating sugar with African slave labour.

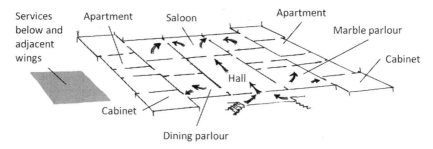

Figure 6.4: Socio-spatial dynamic: Houghton Hall c.1730.
Service provision in grey. (Image: author.)

The house of an aspiring Parliamentarian, Claydon House in Buckinghamshire is an example of the extensive alteration of an existing building for the purposes of enhancement of status in a new elite culture. Ralph, second Earl Verney, who succeeded to the property in 1752 greatly altered the house as part of an ongoing political and social competition between the Verneys and the Temples and Grevilles of neighbouring Stowe House. Having first encased an earlier sixteenth-century house, he then commissioned a London craftsman, Luke Lightfoot, to design a rectangular block containing three major reception rooms – a hall, saloon and library – with an apartment of chambers above. Lightfoot decorated these rooms in the range of contemporary decorative styles, which reflected the emergent culture of sensibility; sinuous rococo, exotic chinoiserie and romantic gothic. The opportunity for circulation in the house, and the affective nature of the decoration suggested a culture of increasingly personal engagement. Having fallen out with Lightfoot, Verney commissioned another architect, Sir Thomas Robinson to augment the house with a great rotunda and a vast dining hall in which Verney on one occasion reputedly entertained two hundred voters. Having largely failed in his political and social ambitions, the rebuilding bankrupted Verney and much was demolished after his death. However, the house represents a prime example of building to enhance political and social status in the mid-eighteenth century.

Victorian upper-middle-class moral probity and material management: Systematised nucleated engagement

As the context for social influence beyond the house continued very much to be an alliance of Parliamentary position and commercial wealth, subjected over the late eighteenth and early nineteenth centuries by increasing penetration by the growing, aspirational and prosperous middle class, it is unsurprising that the social space in the country house continued to consist of a sequence of rooms through which select company could circulate. Predominantly, new country houses were created in a simplified, Grecian form of classicism, but in addition romantic sensibility was given expression in more irregular neo gothic forms, in both cases interior decoration tending to follow these themes. The variety of architectural styles marked the start of a more eclectic historicist referencing of the past in architecture and decoration; selecting a range of architectural and interior decorative styles to evoke certain values. Prime amongst these in the mid-nineteenth century was the gothic, selected to represent affinity with the supposed values of the Middle Ages in faith and social responsibility, at a time of acute change generated by rampant industrialisation. The gradual extension of the male electoral suffrage during the nineteenth century, and the penetration of the elite by the wealthy merchants and industrialists effectively altered the context of social and political influence. Whilst the country house remained an important asset for the cultivation of elite status – the Tory Prime Minister Benjamin Disraeli was assisted in the purchase of a country seat, Hughenden Manor – the country house became increasingly and primarily the *symbol* of that (affluent) status. And whilst the cultivation of status now occurred significantly beyond the country house, the industrialist William first Baron Armstrong built Cragside in Northumberland (designed by Richard Norman Shaw 1863–84) in part for the entertainment of commercial clients.

Whilst retaining its suite of social rooms – the dining room, the drawing room, and the gallery – the Victorian country house tended to reflect middle class values; privacy and probity. In looking back to the Middle

Ages an attempt was made to reinvent the notion of the household community – with an emphasis on physical comfort Victorian elite houses tended to be staffed by large numbers of servants – but one which was subjected to strict moral management, with spatial differentiation underlining the varied status of householder, family, guests and servants; a form of highly regulated and status-conscious association. Tyntesfield (c. 1860s; Figure 6.5), the house of the merchant William Gibbs, ennobled as Baron Wraxall, articulates these values and this sense of spatial organisation. The entrance was made through an intimate passageway and significantly the hall had shifted from impressive entry to the hub of family life – the social rooms and the stairwell to personal accommodation above. A suite of rooms for varying forms of socialisation – frequently with gendered associations – the dining room, drawing room and library – form the core of the social house. There is also extensive provision upstairs for the accomodation of family and guests. Adjacent, but segregated are the extensive service quarters, defined by function and status in the servant corps, with the courtyard reintroduced as a service area – a managerial approach to the extended household. Tyntesfield could be seen a reimagining of an idealised medieval household – complete with its own chapel – but one set in nineteenth-century managerial economic circumstances, and moral and social culture (National Trust 2003).

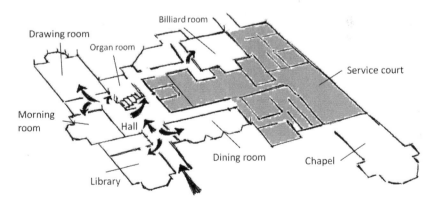

Figure 6.5: Socio-spatial dynamic: Tyntesfield c.1870.
Service provision in grey. (Image: author.)

Conclusion

The country house continued to be a centre of influence in the later nineteenth and early twentieth centuries. Clouds House in Wiltshire, built by
the member of parliament Percy Wyndham (architect Philip Webb 1886)
became the centre of the 'Souls' artistic and political gatherings between
1885 and 1920. Other new country houses, such as Cragside (1863–84) and
Standen (Philip Webb architect 1891–4) in West Sussex for the railway
lawyer James Beale expressed in architecture and interior furnishings a shift
away from early Victorian moralising to Aesthetic sensibility and Arts and
Crafts simplicity and authenticity, but nevertheless retained the sense of a
very grand family residence. In the late nineteenth century income from
agricultural estates slumped due to cheap food imports, and through the
twentieth century the significance of the English country house was diminished by the increasing political marginalisation of the land-owning class,
and economically challenged by inheritance taxation. Where the country
house has survived it has been either largely as a private asset – a place of
private retreat and a manifestation of personal wealth – or preserved by
private trusts and public bodies such as the National Trust as examples of
historical heritage. In such a role it can frequently now be seen as an institution which in the past resisted change in order to maintain inherited status.
This was a significant role it fulfilled with varying success, but arguably a
fuller understanding of its social function (which has been attempted in
a very generalised fashion here) is to see in the country house a potent
built expression of social status which was successfully adapted over several centuries, according to changing economic and political conditions,
and enabled the permeable English elite to maintain their supremacy in a
changing world (Bush 1984: 214–15). As such it reflects both the hidden
role of economic forces which created and maintained the country house
(Marx, Lefebvre 1991: 31)[2] and the changing nature of the wider society,

---

2   'every society ... produces a space, its own space'. 'I say each society, but it would be
     more accurate to say each mode of production, along with its specific relations of
     production ...' (Lefebvre 1991: 31).

broadly expressed by Tönnies as a move from *Gemeinschaft* [community] to *Gesellschaft* [society].[3]

At the outset it was argued that space articulates social status by movement between exclusion and inclusion, and by social proximity. This can be organised horizontally and vertically, or by a combination of both. In addition, spatial dimensions also indicate the exclusiveness or inclusiveness of the company and status. It was also suggested that the enactment of the social dynamic expresses the wider contemporary political, economic and social culture, but as an evolution from past modes of expression. Thus the late Medieval and early Tudor extended household was still centred around the primacy of the lord expressed in the central hall, but complemented by more individualised lodgings around a court; a largely introverted household with a strongly horizontal dynamic reflecting the largely inclusive internal hierarchy. By the late sixteenth century many elite dwellings had become condensed into one extroverted entity, and whilst the hall was retained as a significant entrance – and continuing reminder of medieval estate – elite social engagement had detached and elevated itself from the larger household and centred on a great high chamber; an increasingly differentiated – humanist – ordering of the world thus expressed in a vertical hierarchy. By the late seventeenth century elite status was underpinned by notions of order and discernment, reflected in a structuring of the dwelling which permitted a strict filtering of social engagement – essentially horizontal – with servants as far as possible hidden from sight. However, the marginalisation of the servant corps often in a basement below the *piano nobile*, and the frequent inclusion of an upper 'royal' apartment provide a complementary vertical dynamic. By the mid-eighteenth century, whilst retaining the apartment for private purposes a wider culture of elite assembly was reflected in a freer mode of *peer* association or circulation in

3   Concepts evolved by Ferdinand Tönnies in *Gemeinschaft und Gesellschaft* first published in 1887 in Leipzig, theorising the values underpinning social relationships in pre-modern and capitalist society. In the former, *Gemeinschaft* describes the desire of the individual, directed by ideology, to serve the social group; in the latter *Gesellschaft* the reorientation of social relationships towards self-interest, now regulated by the instruments of law.

interconnected rooms; a circular horizontal dynamic, servants continuing to occupy lower accommodation. By the mid-nineteenth century the
English elite had been permeated by the industrious middle classes, cultivating a moral family centred, but comfortably serviced dwelling, reflected
in select sociability around a number of family rooms. Large numbers of
servants created extended households, but managed within clearly defined
and segregated service areas.

This selective and simplified survey is intended to demonstrate the
way in which the structuring of the English country house, through spatial
differentiation and movement articulated and enacted elite social status,
and thus the manner in which habitation can act as a social asset and representation of such status. As an institution the country house was intended
to provide a statement of the builder's status and provide for continuity
of his or her reputation and lineage. It thus frequently employed as its justification the built form and *habitus* of preceding generations. However,
arguably the success of the country house and its elite inhabitants was due
to their general ability over generations to adapt to changing political and
economic circumstances, demonstrated in the manner in which they built
and adapted their houses to express evolving modes of social engagement.

Bibliography

Ashley-Cooper, A. (second Earl of Shaftesbury) (2004 [1711]). *Characteristics of Men,
    Manners, Opinions, Times.* Edited by Lawrence E. Klein. Cambridge: Cambridge
    University Press.
Bacon, Sir F. (1627 [1669]). *Essays of Francis Bacon or Counsels, Civil and Moral.*
    London.
Barron, D., and West, E. (1991). *Social Space and Group Boundaries: The Theories of
    Pierre Bourdieu and Peter Blau.* <http://eureka.sbs.ox.ac.uk/1219/> accessed
    20 April 2016.
Benveniste, E. (1973). *Indo-European Language and Society.* London: Faber.
Bourdieu, P. (1977). *Outline of a Theory of Practice.* Translated by R. Nice. Cambridge:
    Cambridge University Press.

Bourdieu, P. (1986 [1984]). *Distinction: A Social Critique in the Judgement of Taste.* London: Routledge.

Bourdieu, P. (1990). *The Logic of Practice.* Cambridge: Polity Press.

Bush, M. L. (1984). *English Aristocracy: A Comparative Synthesis.* Manchester: Manchester University Press.

Buxton, A. (2015). *Domestic Culture in Early Modern England.* Woodbridge: The Boydell Press.

Fortes, M. (1958). 'Introduction'. In *The Developmental Cycle in Domestic Groups.* Edited by J. Goody. Cambridge: Cambridge University Press.

Gage, J. G. (1822). *History and Antiquities of Hengrave.* London.

Girouard, M. (1978). *Life in the English Country House.* New Haven, CT, and London: Yale University Press.

Girouard, M. (1990). *The English Town.* New Haven, CT, London: Yale University Press.

Hanson, J. (2003). *Decoding Homes and Houses.* Cambridge: Cambridge University Press.

Harrison, W. (1587 [1994]). *The Description of England.* Edited by G. Edelen. Washington, DC, New York: Folger Shakespeare Library, Dover Books.

Hillier, B., and Hanson, J. (1984). *The Social Logic of Space.* Cambridge: Cambridge University Press.

Huizinga, J. (1924 [1972]). *The Waning of the Middle Ages.* Harmondsworth: Penguin.

Johnson, M. (1999). 'Reconstructing Castles and Refashioning Identities in Renaissance England'. In S. Tarlow and S. West (eds), *The Familiar Past? Archaeologies of Later Historical Britain.* London and New York: Routledge.

Johnson, M. (2002). *Behind the Castle Gate: from Medieval to Renaissance.* London: Routledge.

Langland, W. (1992). *Piers Ploughman.* Translated by A. V. C. Schmidt. Oxford: Oxford University Press.

Lefebvre, H. (1991). *The Production of Space.* Oxford: Blackwell

Lévi-Strauss, C. (1987). *Anthropology and Myth: Lectures, 1951–1982.* Translated by R. Willis. Oxford: Basil Blackwell.

Loades, D. M. (1989). *The Tudor Court.* London: Historical Association.

Merleau-Ponty, M. (1965). *Phenomenology of Perception.* Translated by Colin Smith. London: Routledge and Kegan Paul.

National Trust, The (1995). *Ham House.*

National Trust, The (1997). *Petworth House.*

National Trust, The (2003). *Tyntesfield.*

Rapoport, A. (1990). 'Systems of Activities and Systems of Settings'. In S. Kent (ed.), *Domestic Architecture and the Use of Space*. Cambridge: Cambridge University Press.

Thornton, P. (1978). *Seventeenth Century Interior Decoration in England, France and Holland*. New Haven, CT: Yale University Press.

Thornton, P. (1984). *Authentic Decor: The Domestic Interior 1620–1920*. London: Weidenfeld and Nicolson.

Tönnies, F. (1887). *Gemeinschaft und Gesellschaft*. Leipzig.

West, S. (1999). 'Social Space and the English Country House'. In S. Tarlow and S. West (eds), *The Familiar Past? Archaeologies of Later Historical Britain*. London and New York: Routledge.

Wilson, T. (1553 [1567]). *The Arte of Rhetorique* · iii. f. 92v. London.

Whyte, William. (2006). 'How do Buildings Mean? Some Issues of Interpretation in the History of Architecture'. *History and Theory* 45(2): pp. 153–177.

REBECCA DEVERS

7   Miracle Kitchens and Bachelor Pads: The Competing Narratives of Modern Spaces

ABSTRACT

'Miracle Kitchens and Bachelor Pads' examines the presentation of domestic spaces in early issues of Playboy, particularly the use of narrative techniques in such presentations, arguing that such a practice contributed to a new mythology of masculinity in mid-twentieth-century America. The analysed issues include devoted features on domestic space, specifically the bachelor pad and how one inhabited and furnished it. The essay examines short stories and fables published in these issues (for instance, 'The Amorous Goldsmith', 'Love, Incorporated', 'The Hoodwinked Husband', and 'A Cry from the Penthouse'), contemporary literary texts (John Cheever's 'O Youth and Beauty!' and Arthur Miller's *Death of a Salesman*), and social and literary theorists (including Pierre Bourdieu and Bill Osgerby) – as well as an advertisement for a new kitchen from a 1947 issue of *Good Housekeeping* – to argue that the magazine's successful establishment of the bachelor as a cultural icon depended upon narrative elements like plot, character development and setting, as well as upon conventional structures of myths.

In May of 1954, *Playboy* published its first rendering of a bachelor pad in a two-page cartoon titled 'Playboy's Progress'. It was a hand-drawn aerial plan of an apartment, with a step-by-step map to help the playboy make 'progress' with his 'friend'. A dotted line trails its way through the space with locations marked by numbers that correspond to lines of text in the bottom centre of the image. There is only a perfunctory introduction:

> Scene: *Playboy's penthouse*
> Time: *Shortly before midnight*
> Characters: *Playboy and friend* ('Playboy's Progress' 1954: 22)

Resembling both performance and ritual, the twenty-five steps guide the reader through the apartment and explain how to use the items within it to convince a somewhat reluctant 'friend' that she is, in fact, 'that kind of a girl' ('Playboy's Progress' 1954: 23). For a start, the successful bachelor will have planned ahead to ensure that certain items will be at his disposal. As the night progresses, the playboy 'puts romantic Glenn Miller records on phonograph'; 'mixes cocktails with spiked olives'; 'begins reading aloud from *This Is My Beloved*'; 'reads selected passages aloud from the *Kinsey Report*'; and 'puts on lounging robe' ('Playboy's Progress' 1954: 22). Furthermore, other necessary items, like a large painting of a nude woman and modern furniture appoint the space, and there is no distracting television. *Playboy* publisher Hugh Hefner intended the magazine to serve 'as a "handbook for the young man-about-town"' (quoted in Fratterigo 2009: 60), and 'Playboy's Progress' serves that purpose; here, in a single, hand-drawn image, is a treasure map of seduction.

Intended to be taken humorously, the conflict depicted in these steps is between an eager bachelor and an intoxicated woman who repeatedly asks for food as he serves her more alcohol. On the balcony, she rejects his first reference to the bedroom by slapping him. His response? He 'considers tossing her off balcony' ('Playboy's Progress' 1954: 23). Eventually, he decides instead to find another number in his little black book. The friend decides to stay when she realises it's raining, and when the bachelor feigns disinterest. She is finally swayed after reconsidering his references to the *Kinsey Report*, which announced that 'Females who have relations make better adjustments after marriage' ('Playboy's Progress' 1954: 22).

The playboy's route of seduction takes the couple through every room of the apartment, including the kitchen, bathroom and balcony, images of which are relegated to the margins so that the reader's focus is primarily on the living room. At points, the 'Friend wanders off towards kitchen' ('Playboy's Progress' 1954: 22); 'staggers into kitchen'; and 'refuses passionate embrace' in the bathroom ('Playboy's Progress' 1954: 23). And, when the friend 'follows playboy' as he 'wanders off in the general direction of bedroom', the narrative ends with '*Curtain*' ('Playboy's Progress' 1954: 23). The rest is left to the reader's imagination, even though every step leading up to it has been presented in specific detail. The playboy appears to have needed this entire space – and everything in it – to accomplish his goal (the convenient rain storm was a nice touch, too). Using elements of both design and narrative, 'Playboy's Progress' establishes a habitus of mid-century masculinity, helping to define a domestic space that was at once both believable and mythical, a perfect setting for an alternative definition of masculinity after World War II. These narrative elements allow *Playboy* to create a new fable of masculinity; the instructions presented in design articles like this one, alongside the fictional pieces published in the issues, redefine cultural expectations and establish a new set of ideals in opposition to the dominant narrative of suburban life.

In this chapter I analyse the stories published in the first six volumes of *Playboy* (1953–9) in which also appeared the following devoted 'Modern Living' articles: 'Playboy's Penthouse Apartment' in September and October of 1956; 'Playboy's Weekend Hideaway' in April 1959; 'The Kitchenless Kitchen' in October 1959; and the 'compendium' on the bed itself, including articles on the psychology and physiology of sleep, in November 1959. When read alongside these architectural designs for bachelor pads, the stories help to define what would have been, for most of *Playboy*'s readers, what was always already (and irrevocably) an imagined space.[1] *Playboy* admitted as much in April 1958 in 'Meet the *Playboy* Reader', which acknowledged that many readers were married and lived in the suburbs. The fantasy space of the bachelor pad became a safe, alternative world in which counter-narratives could be enacted. *Playboy* encouraged this mythical identification of the reader with these fictional spaces by using second person pronouns and describing the inhabitant as 'a man very much, perhaps, like you' ('Meet the *Playboy* Reader' 1956: 54).

In the five issues in question, there appeared twenty-one fictional short stories. Of these, five are included under the 'Ribald Classics' heading, in which other cultures' fables of seduction and deception are presented in translation. Three are military stories, which feature US soldiers abroad; only one of these three did not focus on sex. Of the remaining stories, all but one focus on sexual relationships between men and women. Ten marriages are described, seven of which contain infidelities. There are cheating

---

[1] Bill Osgerby sees the bachelor pad as having only ever been 'a mythological construct' since 'only a wealthy élite were able to turn the fantasy into reality' (Osgerby 2005: 110).

husbands and cheating wives (though some of the women are duped into adultery). Only three stories present successful, monogamous relationships, and they do so unironically. All of the stories were written by men.

A few exemplary stories from *Playboy*'s earliest volumes demonstrate the ways in which the magazine engaged in a mythologising or 'enfabling' of the playboy, situating him as a model of aspirant behaviour. Though the fables varied depending on the gender of their target audience, similar fabling strategies also appeared in print advertisements targeting women and in contemporary literary interrogations of the suburban ideal. Eventually, *Playboy* made the bachelor fable transferrable by situating it in a country home for weekend getaways. Many social historians have examined the magazine's impact on American society; Elizabeth Fratterigo (2009), Bill Osgerby (2001, 2005), Beatriz Preciado (2004) and Pamela Robertson Wojcik (2010) provide important cultural context for the living spaces presented in *Playboy* as well as the shifts in definitions of masculinity in postwar America. With especial attention to the literary elements in the magazine, I build on the work of social historians, examining the ways in which literature and narrative enabled the magazine to achieve mythic proportions.

In the issues analysed here, the only non-military story in which no women appear is Henry Slesar's 'A Cry from the Penthouse'. The story appears in the November 1959 issue, which also contains the 'Compendium' on the bed: articles in a scientific tone on the interpretation of dreams and the physical effects of sleeplessness, as well as photos of 'Beds from Other Times and Places' (which includes female models), a short article on the lounging robe and the introduction of the Playboy Bed. This was the first such compendium in *Playboy*'s history, bringing together scientific expertise, imagined design and photographs of female models. The issue's formal attention to the bed makes the bed's absence from Slesar's story even more apparent. In 'A Cry from the Penthouse', Chet Brander visits his friend Frank Coombs to get repaid for a loan. It is a brutally cold winter evening, and Frank lives in a brand new, nearly empty Manhattan building. The narrator, voicing Chet's thoughts, finds the place 'eerie', noting 'an unearthly quiet that was a combination of overcarpeting and underoccupancy' (Slesar 1959: 34). When Chet rings the doorbell of the penthouse, he derisively calls his friend, under his breath, a 'Big shot!'

Chet does not think Frank could afford this swanky new pad without his friends' loans, so the apartment projects Frank's dissimulating character. When Chet enters the apartment, he feels 'warmth': 'Pleasant steamheat-and-fireplace warmth, whiskey warmth, the warmth of geniality. That was Coombs for you: the perennial host, always ready to smile and clap you on the back and make you welcome, and all so smoothly that you hardly even noticed the hand dipping into your pocket to count the contents of your wallet' (Slesar 1959: 34, 36). *Playboy* elsewhere touted the importance of being a good host: Fratterigo points out that 'Thomas Mario's monthly "Food and Drink" columns highlighted the performance of the bachelor chef and linked cooking with seduction and sexual pleasure' (Fratterigo 2009: 93); however, Slesar's story reveals that hosting is really just a performance, a ritual like the one shown in 'Playboy's Progress'. It is a set of actions one might master in order to manipulate someone and therefore obtain a desired outcome.

Chet then sees 'the lavish front room. It was a room rich in textures: furry carpets and nubby upholstery, satiny drapes and grainy wood panelling' (Slesar 1959: 36). The association of space and character continues as the narrator segues from describing the front room to describing Frank himself: 'Coombs had many textures himself: waxen smooth hair, silken cheeks, velvety smoking jacket, roughcut briar'; perhaps channelling Hef, Frank Coombs even 'gesture[s] with the pipe' (Slesar 1959: 36). Frank knows he's living 'the life'. Moreover, this description reinforces our tendency to see a character's domestic space as an extension or projection of his personality or priorities.

Frank lures Chet to the balcony, and then locks him out of the apartment, exposed to the deadly winter weather too far from the street for his cries to be heard. It's clear that Frank intends to kill off his creditor to avoid repayment. He leaves, and Chet must fend for himself. Eventually, Chet is able to scale to the roof of the building and pull out the tenants' television cables, bringing concerned residents to the roof to investigate. After a short recovery, Chet lets himself back into Frank's apartment (Frank had slipped the key into his pocket to make it appear as if Chet had been there alone). When Frank comes back drunk, he checks the balcony and Chet deftly locks him out there to die.

Frank uses his apartment not for sexual exploits, but to seduce his friend into a vulnerable position. One can see in the story a warning against aspiring to the playboy life undeservedly. This story establishes an 'honour code' for the playboy: he may be a rogue with the ladies, but fatal consequences loom should he deal unfairly with his male friends. The occasional military stories support this fraternal standard, as did the one fraternity story in October 1956, in which membership in a male social group was more important than a romantic relationship. Fraternal strength was the titular 'right kind of pride'. Such stories help to develop the character of the imagined, mythical bachelor who might inhabit the fictional spaces of the bachelor pads pictured throughout the magazine. They also establish a society of shared ideals, helping to normalise not only the serial sexual exploits but also the very fact of a heterosexual man living alone. Fratterigo writes, 'In the hetero-normative climate of the 1950s the unmarried man prompted suspicion about his sexual orientation. *Playboy*'s pad emphasised the bachelor's heterosexuality by gearing its technologies for seduction' (Fratterigo 2009: 87). This heteronormativity extends beyond the design features, since the stories often provide examples of seduction. But even stories set within homosocial environments model standards of acceptable behaviour for those who would desire to live in this alternative fantasy space.

Because Frank Coombs's bed is never seen, we can only assume it was either inspired by or aspires to be The Playboy Bed. Osgerby explains, 'More than a piece of furniture, the "Playboy Bed" was a magnificent temple to the ethos of masculine consumerism' (2005: 109). The bed acts as the command centre of the apartment, housing everything from 'an automatic on-off (voice-activated) dictating machine' to 'power amplifiers' and 'two-dozen man-sized plate switches in polished woods for control of your entire apartment' (The Playboy Bed 1959: 104). The magazine made no secrets about its celebration of sex, so of course the bed and the bedroom would be a highlight of any bachelor's apartment.

The dominating narrative of the bachelor space, then, becomes one of seduction. Once he has mastered its conveniences and possibilities, he can use it as a weapon to get whatever he wants, whether that be sex, money, or popularity. The Playboy Bed was the locus of this power, and it could be the command centre of the apartment no matter how many women he shared it with. In terms of spatial design, the shift effectively removes the bachelor pad from the realm of the traditional and the suburban, reinforcing its presumed novelty and dynamism. In fact, the idealised bachelor pad was often so far removed from the realm of the traditional, with all of its push-button technology, that it sounded more like Ray Bradbury's (1950) 'There Will Come Soft Rains' than a design layout. Just as the McClellan home in Bradbury's post-apocalyptic future appears to have made the housewife's role obsolete, performing all the cooking, cleaning and even childcare automatically, 'the bachelor pad itself', to quote Fratterigo (2009: 87), 'took over the wifely duties of greeting and soothing the man returning from the realities of the outside world'. Fratterigo is referring specifically to the 1956 Penthouse Apartment, but certainly the command-centre bed contributes to this house-as-housekeeper image. And while the McClellan Home eventually crumbled without its inhabitants, the bachelor pad thrives on the imagined potential presence of 'a man very much, perhaps, like you'.

Though it was published a little later than the issues examined here, a short story by Bruce Jay Friedman helps to demonstrate how *Playboy* used simple narratives to reinforce the attraction of the mythical bachelor pad. 'The Killer in the TV Set' describes *in extremis* the hegemonic suburban narrative, against which *Playboy* set itself in opposition.[2] The story follows Mr Ordz, an ordinary married man, during the last week of his life. One evening, unable to face another sexual encounter with his wife, he stays up as late as possible watching television. The MC of a variety show addresses him by name, announcing that he has only seven days to kill Mr Ordz. The stalking continues for a week, until Ordz's skepticism turns into frustration. Ordz punches his television screen, the broken glass slices his wrist, and he dies trying futilely to wake his wife. Friedman presents a macabre suburban routine, presumably what one avoided by living in a bachelor pad where one eschewed television (and all ordinary things) altogether, because one could make 'progress' with a different woman every night.

---

2   For a discussion of *Playboy*'s relationship to the suburban mentality, see Osgerby 2001: 61–86; Osgerby 2005, Fratterigo 2009, especially pp. 15–47; Preciado 2004; Wojcik 2010: pp. 91–9.

Through their use of simple, straightforward plots, sympathetic and relatable characters and successful counter-narratives that subverted a monotonous suburban existence, *Playboy* was able to create a modern fairy tale or fable – a 'sharable tale' meant to exemplify idealised and repeatable social behaviours. In *The Irresistible Fairy Tale: The Cultural and Social History of a Genre*, Jack Zipes (2012: 25) explains that fairy tales are influential carriers of moral instruction and that they help to establish new or alternative 'standards of behaviour', whereas fables have a 'civilising' effect because of their capacity to 'establish ethical guidelines or principles of fair play' (Zipes 2012: 10). Leslie Kurke, referring to the work of James Scott, develops this idea in relation to hegemonic narratives, seeing fables as vehicles for 'counterideology' because 'they are "off-stage" – that is, free from the public world whose performances are largely scripted by the dominant' (quoted in Zipes 2012: 11). While one would be hard-pressed to characterise the owner of a penthouse apartment or a weekend hideaway as 'oppressed', one can nevertheless see the playboy lifestyle as a subversive one, one kept 'off-stage' in favour of a stable family life. Because the bachelor pad navigates the permeable boundaries between private and public (see Preciado 2004), it permitted men to, 'according to Hefner, enjoy the privileges of public space without being subjected to its laws and dangers' (Preciado 2004: 219). Stories like Ordz's demonstrate this sanctuary effect, as Ordz's death emphasises by contrast the bachelor pad as a fantasy space, beyond the reaches of tedious social convention.[3]

On its surface, Ordz's fate is a warning to the *Playboy* reader to escape the doldrums of suburbia (including both monotony and monogamy) before it was too late. It sets the bored husband in opposition both to his wife and marriage, and to the trappings of suburbia itself in the metonymic television set, both a marker and progenitor of middle class conformity. A narrative like 'Playboy's Progress', by contrast, establishes the 'alternate reality' in which a new set of standards can be promoted. Just as the first fairy tales from the late seventeenth and early eighteenth centuries provided

---

3   Fratterigo notes that some were afraid of this power of *Playboy*, citing a Reverend who – in 1960 – saw the magazine as 'a sort of bible. Its modern living features carried the weight of the Ten Commandments' (2009: 74).

their authors – primarily French women – with fantasy settings in which safely to oppose both king and church (Zipes 2012: 25), so does *Playboy*'s narrative treatment of space provide a new set of rules for gender relations by couching them in the mythical setting of the bachelor pad. But beyond this, these narratives reinforce the importance of understanding the rules of whatever space one finds oneself in. In 'Playboy's Progress', the modeled seduction is certainly aggressive; in the case of Frank and Chet, the apartment is both a motive for and a tool of homicide; and Ordz's home life is so mundane, he loses touch with reality. In all three stories, domestic space carries a system of expectations – or habitus – that privilege not the woman, the thief, or the suburbanite, but the savvy bachelor.

Pierre Bourdieu defines habitus as the system of expected actions within a particular society which are at once the consequence of repeated actions in the past and the generators of future behaviours. These customs self-sustain, because they create an environment in which they are the valued and desired standards. While the treasure map of seduction presented in 'Playboy's Progress' is more explicit in what Bourdieu might call its 'conscious aiming at ends', it is also the product of *dis-*'obedience to rules' (Bourdieu 1977: 72). Explanations of how these spaces were to be used, coupled with fiction that contributed to the establishment of ideals for the society of bachelors reading *Playboy*, created a set of regular practices that essentially defined the parameters of a new serial, urban, modern masculinity, a counter-habitus to suburban hegemony.

Playboy's use of the bachelor pad as alternative reality allows for the projection of idealised systems of behaviour: there, surrounded by the appropriate (i.e. masculine) consumer goods, the playboy can navigate a habitus more suited to his personal desires, rather than the desires of a society that saw the family as its bulwark against communism.[4] 'Playboy's Progress' presents this system obliquely; in Bourdieu's terms, it is a list of 'things to do or not to do, to say or not to say, in relation to a *forthcoming* reality' (Bourdieu 1977: 76). The promoted examples of seduction – for example, of women, rather than the deception of one's male friends – are

4   For more on *Playboy*'s role in creating a male consumer, see Osgerby 2001 and Osgerby 2005.

hereby institutionalised: through repetition, such behaviours begin to assume the air of the commonplace, rather than the 'off-stage', and, while the setting enabled the behaviours to emerge, their enfablement allows them to be both imitated and transferred. Without narrative, then, the spaces could not have achieved this mythological status. The fabled bachelor – a bachelor with a story, or a collection of stories – was necessary in order for readers to understand the space within a defined system of interactions and expectations. One had to understand how to live as a playboy before one could imagine living in such spaces. Character and setting rely on each other here in order for each to be believable; in Pamela Roberson Wojcik's (2010: 89) words, 'the bachelor pad produces the bachelor as playboy; simultaneously, the figure of the playboy produces the space of the bachelor pad'.

Print media promoted and reinforced the dominant habitus of suburbia as well, targeting women in publications like *Good Housekeeping*. Consider the advertisement for a new kitchen from Crosley.[5] In September 1945, Crosley promoted the ease with which the housewife could modernise her kitchen, even without her husband's help. This full-page advertisement boasts a headline in the voice of its excited narrator: 'This string is all I need to plan my NEW kitchen!' (Crosley 1945: 120). Four hand-drawn images show a series of events: Mother is won over by this new-fangled string method, the kitchen is planned and realised, and – finally – husband Jack gazes approvingly at his wife bent over in front of the range in her (*their*) modern kitchen. A great deal of text accompanies these images, making the advertisement resemble a comic strip in its marriage of narrative and art. This text explains Mother's hesitancy to believe in the simplicity of modernisation. When she sees the young wife's own hand-drawn plans, however, 'Mother says it's a marvel of arranging – and she ought to know, with thirty years of housekeeping!' The kitchen allows for the young wife's 'work [to flow] along just like a war-plant assembly line', and it can be bought in stages. The final image is set in the future, when 'one wonderful day', Jack will return to this new modern space.

5   For more on the use of technology in the Cold War kitchen, see Devers 2014.

The theme of Crosley's narrative is simplicity; no math is required, nor is there any 'bother, upset, or troubles generally considered necessary in kitchen modernizing'. She does not even have to measure or use numbers. All she needs is a string, so that she can mark the spaces available for new appliances. The modern efficiency of war-time assembly lines gets translated to the suburban home as just enough modern masculinity (in the form of manufacturing efficiency) is introduced into what was traditionally a feminine space. The result of this process is that the kitchen becomes a jointly owned space: the wife corrects her claim of ownership of the kitchen, calling it 'my new kitchen – *our* kitchen – for Jack and me'.

Everything about the Crosley advertisement is aspirant. First, it encourages buying the new kitchen in stages, based on what the young couple can afford. They are encouraged to plan ahead with this dream kitchen in mind. Furthermore, only Mother and the young wife are currently home to plan this kitchen. Husband Jack is (presumably) away at war, and because of the war, Crosley themselves do not even have access to this modern kitchen yet. The disclaimer beneath the image of the completed kitchen notes: '(Crosley is still 100 per cent in war production. But we're planning new marvels for you in the finest Crosley Home Appliances ever!)' In connecting a modern kitchen with the war effort, the narrative shifts from a family anecdote to a fable of patriotism. The implied message is that one should look forward to incorporating 'war-plant assembly line' methods in one's home, calling up the association at this time of homemaking and civil defense.[6] The series of steps in 'Playboy's Progress' instructs the young bachelor, the way Crosley instructs the young wife, on how to furnish and navigate a specific space – and a shifting modern habitus – in order to realise a dream. Notably, the Crosley advertisement encourages the same modernisation (even militarisation) of the kitchen that *Playboy* did; but here, it's within the dominant narrative of suburban matrimony, sanctioned by the patriotic myth of national pride.

The message about the bachelor's kitchen was inconsistent. He was, without question, given permission to cook, entertain and host parties in ways that the magazine safely contained within narratives of heterosexual

6   See, for example, McEnaney 2000 and Lichtman 2006.

exploits, and the kitchen he used was definitely modern (see Preciado 2004, especially 229). But when the playboy lifestyle was removed from the city, more traditional gender divisions reemerged. In April 1959, as part of the feature on 'Playboy's Weekend Hideaway' (discussed in greater detail below), the kitchen is marginalised, separated from the central spaces of the house, if only visually. Moreover, in the narrative tour of that hide-away, the kitchen is used only by women. However, in October of the same year, in a feature called 'The Kitchenless Kitchen', the playboy learned of a structure that could disguise his cooking appliances when they werenot in use. The feature shows photos of a 'handsome hunk of furniture' that 'dispenses with a kitchen as such entirely' (53). Meant to allow the playboy to prepare food without interrupting his duties as host (i.e. without missing the party), the peninsula could be more central in the apartment. This ver-sion of a kitchen seems to eliminate or disguise those icons of traditional kitchens – 'it has no use for the usual collection of pots, pans, skillets, oven and other customary kitchen gear' (53) – in the same way that Crosley's kitchen eliminates the hassle of math. In both cases, readers learn how to adapt their kitchen to a gender-specific modern habitus: women make the kitchen modern to please their husbands; playboys avoid marriage by dis-guising the kitchen as much as possible, even if it *is* appropriately modern.

Literature published during these years demonstrates a need for this new playboy habitus. Notably, the 1949 production of *Death of a Salesman* relied on a stage design in which the dimensions of home were defined by characters' actions and mental states. Miller's stage direction tells us: 'Whenever the action is in the present the actors observe the imaginary wall-lines, entering the house only through its door at the left. But in the scenes of the past these boundaries are broken, and characters enter or leave a room by stepping "through" a wall on to the forestage' (Miller 1998: 1). This groundbreaking decision by designer Jo Mielziner allowed the play to make manifest the ways in which the dimensions of the Loman home are subject to the psychological instabilities of the homeowner.[7] But Willy

7   See Mielziner's account of designing this play in Mielziner 1965; the significance of transitioning between the house of the past and that of the present is discussed on p. 35. For more on Miller's use of 'subjective realism' to present to the theatre audi-ence Willy's experience of time, see Murphy 1995: 4–7.

Loman cannot modernise. He has an outdated kitchen with appliances that are falling apart before they're paid for. His stasis is a combination of his refusal to let go of tradition and his inability to sustain a career that would allow him to afford it, and as a result he is left behind. The world moves on without him, with 'a solid vault' of 'angry' apartment buildings towering over his 'fragile-seeming', 'partially transparent' house (Miller 1998: 1). *Playboy* would later take advantage of our tendency to equate space and character, introducing the second part of its Penthouse Apartment feature with the assertion: 'A man's home is not only his castle, it is or should be, the outward reflection of his inner self – a comfortable, livable and yet exciting expression of the person he is and the life he leads' ('Playboy's Penthouse Apartment' 1956: 65; also quoted in Fratterigo 2009: 84). But which version of home should a suburban husband present as his 'outward reflection'? The one with the assembly line kitchen he cannot afford? The extra, just-in-case concrete house in the basement, in which he would ride out the apocalypse? Or the one that was trying to kill him via the television set?

Some fictional men tried to adapt their suburban spaces to suit their needs, a technique *Playboy*'s bachelors would master. It did not work out so well for Cash Bentley in John Cheever's 1953 story 'O Youth and Beauty'. The story was published the same year as *Playboy*'s first issue, signaling the need for the safe space offered by *Playboy*'s bachelor pads. Cash – an erstwhile high school track star – notoriously punctuates suburban dinner parties with a sort of domestic steeplechase, in which he rearranges the living room furniture and – at the sound of the starting gun – runs through the space leaping magnificently over the repurposed furnishings. He becomes depressed when he breaks his leg and can no longer perform this ritual of youth. One night, frustrated and drunk, he decides to run the race in his own living room, with just his wife as audience. She fires the starting gun ineptly, and the bullet kills him in mid-air as he leaps over the couch. Cash may have been more successful than Mr Ordz at adapting his suburban space to suit his needs, but this success is short-lived. Like Ordz, Cash dies in an absurd accident caused by his own desperation and his wife's carelessness. The space portrayed in 'Playboy's Progress', therefore, appears even more mythical. It is already repurposed; there is nothing there superfluous to seduction. Nothing needs be moved or repositioned in order for the Playboy to celebrate his youth.

In Bourdieu's words, what these men needed was a new, more appropriate environment for their desired actions. Bourdieu argues that 'practices are always liable to incur negative sanctions when the environment with which they are actually confronted is too distant from that to which they are objectively fitted' (Bourdieu 1977: 78). Simply put, the pages of *Playboy* presented a new definition of 'the impossible, the possible, and the probable' (ibid.); the bachelor pad presented a setting in which such definitions could be realised. What was idealised in the mythical bachelor pad would have been 'unthinkable or scandalous' (ibid.) in the suburbs. The 'negative sanctions' incurred by Bentley and Ordz suggest that attempts to subvert the dominant narrative from within the suburban setting itself would be ruinous.

The magazine's inclusion of actual fables prepares the reader to consider the playboy's behaviour within the boundaries of such systems. Notably, the fables included in the studied issues do not support the suburban ideal. Instead, these fables reinforce the commodification of women and duplicity within romantic relationships, normalising and contextualising the fable of seduction presented in design articles. For example, in September 1956, *Playboy* printed 'The Amorous Goldsmith'. In this tale, a man falls in love with a woman he sees in a painting. He seeks out the woman who inspired the image, travels to another country to find her, and invents the evidence to have her arrested as a witch. Then he bribes the jailer and takes her home as his own. In this Arabic tale, as in 'Playboy's Progress', an eager bachelor gets what he wants because he has means; the desires of the young woman are of no interest to him. The following month, in the October 1956 issue that included the second part of the Penthouse Apartment feature, 'The Hoodwinked Husband' presents the story of a Venetian man who is so blinded by love for his new wife that he is tricked into paying for sex with her after helping her cuckold him with his own boss.[8] The boss's lesson for the young husband is particularly relevant to a

8   The original author is identified as Masuccio Salernitano; no translator is identified.

discussion of domestic spaces: 'wives, however fair they may be, must be reckoned as part of the regular furniture of the house, something to serve our pleasant uses whenever we may stand in need. But married or unmarried, we lusty men must always be on the look out for some fresh morsel. Nature demands it' (1956: 87). If a man respects his wife enough to think of her as more than 'furniture', then, according to this fable, he is setting himself up to be 'hoodwinked'. This young husband has not yet learned to navigate the appropriate habitus.

That the playboy habitus could be transferred beyond the bachelor pad suggests its ascension to the level of myth or fable. Wojcik, who examines *Playboy*'s bachelor pads as part of her larger study on apartments in popular culture, suggests that 'the bachelor pad raises the possibility that one's identity is not stable or essential but determined by location' (Wojcik 2010: 109); however, the presence of narrative within the design features and the buttressing of such features with fiction and fables, encourages the reader to imbue these spaces with more symbolic significance. The bachelor pad transforms the familiar 'once upon a time, in a land far away' to a setting more immediate and accessible while still providing a safe space in which alternate modes of expression and interaction can be imagined. Once these standards are established, they can be enacted anywhere, as long as all participating parties are conversant in them.

The fabled playboy was so well established as early as 1959 that he could safely take his narrative out of his city apartment. In April 1959, *Playboy* published 'Playboy's Weekend Hideaway', another installment in the Modern Living series. Designed by James E. Tucker and rendered by Robert Branham, the home is presented in seven pages of colourful hand-drawn images, presented as 'plans for a bachelor's haven far from the madding crowd' (Tucker and Branham 1959: 49). The text provides specifics on the bachelor's ideal country home, including how it is furnished and how it might be used to help the bachelor entertain and seduce. The drawings are landscape-oriented, asking the reader to rotate the magazine, flipping pages from bottom to top rather than from right to left. The title page shows a modern house from an aerial view; situated in a bucolic setting by a lake and boasting its own pool and garage, the house is a marvel of modern architecture with a porch and an abundance of floor-to-ceiling windows. The natural setting, 'far from the madding crowd' of the city, enhances the home itself.

Turning the page, the reader sees a new aerial view of the home, this time with the roof removed so the floor plan is visible. The narrative begins with exposition and the establishment of relatability; the reader discovers that what makes this house special is that it is designed for the city-dweller who appreciates nature 'in measured amounts [...] which immediately sets him apart from farmers and commuters' (Tucker and Branham 1959: 50). This man, 'perhaps like you' (Tucker and Branham 1959: 53), desires an escape from the city without escaping from its modern conveniences. Different sections of the house receive this attention: the living room, which is sandwiched between pool and lake; the rec room or 'cave' downstairs, with windows offering an under-water view of the pool – 'luminous living murals' – and an array of games (1959: 53); the master bath and master bedroom. Notably, while the house has a kitchen, that space has no dedicated text here. Instead, the 'food bar and cooking corner' is seen from another view of the living room. While the authors do use the word 'kitchen' in this caption, they focus on the ways in which the space 'is visually separated from the rest of the room' and the fact that there are indoor and outdoor barbecues (Tucker and Branham 1959: 54).

After the setting is established and the pictorial tour is complete, the narrative continues, taking up a full page on the reverse of the final images of the house. The reader would have those images in mind as he followed the plot provided here, imagining himself in the dream house he'd just seen. The narrative is written in second person point of view, demanding the reader's participation: 'As your sports car winds up the last quarter mile of road, you see the hideaway very much as it is pictured on Page 49 [*sic*]' (Tucker and Branham 1959: 53). After the details of the home are reviewed, a specific series of events unfolds. 'Let's say that you, as proud possessor of this bachelorly domain, have driven up from the city with your dinner companion on a Friday night; Saturday morning finds you stretching luxuriously in the master bedroom's huge double bed' (56). This fantasy continues, with guests arriving and enjoying the hideaway with the owner. The fantasy culminates in the reader's realisation: 'within these walls you are, literally, an irresistible host' (56).

What distinguishes this from a suburban home is the sophistication of its gadgets, its prioritisation of leisure activities,[9] and the seriality of the guests; otherwise, the gender divisions of the suburbs remain. 'Soon other guests arrive and while the girls all go do a spot of cooking, you take the men down to the rec room to show them the underwater windows facing the pool, the bar, the juke box and the large circular card table where, from time to time, there are stag poker sessions that last almost the entire weekend. And then you go back upstairs to join the girls' (Tucker and Branham 1959: 56). Moreover, the bachelor is comfortable in this space: he is not fighting it the way Ordz, Loman and Bentley did; and he did not attain it nefariously the way Frank Coombs did. This 'hideaway', then, becomes the ultimate success of the fabled playboy: his myth is transferrable and no longer merely another possibility afforded by city life. More than being, as in Fratterigo's construction, 'a state of mind' (2009: 102–3), the bachelor's home was defined by a system of acceptable and expected behaviours, a mode of communication among like-minded men (and willing women) that allowed for expressions of identity and desire that the language of the suburbs could not approximate.

To conclude, the establishment of the bachelor pad as a mythic space was propelled by narrative tours of fictional spaces, as well as fictional short stories, which reinforced through repetition the characteristics, settings, actions and concerns of the man who might live there. *Playboy* could present this imagined space alongside possible characters and plots that helped bring a believable, relatable dimension to otherwise static design drawings. The fable of seduction associated with the playboy contributed to a new habitus of mid-century masculinity, opposing a stifling, monotonous

---

9   See Preciado 2004 for a discussion of ways that *Playboy* helped men reclaim domestic space through sex; she writes, '*Playboy* magazine's most urgent mission was to take back the house, because only the interior space, as a gender performative machine, could effectuate the transformation of the man into the Playboy' (p. 226). Furthermore, Fratterigo's phrasing when describing the magazine's view of family life recalls the militarisation seen in modernising narratives: '*Playboy* jettisoned the family and instead forged a combination of domesticity and masculinity in the figure of the consumption- and pleasure-oriented bachelor' (2009: 103).

narrative that celebrated the family and the suburbs. Recognising this
mythologising of the bachelor allows us to recognise the ways in which
domestic space becomes an agent of oppression and power. In many of these
stories, women's choices are marginalised and (in one fable) seduction is
tossed aside in favour of false arrest and kidnapping. The list of dead men
in the narratives discussed here – Coombs, Ordz, Bentley, Loman – also
suggests that failure to adapt to a changing habitus, or trying to live within
the wrong one, is dangerous and destructive, regardless of gender or locale.
This undercurrent of warning lends urgency to the magazine's message,
helping *Playboy*, in a sense, to write itself into importance. It also reveals
to us our essential need for narrative – for plots that exemplify standards,
for themes that convey memorable lessons and for relatable characters in
familiar (or enviable) situations – in our formation of our understanding
of ourselves.

Bibliography

Arberry, A. J. (translated 1956). 'The Amorous Goldsmith'. *Playboy* 3(9): pp. 37, 77–8.
Bourdieu, P. (1977 [1972]). *Outline of a Theory of Practice*. Translated by R. Nice.
    Cambridge: Cambridge University Press.
Bradbury, R. (1979 [1950]). 'There Will Come Soft Rains'. In *The Martian Chronicles*.
    New York: Bantam: pp. 166–72.
Cheever, J. (2000 [1953]). 'O Youth and Beauty!' In *The Stories of John Cheever*. New
    York: Vintage: pp. 210–18.
Crosley Inc. 'This string is all I need to plan my NEW kitchen!' Advertisement, *Good
    Housekeeping*, September 1945: p. 120.
Devers, R. (2014). '"You Don't Prepare Breakfast … You Launch It Like a Missile": The
    Cold War Kitchen and Technology's Displacement of Home'. *Americana: The
    Journal of American Popular Culture (1900-Present)* 13(1). <http://www.ameri-
    canpopularculture.com/journal/articles/spring_2014/devers.htm> accessed
    10 May 2015.
Fratterigo, E. (2009). *Playboy and the Making of the Good Life in America*. Oxford
    University Press, Oxford.
Friedman, B. J. (1994 [1961]). 'The Killer in the TV Set'. In *Playboy Stories*. Edited by
    A. K. Turner. New York: Penguin: pp. 77–85.

Lichtman, S. A. (2006). 'Do-It Yourself Security: Safety, Gender, and the Home Fallout Shelter in Cold War America'. *Journal of Design History* 19(1): pp. 39–55.

McEnaney, L. (2000). *Civil Defense Begins at Home: Militarization Meets Everyday Life in the Fifties*. Princeton, NJ: Princeton University Press.

Mielziner, J. (1965). *Designing for the Theatre: A Memoir and a Portfolio*. New York: Atheneum.

Miller, A. (1998 [1949]). *Death of a Salesman*. New York: Penguin.

Murphy, B. (1995). *Miller: Death of a Salesman*. Cambridge: Cambridge University Press.

Osgerby, B. (2001). *Playboys in Paradise: Masculinity, Youth and Leisure-style in Modern America*. Oxford: Berg.

Osgerby, B. (2005). 'The Bachelor Pad as Cultural Icon: Masculinity, Consumption and Interior Design in American Men's Magazines, 1930–65'. *Journal of Design History* 18(1): pp. 99–113.

Playboy Magazine. (1954). 'Playboy's Progress'. *Playboy* 1(6): pp. 22–3.

Playboy Magazine. (1956). 'Playboy's Penthouse Apartment' [part I]. *Playboy* 3(9): pp. 53–60.

Playboy Magazine. (1956). 'Playboy's Penthouse Apartment' [part II]. *Playboy* 3(10): pp. 65–70.

Playboy Magazine. (1958). 'Meet the Playboy Reader'. *Playboy* 5(4): p. 54.

Playboy Magazine. (1959). 'The Kitchenless Kitchen'. *Playboy* 6(10): pp. 53–8.

Playboy Magazine. (1959). 'The Playboy Bed'. *Playboy* 6(11): pp. 66–7, 104.

Preciado, B. (2004). 'Pornotopia'. In *Cold War Hothouses: Inventing Postwar Culture From Cockpit to Playboy*. New York: Princeton Architectural Press: pp. 216–53.

Salernitano, M. (1956). 'The Hoodwinked Husband'. *Playboy* 3(10): pp. 52, 87.

Sheckley, R. (1956). 'Love, Incorporated'. *Playboy* 3(9): pp. 16–18, 62, 76–7.

Slesar, H. (1959). 'A Cry from the Penthouse'. *Playboy* 6(11): pp. 34, 36, 40, 105.

Tucker, J. E., and Branham, R. (1959). 'Playboy's Weekend Hideaway'. *Playboy* 6(4): pp. 49–56.

Wojcik, P. R. (2010). '"We Like Our Apartment": The Playboy Indoors'. In *The Apartment Plot: Urban Living in American Film and Culture, 1945 to 1975*. Durham: Duke University Press: pp. 88–138.

Zipes, J. (2012). *The Irresistible Fairy Tale: The Cultural and Social History of a Genre*. Princeton, NJ: Princeton University Press.

PART III

Diminished Habitation

DAMIAN ROBINSON

8 A Home on the Waves: The Archaeology of Seafaring and Domestic Space

ABSTRACT

For the people who live and work aboard ships on voyages far from their terrestrial homes, they become much more than pieces of technology. Through the agency of the crew and their material culture domestic spaces are created allowing ships to become transitory homes away from homes. This chapter investigates this phenomenon in contemporary seafaring, where domesticity is related to the welfare of the crew and is a matter of avoiding fatigue and improving safety through regulation. Homes on the waves can also be detected in the archaeology of ancient shipwrecks through the same distinct combination of meaningfully patterned material culture set within the spatial structure of the vessel that is seen in seafaring today. The *Mary Rose*, a Great Ship from the English navy of Henry VIII, and the glass wreck from the anchorage of *Serçe Limanı*, Turkey, are used as case studies to illustrate how such homes can be reconstructed. At the heart of this investigation are the ship's crew – be they ancient or modern – and the active role that they play in making spaces habitable and in doing so creating homes upon the waves.

> She's not a machine. She's far more than a machine. She's a home.
>
> — CAPTAIN 'GRIFF' GRIFFITHS, HMS TIRELESS
> (Hennessy and Jinks 2015: 34)

Introduction

In a volume that deals with the concepts of the domestic environment, this chapter may stand out as something of an anomaly, being concerned as it is with seafarers whose terrestrial homes may be hundreds or perhaps thousands of miles away from the vessel on which they serve and which they may rarely visit. Yet the centrality of the domestic environment is such to our physical and mental well being that even in such transient maritime

communities everyday material culture is deployed in combination with the
structure of the ship and its rules, hierarchies and conventions (Weibust
1958, 1969) to create domestic spaces to which the mariner can retreat to
for rest and relaxation from the rigours of their lives on the waves. Such
maritime domestic spaces can be traced from the earliest trading vessels
archaeologically excavated through to anthropologies of contemporary
and near contemporary seafaring communities. Their continual construction across time and space would suggest that such domestic spaces are
closely inculcated with the practice of long-distance seafaring. As Captain
Griffiths of the submarine HMS Tireless succinctly puts it, for the mariner,
the ship is a home.

Performance, safety and transient domestic space

Why though should it be important to create such a sense of domestic
space aboard a ship? In the world of professional cycling such issues have
recently come to the fore with respect to those riders participating in the
'Grand Tours', the three major twenty-one day-long races around Italy,
France and Spain. During such events riders move from hotel to hotel,
rarely spending consecutive nights in the same bed. The effect upon athletic performance of such constant changes in environment is thought to
be considerable and drawing upon a body of research in sports science (for
example Cummiskey et al. 2013; Samuels, 2008), Team Sky Pro Cycling
have been attempting to ameliorate this through the creation of an impression of stability and continuity in these changing domestic environments
(<http://www.teamsky.com/> accessed 21 March 2016). The team and its
head, Sir David Brailsford, are widely known for their attention to detail and
the cumulative competitive advantages that can be derived from 'marginal
gains' in which the materiality of domestic space has a key role to play.[1]

---

1   See point 7 in Denyer 2013: <http://www.som.cranfield.ac.uk/som/dinamic-content/
     news/documents/manfocus35/management_focus_issue_35_15_steps.pdf > accessed

Initially, this was manifested by Team Sky's attempt to create similar sleeping environments through each rider having their own mattress, bedding and pillows that were transported and set up in that night's hotel room prior to the arrival of the riders.[2] The culmination of this came at the *Giro d'Italia*, the Tour of Italy, in 2015 when the team used a large truck-style motorhome for its leader, Richie Porte, to sleep in.

> It's good to have your own space and not have to pack and unpack your suitcase everyday. It's also nice to be able to get away from the race a little. It's also a sanctuary in there … The most important thing for me is that it had a good bed. Come ten o'clock I can go to bed and sleep well.[3]

The qualities that Porte is describing for the motorhome are essentially the same as those that could be ascribed to domestic space and it clearly became his 'travelling home' for the duration of his participation in that particular Grand Tour. For Brailsford and Team Sky the advantages of the motorhome experiment at the *Giro* was sufficient for them to consider using it in the next Grand Tour of the year, the *Tour de France*.[4] This was, however, something of a marginal gain too far for the UCI, the governing body of the sport, who moved quickly to amend its regulations (article 2.2.010) to state that: 'riders must stay in the hotels provided by the organiser throughout the entire duration of the race' on the basis of fairness to all riders.[5] For the UCI the threat was clear, teams with sufficient resources could afford

---

21 March 2016; also Slater 2012 for a discussion about the concept and how it resulted in the dominance of the Great Britain cycling team at the London Olympics <http://www.bbc.co.uk/sport/olympics/19174302> accessed on 21 March 2016.

2   Scott 2012 <https://roadcyclinguk.com/news/massage-mark-cavendish-and-team-morale-mario-pafundi-on-being-a-soigneur-with-team-sky.html#RmLx7SXFlvJyxEOU.97> accessed 21 March 2016.

3   Richie Porte quoted in Ferrand 2015 <http://www.cyclingnews.com/news/porte-says-marginal-gains-motorhome-at-the-giro-ditalia-is-a-sanctuary/> accessed 21 March 2016.

4   <http://www.teamsky.com/teamsky/sky%20sports%20news/article/54170#ctzJD TSsdOHAZPYd.97> accessed 21 March 2016.

5   <http://www.uci.ch/pressreleases/uci-management-committee-welcomes-progress-implementing-strategic-plan/> accessed 21 March 2016.

to create quiet and stable domestic environments for their riders, who
would reap a performance advantage. Instead the changes to the regulations ensured the continuation of the 'level playing field' whereby Grand
Tours would be won not only through a rider's ability to out perform the
rest of the peloton on the bicycle, but also in their ability to adapt the best
to their transient lives in hotel rooms of varying quality.

The science behind Brailsford's decision to invest in a 'marginal gains
motorhome' makes interesting reading from a seafaring perspective, as much
of the literature is concerned with physical performance and the mental
perception of effort. The debilitating effects of poor sleep can have serious
repercussions for the safety of a vessel at sea. Although the ability to function varies from person to person, sleep deprivation reduces the ability to
maintain exercise, as well as the tolerance for it, alongside elevating psychological states, such as neurosis, anxiety and depression (Martin 1981).
Indeed, sleep deprivation can lead to an inability to maintain attention
and alertness as well as significantly affecting reaction times, resulting in a
greater risk of accidents due to a reduced capacity to respond quickly (Scott
et al. 2006). The necessity for a crew to have sufficient rest, relaxation and
sleep is a feature of fundamental importance as it allows them to recover
both physically and mentally from the rigours of the voyage. This would
be of particular importance during the course of an arduous long-distance
sailing passage (or for that matter a cycling Grand Tour) when physical
and mental performance may also drop off through insufficient recovery
and the building up of a 'sleep debt' (Reilly and Edwards 2007). For Team
Sky, the emphasis is on rider comfort and the creation of a stable domestic
environment as a way to alleviate the worst excesses of fatigue and in doing
so aid athletic performance. The contemporary maritime community is
similarly interested in the impact of fatigue upon seafarers, although here
the emphasis is on crew safety and on mitigating against fatigue on-duty as
opposed to crew comfort and the creation of restful domestic spaces. This
is a relatively recent research area in the maritime literature,[6] where fatigue
is defined by the International Maritime Organization as:

6   Allen et al. 2008: 82. Also see Wadsworth et al. 2006; Wadsworth et al. 2008; Project
     Horizon 2011; Jepsen et al. 2015

A reduction in physical and/or mental capability as the result of physical, mental or emotional exertion which may impair nearly all physical abilities including: strength; speed; reaction time; co-ordination; decision making; or balance. (International Maritime Organization, MSC/Circular 813)

The economic impact of fatigue is clearly illustrated in first point of Marine Guidance Note 505(M), from the UK's Maritime and Coastguard Agency:

Fatigue kills: careers, clients, crew. Fatigue amongst seafarers is recognised to be a serious issue affecting maritime safety. Objective evidence consistently shows fatigue to be a contributory cause of accidents, injuries, death, long term ill health, major damage, loss of vessels and enormous environmental harm. (Maritime and Coastguard Agency, MGN 505 (M), 1.1, 2)

The extent to which fatigued crews contribute to accidents and losses is now becoming clearer as ship design and navigational improvements have reduced the frequency of shipping incidents caused by technological failures, highlighting the importance of the 'human element' in them (Hetherington et al. 2006, 402). For example, a review of deaths of British fishermen demonstrated that 74 per cent were due to accidents at work (Roberts 2004). The role that human error may have played in these accidents can, perhaps, be inferred from figures from the US Coastguard, which suggest that errors are responsible for somewhere between 75–96 per cent of all marine casualties.[7] Furthermore, 43 per cent of all accidents reported to the US Coastguard cite human error as the primary cause, a figure that in reality may rise to as high as 80 per cent.[8] The role that fatigue plays in this can be clearly seen in a report on 1,647 collisions, groundings, contacts and near collisions by the British Marine Investigations Branch (Marine Accidents Investigation Branch 2004: 4). This demonstrated that

---

7   Ibid. using data from a paper 'Human Error and Marine Safety' by Anita F. Rothblum (2000), US Coast Guard Research and Development Center <http://bowles-langley.com/wp-content/files_mf/humanerrorandmarinesafety26.pdf>.

8   Hetherington et al. 2006: 402 using data from a conference presentation by Ebsen et al. 1985. See also Project Horizon (2011: 5), which gives slightly different statistics notes that marine accident statistics show that 'human error' was the key contributory factor in 60 per cent of accidents and in 80–90 per cent of collisions.

a third of all groundings involved a fatigued officer alone on the bridge at night and that two thirds of vessels involved in collisions were not keeping a proper lookout. This report clearly outlined the contributory factors seen in the grounding of the general cargo vessel the Antari near Larne, Northern Ireland, on 29 June 2008, four years *before* the accident happened (Marine Accident Investigations Branch Report No. 7/2009). Here the fatigued officer of the watch fell asleep shortly after midnight and failed to make a necessary navigational course alteration that resulted in the ship grounding on a beach on a clear moonless night in calm seas with good visibility. There was also no additional lookout posted – despite it being a policy of the company, the flag state and the Maritime and Coastguard Agency – because the able seaman who would have done this duty was tired. Furthermore, the watch alarm was turned off so that it would not disturb the sleep of the off-duty officer. There was clearly a catalogue of failures that resulted in the grounding of the Antari, but the level of fatigue in the crew underpinned all these.

The Maritime and Coastguard Agency recommends that a 'Fatigue Management Plan' be put in place for every vessel, as 'organisations which manage fatigue effectively are shown to experience significantly reduced levels of accidents, injuries and staff turnover' (Maritime and Coastguard Agency, MGN 505 (M), 2.2: 2). Enshrined within this, amongst other things, is the concept of the 'Habitability' of the vessel, which is also seen in national laws, such as the UK's Merchant Shipping Act (1995, section 43), legislation from Classification Societies, such as the American Bureau of Shipping (American Bureau of Shipping 2002), and conventions of United Nations agencies (International Labor Organization 1953, Convention 92). These require vessels to have and maintain certain minimum standards with regards to crew accommodation, including berthing, sanitary, food, recreation, laundry and medical provision. Effectively these quantify and create the physical spaces for a domestic environment on board a vessel, as well as reinforcing the social and economic hierarchy between the officers and the rest of the crew. In dealing with crew accommodation requirements Article 6 of Convention 093 of the International Labor Organization says that: 'The location, means of access, structure and arrangement in relation to other spaces of crew accommodation shall be such as to ensure adequate security, protection against weather and sea, and insulation from heat and cold, undue noise or effluvia from other spaces'. Article 10.4 unpacks this in more detail and deals specifically with the floor area per person of sleeping rooms intended for ratings in vessels of different sizes ranging from 1.85 square metres per person on vessels of less than 800 tons, up to 2.78 square metres in vessels over 3,000 tons. Within this figure is included the space occupied by berths and lockers, chests of draws and seats,[9] the requirement for which are also specified.[10] The regulations denote that no more than four ratings should be berthed per room in individual beds, although in certain cases in passenger ships, permission may be granted to accommodate up to ten ratings per sleeping room.[11] Here it should also be noted that this does not apply to officers, who only need to share with at most one other person.[12] Such hierarchies are also carried over in to the requirements for mess room accommodation where the master and officers have a separate room from petty officers and other ratings, and also into recreational space.[13]

Whether approached from the perspective of performance or safety, it is clear that the creation of adequate domestic spaces is a major part of vessel design and shipboard life. The importance of making a 'home on the waves' therefore helps to ensure that crews are alert and capable of working *and* living at on board a ship at sea. These are fundamental issues that would also have concerned our seafaring ancestors, particularly those who undertook longer distance voyaging on vessels of a size that allowed the delineation of living space. It is clear though that in modern vessels while habitability regulations create domestic spaces for crews, it is through the agency of the crew that these sometimes extremely meagre spaces are transformed into 'homes'. Through working, eating and sleeping together on a ship, its crew

---

9   Ibid. article 10.6
10 Ibid. articles 10.22, 25, 27.
11 Ibid. article 10.10.
12 Ibid. article 10.9. Note also that in Team Sky, only the team leader lived in the motorhome, with the rest of the team staying in the designated hotel.
13 Ibid. articles 9, 11 and 12.

can be regarded as being part of a 'total institution',[14] or a community of practice (Acejo 2012: 78.). Through life on board the crew learn particular behaviours that allows them to cope with and participate in its smooth running. These can take the form of semi-formalised induction and training that habituate a new sailor to maritime life (Zurcher 1965), which in turn result in their acceptance of and participation in informal phenomena such as rituals, traditions, and shipboard customs (Acejo 2012, 78–9; Zurcher 1965). A good example is the ceremony of 'Crossing the Line', whereby those sailors who have never crossed the equator undergo a light hearted ritual initiation that helps to integrate them into the crew (Zurcher 1965: 396–7).

For Filipino sailors on board contemporary vessels,[15] effective crew membership involves developing good *pakikisama* skills (getting along), which are needed to be part of the community (Acejo 2012: 79). This is promoted through shared mess and entertainment areas where they socialise together, talk, watch Filipino films, play games from home and so on. Such interactions in shared spaces and in a familiar language (the working life on ships with multi-ethnic crews is generally English; Sampson 2003, 266; Acejo 2012: 80) and with familiar material culture enable the seafarers to cope with the isolation from their homeland and families and to crucially 'acquire a sense of sociability similar to that found at home' (Acejo 2012: 81).[16] In this situation, the rigid spatial and social structure of a vessel that enforces the separation of the crew from the officers may be something of a comfort, allowing both groups to relax separately in their own familiar shipboard communities.[17] These feelings are neatly summarised by a

14 Goffman 1961: xiii defined the total institution with regards to asylums. See Zurcher 1965 and also Lamvik 2012: 25–7 on the use of the prison metaphor by Filipino seafarers to refer to their lives on board ship and the 'sentence' of their contracts.

15 Filipino sailors make up roughly one in every four workers at sea, the largest national group, and work primarily as ratings aboard container ships, tankers and cruise liners (McKay 2007: 617–18).

16 Although most Filipino seafarers would identify themselves as 'belonging' in the Philippines rather than on the ship (Sampson 2003: 272–3).

17 See Østreng 2001, although Sampson (2003: 276) suggests that ships can be thought of as a deterritorialised mundane 'hyperspaces' and their multinational crews miniature 'global communities'. For naval vessels, see Zurcher 1965: 391.

deck-hand on a research vessel who definitely did not want to share his cabin with a visiting scientist: 'this is my house and the people who I bunk with are my buddies' (Bernard and Killworth 1973: 151).

For the archaeologist, it is notable that these domestic activities are both physically situated in definable spaces aboard ship and often involve material culture. In a modern vessel, for example, the karaoke machine is an important object in the messes of ships with a large Filipino crew (Clare 2014: 192). Singing alongside other sailors demonstrates good *pakikisama* skills and helps to create and maintain a sense of crew togetherness and moral: a 'happy-ship' (Weibust 1969: 451). Crucially, both the mess and the machine are things that the maritime archaeologist would normally be able to identify in the remains of the ships that they are excavating and while we may not be able to infer all, or indeed many, of the myriad social relationships entwined with them, a careful consideration of objects recovered from particular spaces, offers a way into the interpretation of ancient shipboard domestic space. For example, even in the most degraded British merchant shipwreck from the nineteenth and twentieth centuries, the location of the mess would be evident from concentrations of 'domestic' china and crockery in particular parts of the wreck. Such pottery can also be highly diagnostic as it was often overprinted with the name of the shipping company, or with their monograms or house flags (Laister 2006). Furthermore, some companies had specific types of china produced for the different classes on board the vessel and consequently, the distribution of these around the wreck could also give indications of the locations of, for example, the first-class dining room, compared to those of the second and third classes.[18] Through providing the name of the shipping company, a piece of china could also help to suggest the route that the vessel was embarked upon, provide an approximate date for the ship and even its name. The find location of particular pieces of 'domestic' material culture, as opposed to objects that would have formed parts of the cargo or fittings of the vessel, are thus of primary importance in the interpretation of shipboard domesticity.

18   Ibid. 76–7 for examples of first- and second-class china used on Red Star Line.

Domestic space and maritime archaeology

The Mary Rose

In the archaeology of seafaring, domestic spaces can be most easily recognised in the larger, well-excavated and published vessels. An example of
which is the warship the *Mary Rose*, which sank on 19 July 1545 in battle
against the French and which was raised in 1982 following its careful excavation and meticulous recording (Marsden 2003). The *Mary Rose* was a Great
Ship in Henry VIII's navy; it was a large, multi-decked, complex vessel. At
a little over 500 tons, she was around 50m long and 12m in breadth and
would have been an imposing sight (McElvogue 2015: 9).

On the Main deck of the ship three cabins were discovered and from
the artefacts recovered within them interpretations were made regarding
the on board roles of their occupants. In the forwardmost cabin a well-
made elm chest contained a gimballed compass, near to which was found
an ash case with two pairs of dividers (Marsden 2003: 118).[19] The presence
of these navigational instruments has led to the suggestion that this would
have been the cabin of the ship's pilot or Master. Furthermore, the location
of other pieces of navigational equipment on the Upper deck or within
the Sterncastle also suggests the presence of pilots in this area of the vessel,
which would have been 'the command-and-control nexus of the ship when
entering battle' (Hicks 2005: 266). The same types of artefacts can therefore
be seen in the *Mary Rose* in both their 'working' location and also stored in
their 'domestic' space. This clearly highlights the importance of the spatial
context of the find within the ship when it comes to the interpretation of
the different types of activities that could have taken place in the space.

Amidships on the starboard side of the Main deck were the two cabins
of the Barber-surgeon; one probably served as his quarters, the other his sur-
gery, inside of which was a chest containing medicinal materials (Marsden

---

19   See Gardiner 2005, chapter 7 for more information about the navigational instru-
      ments aboard the *Mary Rose*.

2003: 119).[20] This exceptional find contained more than sixty objects including pottery jugs and wooden canisters that would have contained medicines and/or ointments and glass phials for the storage of volatile or caustic/corrosive liquids, or scented waters or oils for shaving officers. Inside the chest and within the cabin were also found the other medical instruments, including pewter bleeding bowls, two syringes in brass and pewter that were either used for urethral irrigations or for introducing lotions into open wounds, and the turned wooden handles of surgical instruments and grooming equipment (Castle and Derham 2005).

A little further aft is the surviving third cabin on the Main deck. This contained a considerable number of woodworking tools, which suggests that it was most likely occupied by the ship's carpenter (Marsden 2003: 119).[21] The tools were stored within two chests found inside the cabin, or out and ready for use in wicker baskets, or on racks or hooks on the walls. Outside of the carpenter's cabin, was a simple crate that contained the largest variety and greatest numbers of woodworking tools. This suggests that there was a difference between tools that might have been personal possessions that were packed carefully in chests and those in the crate that were more likely to be ship's issue (McKewan 2005: 296–9).

While the interpretation of the profession of the occupants of each cabin was based upon the presence of the tools of their trades, each cabin and the chests within which so many of the tools were stored also contained personal possessions, which alongside evidence for sleeping platforms and straw-filled mattresses enabled the cabins to be regarded as a form of domestic space. For the Barber-surgeon and the carpenters, their cabins were both places of work and also rest and recreation. A *tabula* or tables set was found in the Carpenter's cabin, for example. This was a popular race game in Medieval Europe that eventually became known as Backgammon. Furthermore, eleven bone dice were also found in personal chests mostly in the vicinity of the Carpenter's cabin (Redknap 2005). Fishing gear was

20 See Gardiner 2005, chapter 4, for more information about the medical treatments and equipment aboard the *Mary Rose*.
21 See Gardiner 2005, chapter 8, for more information about the maintenance equipment aboard the *Mary Rose*.

also recovered from this cabin and, like the dice and games, this would have been used to while away the hours as a leisure activity (Every 2005). The occupants also owned two of the nine books discovered on the ship, with one of the others being found in a chest in the Pilot's cabin. These would have been expensive items in 1545 and the valued personal possessions of educated and wealthy men (Richards and Gardiner 2005). The other artefacts in the chest from the Carpenter's cabin within which the book was found were also of high quality and included silver coin and rings, pewter plate, a rare leather-encased sundial (Gardiner and Cowham 2005: 167), all of which helps solidify the impression of the ship's carpenter place in the socio-economic hierarchy of the vessel. These leisure-related artefacts also clearly demonstrate that even though the *Mary Rose* was a ship of war and was sailing out to do battle, its crew were also prepared for whiling away the long hours of off-duty inactivity that accompanied a life on the waves.

The Pilot, the Barber-surgeon and the Ship's carpenter were clearly important figures on the *Mary Rose* and through the combination of the surviving architecture of the ship and distinctive material culture their domestic spaces are identifiable. Such men, however, are a rarity and it is much more difficult to recreate domestic spaces for the majority of the 400 plus men aboard the vessel (Knighton and Loades 2000: 43). The widespread distribution throughout the remains of the ship of eighty-two combs may, however, provide an insight. Combs are very personal pieces that each sailor would most likely have owned; nine were found in association with human remains, one of which demonstrates that it was being carried about their person at the time of death (Richards 2005: 156–9, Figure 3.47). The same can also be said for the distribution of small multi-purpose knives that would have been essential items of kit for each man, of which fifty were found throughout the ship (Every and Richards 2005: 144–5, Figure 3.36). The widespread distribution of these personal items is also mirrored in that of the 'messing' items and eating and drinking utensils (Weinstein 2005a: 440–8, Figure 11.20; 2005b: 448–58, Figure 11.29), which were similarly widely distributed and may have been either personal property or standard issue items that were personalised (Weinstein, Gardiner and Wood 2005: 496). Importantly, the pewter plates that probably belonged to Sir George Carew (Weinstein 2005b, Figure 11.20), the

Vice-Admiral who flew his flag aboard the *Mary Rose* and went down with the ship, were stored in the galley. This would indicate that the ship sank between mealtimes with most of the cooking and serving equipment stored ready for their next use, which is only to be expected since the ship was sailing into battle. The wide distribution of messing items – 50 per cent of bowls recovered were found on the gun decks – would suggest that they were stowed where then men ate and slept (Gardiner and Wood: 497). Consequently, here amongst the guns of the Main deck and separated off from the cabins of the ship's officers would be the small domestic spaces of many of the sailors. A further concentration of chests and general material culture from the fragmentary remains of the Upper deck beneath the Sterncastle, would indicate another domestic area that could have accommodated up to 160 men (Gardiner and Wood: 498).

The Serçe Limanı ship

Domestic spaces can also be discerned in smaller shipwrecks through the same combination of the surviving architecture of the vessel and the associated material culture. A good example of this is the so-called glass wreck that was lost in the anchorage of *Serçe Limanı* on the southwest coast of Turkey around AD 1025. This vessel was meticulously excavated and recorded between 1977 and 1979 by the Institute of Nautical Archaeology at Texas A&M University (Bass and van Doorninck Jr 2004a).

The *Serçe Limanı* vessel was returning to somewhere in the region of Constantinople from a voyage to a port in the Fatimid caliphate. Here it had laded a cargo of 3 metric tons of cullet, which included over a ton of broken Islamic glass vessels, pieces of intact glassware, glazed Islamic bowls, red-ware cooking vessels, copper cauldrons and buckets, sumac and raisins (Bass 2004a: 3–4). After taking shelter in the seemingly safe anchorage of *Serçe Limanı*, the ship was blown upon the rocky shore after the iron shank of its starboard bower anchor snapped and was lost.

The hull of the ship was approximately 15m long with a beam of just over 5m. It was quite box-like in shape, which allowed it to carry a cargo of 35 metric tons. Three distinct domestic spaces can be identified from the remains, which provided accommodation for passengers and crew of different socio-economic status. At the bow of the ship was a compartment in which was found a small cache of Islamic glazed bowls and glass vessels alongside a now-perished box or bag that would have contained a personal grooming set – a wooden comb, pair of scissors, a razor and knife all in iron and the wooden handle perhaps of a mirror (Bass 2004b: 275) – alongside four Byzantine copper coins (Bass and van Doorninck Jr 2004b: 266). The presence of the grooming kit as well as food (sheep/goat and possibly pork suggesting Christian occupant(s) (Armitage 2004: 487–8)) in this compartment suggests that this was likely to have been a domestic space that was inhabited either by one of the merchants or a passenger/member of the crew who had purchased the Islamic objects in the bundle of goods perhaps to sell upon their return.

On the deck between a stack of five spare anchors and the main mast of the *Serçe Limanı* ship, a second domestic space was discovered. The workaday finds from this area would suggest that it was more likely for the crew or perhaps lower-class passengers.[22] These included storage, cooking and serving vessels in pottery and metal (Bass and van Doorninck Jr 2004b: 266–7), along with sheep/goat bones indicating the consumption of food here. Fishing net lead sinkers were also found in this mid-ship area, alongside spindle whorls and bronze net needles, which indicates that the crew may have whiled away some of their time spinning thread and sewing/repairing their nets. Three nets in total were found on board, which would have been set when the ship was moored: they may well have provided the fish consumed on the ship (Piercy and Bass 2004: 424–5). While fishing may have been more of an occupational task than a recreational pursuit, the remains of a Backgammon set found in this domestic area provides an insight into the kinds of activities in which the crew may have engaged.

The third domestic area of the *Serçe Limanı* ship was located at the stern where there was another large compartment separated from the cargo hold by a bulkhead (Bass and van Doorninck Jr 2004b: 268–70). In here were stored many of the personal possessions of the crew, merchants and

22   See Prior 1984.

passengers. These included a wicker basket containing a wide selection of woodworking tools with a sharpening stone and nails (Hocker 2004). These would have belonged to the ship's carpenter and it is interesting to note that the basket also contained a Byzantine steelyard, nearby which were two balance pans and a set of balance pan weights, perhaps suggesting that he also undertook some trading activities. Below the floor of the compartment was a small hold where personal cargoes and goods were stored, including fifty-one wine amphora that belonged to M(ichael), possibly the Captain of the ship (Bass and van Doorninck Jr 2004b: 270). It is notable that it is in this area at the stern of the vessel where the most expensive objects, such as the jewellery (Jenkins-Madina 2004), were discovered, along with most of the tools, weapons and mercantile equipment, suggesting that this was the domestic space for the most important people on board. The food remains reinforce this interpretation with a greater variety of meat and fish bones being recovered here than in the other domestic spaces, suggesting the higher social class of the people eating at the stern (Armitage 2004: 489). The types of games played aft were also different than those amidships, with the remains of a chess set being recovered. This was an intellectual game played by the upper classes, as opposed to the simple race game of Backgammon, which was played by the crew in the domestic space in the centre of the vessel (Cassavoy 2004: 337).

Conclusion

The *Mary Rose* and the ship from *Serçe Limanı* were deliberately chosen to exemplify how maritime domestic space is observable in the archaeological record, but they are not isolated examples.[23] Indeed a concern to understand the lading of a ship and to differentiate cargo from crew-use objects is seen from the very first scientifically excavated ancient shipwreck off

23   See Beltrame 2015 for a brief survey.

Cape Gelidonya in Turkey (Bass 1967a). While little of the hull survived, from the distribution of artefacts around the wreck site, it was possible for the excavator to confidently assert where the living quarters of the ship – assumed to be in the stern – came to rest and subsequently decayed (Bass 1967a: 45). Through the recognition that the spatial pattern of material culture from the wreck could be interpreted, George Bass was able to conclude that for this particular vessel from the Late Bronze Age:

> At least the more important members of the crew lived near to the stern, in an area lit at night by a single oil lamp. Their meals were supplemented ... [with] perhaps fish which they had caught with lead-weighted lines. ... On board a merchant was prepared to trade in almost any Eastern Mediterranean port ... For official transactions he carried his personal cylinder seal, which seems to have been an heirloom ... He, or perhaps members of the crew, also carried five scarabs as seals, souvenirs or religious talismans ... an astragal ... if it was not used to while away the hours in the game of knucklebones, offered divine guidance to the captain when he was in doubt. (Bass 1967b: 163)

The recognition of domestic spaces in the fragmentary archaeological remains of any the vessels are works of interpretation extrapolated from patterns and associations. We can never really know whether our Late Bronze Age, Byzantine or Medieval sailors really regarded their vessels as 'homes on the waves'. But what can be said with some confidence is that the anthropology of seafaring would certainly suggest that shipboard domestics spaces would have been something more that *just* a place for a mariner to sleep or to rest at the end of a long day at sea or a watch, or to store their possessions.

The importance of adequate rest for the crew of a sailing ship is clear from the literature on athletic performance and on the focus on fatigue in the modern maritime industry. Restful places are necessary to ensure that crews can repeatedly endure the harsh conditions that a working life at sea entails and one wonders at just how many ancient shipwrecks would have been caused by a desperately fatigued crew making the wrong decision or not reacting with sufficient speed when danger presented itself? If modern statistics can be any guide at all, the answer is likely to be a large proportion of them.

Maritime domestic space, however, is more than about simply getting sufficient sleep for a person to be able to adequately function. Mental relaxation is also of key importance and the consistent association in ancient shipwrecks of the spaces in which crews lived, with personal objects, such as pocket knives, combs and other grooming equipment, 'messing' items and drinking wares, games and other recreational pursuits, provide an insights. Through eating and drinking and playing games – as well as perhaps maintaining an acceptable standard of personal hygiene – crews would have bonded together, becoming part of a shipboard community rather than a disparate group of individuals. Given the associations of rest and relaxation with companionship and the safety from the perils of the sea that the ship brings, the extension of the metaphor of 'home' to a place of work potentially far from a mariner's actual home, is entirely understandable. Ships become more than just machines and through the social actions of their crews and through the use of material culture homes on the waves are created.

Acknowledgements

My interest in the domestic lives of seafarers began on board the research vessel Princess Duda during our annual missions to excavate the submerged port city of Thonis-Heracleion, Egypt. My thanks must therefore go to Eric Smith and also to Captain Mike Archer and Dick Stower for putting up with my innumerable questions about a sailor's life during our time in Aboukir Bay, Egypt. I would also like to thank Franck Goddio and the Hilti Foundation for allowing me to ask these questions in the first place.

Bibliography

Acejo, I. (2012). 'Seafarers and Transnationalism: Ways of belongingness ashore and aboard'. *Journal of Intercultural Studies* 33(1): pp. 69–84.
Allen, P., Wadsworth, E., and Smith, A. (2008). 'Seafarers' fatigue: a review of the recent literature'. *International Journal of Maritime Health* 59: pp. 81–92.

Armitage, P. L. (2004). 'Faunal Remains'. In G. F. Bass, S. Matthews, J. R. Steffy and
F. H. van Doorninck Jr, *Serçe Limanı. An Eleventh Century Shipwreck. Volume
1: The Ship and its Anchorage, Crew and Passengers*. Texas: A and M University
Press: pp. 471–92.

Bass, G. F. (1967a). 'Cape Gelidonya: A Bronze Age Shipwreck'. *Transactions of the
American Philosophical Society*. The American Philosophical Society: pp. 57–8.

Bass, G. F. (1967b). 'Conclusions'. In G. F. Bass (ed.), *Cape Gelidonya: A Bronze Age
Shipwreck. Transactions of the American Philosophical Society* 57(8). The American Philosophical Society.

Bass, G. F. (2004a). 'Introduction and Explanations'. In G. F. Bass, S. Matthews, J. R.
Steffy and F. H. van Doorninck Jr, *Serçe Limanı. An Eleventh Century Ship-
wreck Volume 1: The Ship and its Anchorage, Crew and Passengers*. Texas: A and
M University Press: pp. 3–9.

Bass, G. F. (2004b). 'Personal Effects'. In G. F. Bass, S. Matthews, J. R. Steffy and
F. H. van Doorninck Jr, *Serçe Limanı. An Eleventh Century Shipwreck Volume
1: The Ship and its Anchorage, Crew and Passengers*. Texas: A and M University
Press: pp. 275–87.

Bass, G. F., and van Doorninck Jr, F. H. (2004a). 'Discovery, Excavation and Conser-
vation'. In G. F. Bass, S. Matthews, J. R. Steffy and F. H. van Doorninck Jr, *Serçe
Limanı. An Eleventh Century Shipwreck Volume 1: The Ship and its Anchorage,
Crew and Passengers*. Texas: A and M University Press: pp. 49–70.

Bass, G. F., and van Doorninck Jr, F. H. (2004b). 'The Ship, Its Lading and Its Living
Spaces'. In G. F. Bass, S. Matthews, J. R. Steffy and F. H. van Doorninck Jr, *Serçe
Limanı. An Eleventh Century Shipwreck Volume 1: The Ship and its Anchorage,
Crew and Passengers*. Texas: A and M University Press: pp. 265–72.

Beltrame, C. (2015). 'The Contribution of the Yassiada Shipwreck Excavation to the
Knowledge of Life Aboard Ancient Ships'. In D. N. Carlson, J. Leidwanger and
S. M. Kampbell, *Maritime Studies in the Wake of the Byzantine Shipwreck at
Yassiada, Turkey*. Texas: A and M University Press: pp. 63–70.

Bernard, H. R., and Killworth, P. D. (1973). 'On the social structure of an ocean-
going research vessel and other important things'. *Social Science Research* 2:
pp. 145–84.

Cassavoy, K. (2004). 'The Gaming Pieces'. In G. F. Bass, S. Matthews, J. R. Steffy and
F. H. van Doorninck Jr, *Serçe Limanı. An Eleventh Century Shipwreck Volume
1: The Ship and its Anchorage, Crew and Passengers*. Texas: A and M University
Press: pp. 329–43.

Castle, J., and Derham, B. (2005). 'The Contents of the Barber-Surgeon's Cabin'. In
J. Gardiner (ed.), *Before the Mast – Life and Death Aboard the Mary Rose*. The
Mary Rose Trust: pp. 189–219.

Clare, H. (2014). *Down to the sea in ships*. London: Chatto and Windus.

Cummiskey, J., Natsis, K., Papathanasiou, E., and Pigozzi, F. (2013). 'Sleep and Athletic Performance'. *European Journal of Sports Medicine* 1(1): pp. 13–22.

Every, R. (2005). 'Fishing Gear'. In J. Gardiner (ed.), *Before the Mast – Life and Death Aboard the Mary Rose*. The Mary Rose Trust: pp. 141–4.

Every, R., and Richards, M. (2005). 'Knives and Knife Sheaths'. In J. Gardiner (ed.), *Before the Mast – Life and Death Aboard the Mary Rose*. The Mary Rose Trust: pp. 144–53.

Gardiner, J. (2005). *Before the Mast – Life and Death Aboard the Mary Rose*. The Mary Rose Trust.

Gardiner, J., and Cowham, M. (2005). 'Timepieces'. In J. Gardiner (ed.), *Before the Mast – Life and Death Aboard the Mary Rose*. The Mary Rose Trust: pp. 162–70.

Gardiner, J., and Wood, R. (2005). 'Feeding the Crew'. In J. Gardiner (ed.), *Before the Mast – Life and Death Aboard the Mary Rose*. The Mary Rose Trust: pp. 496–8.

Goffman, E. (1961). *Asylums*. Doubleday and Co.

Hennessy, P., and Jinks, J. (2015). *The Silent Deep – The Royal Naval Submarine Service since 1945*. Allen Lane.

Hetherington, C., Flin, R., and Mearns, K. (2006). 'Safety in Shipping: The human element'. *Journal of Safety Research* 37: pp. 401–11

Hicks, R. (2005). 'The Role of the Pilot'. In J. Gardiner (ed.), *Before the Mast – Life and Death Aboard the Mary Rose*. The Mary Rose Trust: pp. 264–7.

Hocker, F. M. (2004). 'Tools'. In G. F. Bass, S. Matthews, J. R. Steffy and F. H. van Doorninck Jr, *Serçe Limanı. An Eleventh Century Shipwreck Volume 1: The Ship and its Anchorage, Crew and Passengers*. Texas: A and M University Press: pp. 297–326.

Jenkins-Madina, M. (2004). 'Jewelry'. In G. F. Bass, S. Matthews, J. R. Steffy and F. H. van Doorninck Jr, *Serçe Limanı. An Eleventh Century Shipwreck Volume 1: The Ship and its Anchorage, Crew and Passengers*. Texas: A and M University Press: pp. 289–95.

Jepsen, J. R., Zhao, Z., and Leeuwen, W. M. A van. (2015). 'Seafarer fatigue: a review of risk factors, consequences for seafarers' health and safety and options for mitigation'. *International Journal of Maritime Health* 66(2): pp. 106–17.

Knighton, C. S., and Loades, D. M. (2000). *The Anthony Roll of Henry VIII's Navy*. Ashgate.

Laister, P. (2006). *Mariner's Memorabilia – A guide to British shipping company china of the 19th and 20th centuries*. Peter and Pam Laister Publishing.

Lamvik, G. M. (2012). 'The Filipino seafarer: A life between sacrifice and shopping'. *Anthropology in Action* 19(1): pp. 22–31.

McElvogue, D. (2015). *Tudor Warship Mary Rose*. Conway.

McKay, S. C. (2007). 'Filipino Sea Men: Constructing masculinities in an ethnic labor niche'. *Journal of Ethnic and Migration Studies* 33(4): pp. 617–33.

McKewan, C. (2005). 'The Ships' Carpenters and Their Tools'. In J. Gardiner (ed.), *Before the Mast – Life and Death Aboard the Mary Rose*. The Mary Rose Trust: pp. 293–319.

Marsden, P. (2003). *Sealed by Time – The loss and recovery of the Mary Rose*. The Mary Rose Trust.

Martin, B. J. (1981). 'Effect of sleep deprivation on tolerance of prolonged exercise'. *European Journal of Applied Physiology and Occupational Physiology* 47: pp. 345–54.

Østreng, D. (2001). 'Does togetherness make friends? Stereotypes and intergroup contact on multi-ethnic-crewed ships'. *Vestfold College Publication Series*/Paper 2000–2001. <http://www-bib.hive.no/tekster/hveskrift/notat/2001-02/index. html > accessed 20 April 2016.

Piercy, G. V., and Bass, G. F. (2004). 'Fishing Gear'. In G. F. Bass, S. Matthews, J. R. Steffy and F. H. van Doorninck Jr, *Serçe Limanı. An Eleventh Century Shipwreck Volume 1: The Ship and its Anchorage, Crew and Passengers*. Texas: A and M University Press: pp. 399–435.

Prior, J. H. (1984). 'The Naval Architecture of Crusader Transport Ships'. *Mariners Mirror* 70: pp. 277–84.

Project Horizon. (2012). 'Fatigue at Sea'. *Research Report 2011*. European Union 7th Framework Programme.

Redknap, M. (2005). 'Recreation: Games and Gaming'. In J. Gardiner (ed.), *Before the Mast – Life and Death Aboard the Mary Rose*. The Mary Rose Trust: pp. 133–40.

Reilly, T., and Edwards, B. (2007). 'Altered sleep-wake cycles and physical performance in athletes'. *Physiology and Behaviour* 90: pp. 274–84.

Richards, M. (2005). 'Grooming and toilet items'. In J. Gardiner (ed.), *Before the Mast – Life and Death Aboard the Mary Rose*. The Mary Rose Trust: pp. 156–62.

Richards, M., and Gardiner, J. (2005). 'Books and Writing Equipment'. In J. Gardiner (ed.), *Before the Mast – Life and Death Aboard the Mary Rose*. The Mary Rose Trust: pp. 127–33.

Roberts, S. E. (2004). 'Occupational mortality in British commercial fishing, 1976–95'. *Occupational Environmental Medicine* 61: pp. 16–23.

Rothblum, Anita F. (2000). 'Human Error and Marine Safety'. <http://bowles-langley.com/wp-content/files_mf/humanerrorandmarinesafety26.pdf> accessed 20 April 2016.

Sampson, H. (2003). 'Transnational drifters or hyperspace dwellers: an exploration of the lives of Filipino seafarers aboard and ashore'. *Ethnic and Racial Studies* 26(2): pp. 253–77.

Samuels, C. (2008). 'Sleep, recovery and performance: The new frontier in high-performance athletics'. *Neurologic Clinics* 26: pp. 169–80.

Scott, J. P. R., McNaughton, L. R., and Polman, R. C. J. (2006). 'Effects of sleep deprivation and exercise on cognitive, motor performance and mood'. *Physiology and Behaviour* 87: pp. 396–408.

Wadsworth, E. J. K., Allen, P. H., Wellens B. T., McNamara, R. L., and Smith, A. P. (2006). 'Patterns of fatigue among seafarers during a tour of duty'. *American Journal of Industrial Medicine* 49: pp. 836–44.

Wadsworth, E. J. K., Allen, P. H., McNamara, R. L., and Smith, A. P. (2008). 'Fatigue and health in a seafaring population'. *Occupational Medicine* 58: pp. 198–204.

Weibust, K. (1958). 'The Crew as a Social System'. *Skrift* 40. Båtgransking Norsk Sjøfartsmuseum.

Weibust, K. (1969). 'Deep Sea Sailors: A Study in Maritime Ethnography'. *Handlingar* 71. Nordiska Museets

Weinstein, R. (2005a). '"Messing" Items'. In J. Gardiner (ed.), *Before the Mast – Life and Death Aboard the Mary Rose*. The Mary Rose Trust: pp. 440–8.

Weinstein, R. (2005b). 'Eating and Drinking Vessels and Utensils'. In J. Gardiner (ed.), *Before the Mast – Life and Death Aboard the Mary Rose*. The Mary Rose Trust: pp. 448–58.

Weinstein, R., Gardiner, J., and Wood, R. (2005). 'Official Issue or Personal Possession?' In J. Gardiner (ed.), *Before the Mast – Life and Death Aboard the Mary Rose*. The Mary Rose Trust: pp. 489–96.

Zurcher, L. A., Jr (1965). 'The sailor aboard ship: a study of role behaviour in a Total Institution', *Social Forces* 43(3): pp. 389–400.

RACHAEL KIDDEY

9 Homeless *Habitus*: An Archaeology of Homeless Places

ABSTRACT

It has been suggested that, without 'homelessness', we would not be concerned by what 'home' means (Dovey 1985). Such is the primal nature of 'home' that the concept resists definition, like 'love' or 'landscape', 'home' is subjective and phenomenological. 'Home' involves 'systems of settings' (Rapoport 1995) – shelter, most probably, and intra-psychic relationships between people and things that are constructed differently for everyone. There exists no legal definition of 'home' yet 'homeless' is a social status defined and rationalised by legal discourse, the historical development of which has its roots in English medieval vagrancy statutes. It could be argued that homelessness is landlessness, a legacy and contemporary expression of the product of capitalism and enclosure. Homelessness has come to symbolise the archetypal 'Other' – a good example of Husserlian inter-subjectivity (Steinbock 1994). However, homeless people, like all other people, must exist and meet basic human needs *somewhere*, whether or not their appropriation of space is constructed as 'illegal' or 'inappropriate' behaviour. So how do homeless people make 'home space' in the city?

Drawing on archaeological fieldwork conducted collaboratively with homeless people as colleagues (rather than 'participants'), this chapter examines four homeless places from the cities of Bristol and York. Using Lefebvre's (1991) definition of 'place' as space defined by social activity, two sleeping places and two social places are encountered and interpreted according to the homeless people to whom each place is significant. Viewing landscapes, places and things from the perspective of homeless people, contemporary homeless *habitus* is revealed diverse and creative. This approach prioritises the individual humanity of homeless people (Somerville 2013) and destabilises dominant stereotypes of 'the homeless'.

Introduction

The etymological origins of the English word 'home' suggest that the word – *heim* in German, *hjem* in Swedish, *hem* in Norwegian – originates from Germanic languages. The German word *heim* itself derived from the

Indo-European notion *kei*, meaning 'something precious' (Reinders and van der Land 2008: 4). In Britain we see derivations of the word 'home' in place names, for example, Birming*ham* and Chelt(en*ham* (denoting a collection of dwellings), Old German *heima* (meaning home, world) and Viking nifel*heim* (one of the nine Norse worlds, this being a dark world inhabited by giants). The Irish word *coim* means beloved or loved and is also associated with early European meanings of home (cf. Brink 1995). The word 'home' but perhaps more insistently the concept runs deeply within the human experience and psyche, expanding from and within different peoples, crossing temporal and cultural borders for as long as humans have existed. Such is the primal nature of the concept of home that it resists definition. Like 'love' or 'landscape', 'home' is subjective and phenomenological, involving sets of relationships in particular settings (Rapoport 1995). Shelter is the feature that probably comes most quickly to mind but home also involves intra-psychic relationships between people, animals and things, making it different for everyone. There exists no legal definition of home (Fox 2002) yet homeless is a legally defined social status, rationalised by political discourse that has its roots in English medieval vagrancy statutes (Chambliss 1964). Homelessness then may be considered landlessness, a contemporary expression of the sixteenth- and later eighteenth-century enclosure movements and a product of capitalism. However, as fellow human beings, homeless people must exist and meet basic human needs *somewhere* regardless of whether or not their appropriation of space is constructed as 'illegal' or 'inappropriate'.

This chapter draws on fieldwork conducted during the Homeless Heritage project (Kiddey 2014) which used established archaeological methodologies to document how homeless people made home spaces in two British cities, Bristol and York. After briefly situating the practice of Contemporary Archaeology in theoretical context the Homeless Heritage project (2009–14) is introduced. Two contemporary homeless sleeping places are interpreted according to collaborative ethnographic fieldwork undertaken with homeless people. In viewing landscapes, places and things from the perspective of homeless people, contemporary homeless *habitus* is revealed to be diverse and creative. But first, in order to better understand what is meant by the term home*less* it is necessary to unpack more fully what is meant by 'home'.

What do we mean by 'home' and 'homeless'?

Disagreement over what constitutes 'home' may be explained by its subjectivity and individual construction. Home is often understood to involve certain characteristics in varying combinations. Such characteristics might include, '... privacy, space, control, personal warmth, comfort, stability, safety, security, choice, self-expression and physical and emotional well-being' (Neale 1997: 54). Stasis of some kind is an often implied, taken-for-granted feature of the modern Euro-American concept of home, a claim that warrants closer attention before we proceed to understand home as a phenomenological set of relationships.

In reference to hunter-gatherer communities, anthropologist Marshall Sahlins (1974) suggests that, contrary to axiom, it is actually *modern* economic systems that invent scarcity of resources because the capitalist mode requires that production continues to expand or the model fails. As Sahlins notes, '... Free from market obsessions of scarcity, hunters' economic propensities may be more consistently predicated on abundance than our own' (Sahlins 1974: 2). A neat, if reductive, explanation of capitalism is simple inequality or the unfair distribution of wealth (unfair access to natural resources). Implicit within the capitalist mode is greed, a central feature of which is that it can never be fully satiated. This is the economic system that gathered force throughout Britain from the sixteenth century forward, a system by which some (poor) people's access to natural resources – woodland, water, hunting grounds – was fundamentally ruptured by the privatisation of common lands through movements that have come to be known in British history as enclosure. In parallel, those who attempted to access what had previously been 'common land', were increasingly criminalised until common rights were eroded to little more than the right to be detained or exported across the ocean for the 'social crime' of being found vagrant (we might say 'homeless') (Beier 1985: xxii). This practice of forcibly exporting poor people to less desirable places continues to the present day in Britain, rationalised by current homelessness policy (cf. Kiddey 2014: 319–31).

Home then is more than simply a building or place. Home is 'generated developmentally, concordantly and inter-subjectively, and experienced as such from the perspective of the participants' (Steinbock 1994:

218–19). Home is an individual system of relationships between humans and non-humans, likely incorporating aspects of shelter and privacy but also other people, animals, natural features such as trees, gardens, beaches or rivers and also memories and things. The result of the shift in the majority of home living arrangements, from essentially transient hunter-gatherer lifestyles to forcibly settled ones, is that the places that we are able to call home have been commoditised and therefore our 'choice' over where we live is dependent upon our access to resources, that is, money or increasingly debt (cf. Graeber 2011). Those who have responded to this 'choice' by living transient lifestyles (for example, gypsies, travellers and tramps) have been unremittingly criminalised in Britain (Kiddey 2014: 316–19). Home, in the Euro-American context, must now involve stasis, a building or place that can be fenced around, however small or ill equipped it is to function as home – because it must be taxed. 'Rootedness', as a key feature of home, articulates a peculiarly modern and predominantly 'western' fear – fear of losing our place, fear of becoming homeless (Wikstrom 1995; cf. Somerville 1992). Indeed, psycho-analyst Carl Jung argued that 'home' was essential to developing and sustaining personal identity (Jung 1967). If we accept this, what does it mean to be home*less*?

Perhaps the first thing to observe is that homeless people, like N.E.E.T.s (people Not in Employment, Education or Training), are defined negatively by something they lack – home*less*. Problems associated with homelessness, such as social deprivation, abuse and addition combined with the perceived pathological failure of homeless people, make the subject of homelessness particularly politically charged (for example, Saunders 1989; Somerville 1992; Neale 1997; van der Horst 2004; Quilgars, Johnsen and Pleace 2008, Ocobock 2008). Often, homelessness is more visible in the city – shopping trolleys with possessions strapped to them, sleeping bags in doorways, people begging – but homelessness in Britain is by no means an exclusively urban problem. It exists all over Britain and rural homelessness and over-crowding are growing problems. For example, Cornwall, the south-westernmost county in England, has one of the highest rates of social deprivation in the country and barriers to housing are extreme.[1] Cornwall's neighbouring

1   <http://neighbourhood.statistics.gov.uk/HTMLDocs/AtlasOfDeprivation2010/index.html>.

county, Devon, is not much better. Until recently my husband and son and I lived with my parents. We were lucky. My parents' family house was big enough to accommodate us all but we lived together out of financial necessity rather than choice. Much homelessness and overcrowding is therefore rendered less visible to researchers but it is estimated that 2.23 million people are currently 'hidden' homeless, that is, living unofficially with other households, a practice often called 'sofa surfing' (Fitzpatrick *et al.* 2015). A further estimated 685,000 people are enduring unacceptable overcrowded housing conditions in the UK (ibid.). While it is important to recognise the full scale of the problem of homelessness, in this paper, I focus on two sites of street homelessness – that is, places where homeless people live on the street and in other semi-public places (for a fuller discussion see Fitzpatrick and Jones 2005).

What is street homelessness?

The physical realities of street homelessness are, of course, most keenly felt by those people who find themselves 'roofless' – cold, uncomfortable, excluded and exhausted. As Somerville points out, homelessness is not the converse of the ideal of home because some elements of the ideal concept can remain with homeless (roofless) people (for example, a person may be lacking shelter, privacy, comfort and even safety but they may retain some aspect of emotional well-being, autonomy or caring social relationships) (Somerville 1992). In some cases, reciprocal love and a sense of 'belongingness' (Maslow 1987) might not completely elude homeless (roofless) people rather they are sometimes engendered through relationships between other people or pets. At times, interactions between homeless people and urban wildlife such as pigeons and foxes can generate feelings of compassion.

Despite the subjectivity and inherent inconsistencies with the concept of homelessness, to be homeless is to occupy a statutorily defined social status in Britain and a person must be verified homeless according to legal criteria before they may be considered eligible for housing assistance. In this way, the legal and political definition of homelessness serves the purpose not just of defining a social status but also of rationalising it (Neale 1997). The legacy of the historic development of the concept and individual reality of homelessness is that current housing and homeless policy remains haunted by associated ideologies and related assumptions. Or as Steinbock puts it: 'Those who become homeless are those swept into the vortex of political practices, socioeconomic assumptions, values and expectations bearing on the phenomenon of "home" as we understand it today, and negatively put on "homelessness"' (Steinbock 1995: 205).

Contemporary archaeology: An approach to modern material heritage

The ways in which homeless people appropriate spaces in the city leaves material traces. Such human/non-human interventions may be approached using established archaeological methodologies such as those commonly applied to material remains from the deep or historic past (Foucault 1972). This practice has come to be known as Contemporary Archaeology or archaeologies of the contemporary world (Graves-Brown 2000, Buchli and Lucas 2001, Graves-Brown, Harrison and Piccini 2011). As a methodology, Contemporary Archaeology has significant advantages over other social scientific approaches (Graves-Brown 2000; Holtorf and Piccini 2011). These include that archaeology starts not with social constructions or *ideas* about how society functions but by recording what empirically exists, no matter how alien or hard to understand. As a branch of its parent discipline, Contemporary Archaeology may be considered an 'ecology of practices' (Stengers 2005) that encompass '… the mundane and the material; its work is the tangible mediation of past and present, of people and their cultural fabric …' (Olsen *et al.* 2012: 2). Two further advantages include that there exists a disciplinary preoccupation with time-depth and a familiarity with the concept that everything changes over time. Further to this, contemporary archaeological work directly affects living populations and as such should be firmly located within anthropological ethics which demand that practitioners recognise and take responsibility for their actions (Graves-Brown and Kiddey 2015; see also Tax 1975). This is also what makes Bourdieu's theory of *habitus* so pertinent.

Habitus in relation to contemporary archaeology

French sociologist Pierre Bourdieu (1930–2002) developed his theory of *habitus* based upon social strategies which were largely lineage-based (Bourdieu 1977). *Habitus* can best be understood as a general theory of practice, a way of explaining how people act in relation to specific social relations and structures. Bourdieu's theory does not suggest that social action is the result of oppressive state structures or specifically shaped by individual creativity, rather he explores more broadly what he sees to be the dialectical nature of individuals and the social contexts in which they operate, their networks – *habitus*. Bourdieu's theory of *habitus* is useful in thinking about homelessness because it facilitates a way of showing '... how some sectors of the population are systematically excluded from the centres of social power' (Gosden 1994: 115). Bourdieu's theory recognises that what constitutes 'decent' behaviour is constructed according to class based *habitus* – or what might more loosely be translated as 'manners' (Shanks 2012: 68). *Habitus* is useful in thinking about the observer, their viewpoint from within the network and their influence upon how what they perceive is interpreted and understood. In seeking to work collaboratively on the material constitution of contemporary society with members of a particular social group (homeless people) debates around rights and responsibilities that were central to anthropology in the 1990s are reinvigorated (Bennett 1996). What right do archaeologists have to go poking around in other peoples' lives? Who are archaeologists to impose meaning or make judgments on material culture? What qualifies archaeologists to convey how a particular group of people think or do? Archaeologists have no more special access to the past – even the very recent past – than anyone else. Collaboration with the people whose material culture is under study makes the practice of Contemporary Archaeology explicitly political – a material practice that is conscious of itself as an active network bearing influence (McGuire 2008, Little and Zimmerman 2010, Gokee and De Leon 2014).

The Homeless Heritage project 2009–14

Using Lefebvre's (1991) definition of place as space defined by social activity it was conceived that homeless people make places and give them character as much as any other social group and that therefore the ways in which homeless people manipulated and adapted the landscape could be approached using established archaeological methodologies. This served as the initial hypothesis and in 2009 I undertook a pilot fieldwork project.[2] To start with, it was important to see whether homeless people would be at all interested to work collaboratively with a team of academics and students on an archaeology of contemporary homelessness. The pilot fieldwork was successful and the longer term plan to work collaboratively with homeless people to map and document their heritage became the subject of my doctoral research (Kiddey 2014). Supported by the Department of Archaeology and Anthropology at the University of Bristol and the Department of Archaeology at the University of York, I developed a doctoral project in which I intended to undertake participatory fieldwork with homeless people and students to map the cities of Bristol (and later, York) using archaeological and ethnographic methods.

Drawing on previously established contacts within the homeless population in Bristol, I made contact with other homeless people and prepared to work with everyone who expressed interest in the project. It is important at this early stage to explain that because I wanted to work collaboratively

---

2   Pilot fieldwork was conducted with John Schofield who later became my PhD thesis supervisor.

with homeless people I adopted the term 'colleague' rather than the terms 'respondent' or 'participant' which are more common to social scientific work. This was because the word 'colleague' more accurately represented the relationship – we brought different skills and experience to the project but we worked as equals. I explained that, as the Homeless Heritage team comprised of homeless people, students and academics, we would use a variety of archaeological and ethnographic methodologies to map and record colleagues' experiences of homelessness. For example, we would walk around the city noting down places of significance and names for particular areas and places. We would make and annotate maps – memory maps and counter-maps. We would take photographs, record audio clips and film and through these materials our aim would be to show continued or historic use of the city by homeless people. In so doing, we would literally put contemporary homelessness in Bristol (and later York) 'on the map'. I explained that this work could, if colleagues wished it to, usefully counter stereotypes of homelessness by offering new, alternative views of this familiar yet alien social status.

Agreeing upon methods of recording took time. For example, I had anticipated that some people might not want to be photographed but I had not expected most homeless people to be uncomfortable writing things down. It was important to respect colleagues' wishes and so, in order for us proceed with the aim of genuinely documenting homeless heritage in words and ways meaningful and accessible to colleagues, we made heavy use of the Dictaphone and camera and I noted down what people said about places on a paper map. Later, in a café, I worked with individual colleagues to further annotate maps, create memory maps and add to these, information about places, objects and available resources. Overlaid, these individual maps showed how homeless people perceived the landscape and revealed where homelessness materialised in each city. Some distinct routes became detectable, certain areas of the city were characterised by homeless use more heavily than others. Landscapes of contemporary homelessness emerged dotted with places that were identified as significant to homeless individuals or groups of homeless people. In Bristol and later York, two contemporary homeless sites were archaeologically excavated using stratigraphic methods by teams comprising homeless colleagues, local

police women (Bristol) and archaeology students from the University of
Bristol and the University of York. The public archaeology aspects of the
Homeless Heritage project have been written about elsewhere (Kiddey
and Schofield 2009, 2010 and 2011, Kiddey 2014a and 2014b, Crea *et al.*
2014). Places identified by homeless colleagues included social spaces,
recreational spaces and sleeping spaces. For the purposes of this chapter I
focus on two sleeping spaces, these being more readily associated with the
concept of home by colleagues.

Case studies: Two homeless 'home' places

Jane's Hot Skipper

Figure 9.1: Jane at Hot Skipper. (Image: author.)

Jane was one of the first street homeless women I met. She often spoke of a 'skipper' that she called her 'Hot Skipper'. The word 'skipper' has some historic legacy as homeless parlance meaning 'a place to sleep rough' (cf. Orwell 1933, Kiddey and Schofield 2011). It was located slightly away from Bristol city centre in Berkeley Square and surrounded by solicitors' offices that overlook a grassy square. Late one afternoon in October 2010, as we prepared for our forthcoming presentation at the Theoretical Archaeology Group (TAG) conference, Jane and I went to record the Hot Skipper. She laughed as we walked up Park Street towards the site and said in a mock posh British accent, 'I always insist on the best address!' An observation I have made during the time I have spent working with homeless people is that people tend to speed up as they reach their destination, glance quickly around and then disappear. This was the case with Jane's Hot Skipper. She moved quickly around the corner and as I turned left to follow her, she was gone. I have since established from conversations with homeless colleagues that this 'losing' tactic is a safety strategy, hard to shake off. From below the pavement where I stood, I became aware of stone cellar steps. To my left was the back of a pizza restaurant, down to my right, where I noticed Jane standing, were three recessed stone arches. Jane explained:

> When I used this place [2003/6] I wouldn't show no-one. You can't, right, because soon as someone knows where you kip, it's ruined. They'll want to come too and you'll get moved on because there's too many of you or they'll bring people back with them or you'll get back one night and find it full ... In them days, the staff who worked here would sometimes leave me out a bowl of Spaghetti Bolognese or a bit of pizza on a plate, with cling film over it. It was kind actually. Sometimes there would even be a whole cigarette for me too. But if there wasn't, I used to pick up the ones they'd only half smoked because they didn't have time to finish it. This was a good place.

In front of us were three dimly lit arches, at the time we ventured there these spaces were crammed with bins and catering crates. The last of the arches faced a vent that extracted hot air from the back of the pizza restaurant. It was grilled off with a metal fence, a now familiar practice of shutting homeless people out of the city (cf. Dixon 2009; cf. Kiddey 2014: 137–40).

Jane continued telling me how she used the site. She pointed to the grilled off arch:

> I slept in this one because the hot air vent blows right into the archway and it keeps you warm. Honestly, I could take my clothes off in this skipper and sleep just in my sleeping bag and PJs! With that vent blowing hot air and Patch [Jane's dog] curled up with me, I was warm. In winter, I wear my PJs under my clothes. Extra layer of warmth. The best thing about this place is that I could put dry clothes on the next day.

Jane explained that the site was 'safe' because it was uphill, away from the central Bristol area where Jane said homeless people are much more at risk from physical attack by people who have been drinking on a night out. Data on such attacks are hard to come by. Conversations with homeless charity St Mungo's revealed that no-one disputes that such attacks happen but data are difficult to collate because both terms 'homeless' and 'attack' are difficult to define and therefore attacks on homeless people are statistically hard to prove. Added to this is the complication that with nowhere safe to go homeless people are far less likely to report attacks upon their person because they are at risk from reprisals. The reason that Jane described the 'Hot Skipper' as a 'good' place extend beyond its location uphill, the presence of the hot air vent, the fact that food and sometimes even cigarettes were left for her. The 'Hot Skipper' offered Jane a sense of being needed as Jane recalled by telling me about a pigeon that shared her space:

> She made her nest in the corner. Up there. If I got a sandwich in the day, I would save her little bits and pieces, seeds and that, and feed her. She was like my little pet. People will think that's disgusting, you know, 'pigeons are rats with wings', but I liked her … It was nice to have someone else there. I used to talk to her. She cheered me up and made me keep telling myself 'it's a beautiful world really'.

Jacko's multi-storey car park sleeping place

The Stonebow National Car Park is a concrete multi-storey construction of the sort familiar to most British cities. Located in historic York, the car park is situated just outside the old city centre opposite the Methodist church. I visited the site with Jacko in June 2011. 'I used to sleep here,' Jacko pointed

Figure 9.2: Jacko at Saviourgate. (Image: author.)

to an area underneath the return of a staircase on the lowest floor of the car park but one floor up from street level. He explained that he used to sleep under the return of the staircase because it offered some protection from wet drips from the ceiling and gave the illusion of being slightly cosier, a bit like a cave. But the car park owners closed off the area where Jacko slept with a metal grille and so, in Jacko's words, 'I'd sleep just next to it [next to the metal grille]. Cars park just a bit further out'. Jacko called the car park 'Saviourgate multi-storey' and said it was convenient to him because directly across the road was Carecent, a York based service offering hot drinks, snacks and pastoral care intended to support unemployed people and used by many homeless people in York. Jacko (and other homeless people in York) fondly refer to Carecent as 'Care Bears' and he used the centre every morning it was open as a place to have breakfast and meet people.

Jacko explained that when he had first started using the Saviourgate multi-storey car park site in the late 1990s, it had been monitored by a security guard. The security guard knew that Jacko slept rough in the car park. 'He didn't bother me. I'm not a drinker so I didn't cause any fuss. Just came up here when I was ready to sleep and I was gone in the morning. Tried not to make a mess or leave any of me stuff around'. I asked Jacko if he felt safe sleeping under the stairs in the car park, 'safer than I would be out there in a doorway. It had a security guard when I was using it'.

Discussion

The case studies above come from two very different British cities and yet similarities can be drawn between the sites and also the ways in which they are used by contemporary homeless people to make home space. In both cases, we might agree that each site meets some of the basic attributes that a person requires in order to feel 'at home'. Both the Hot Skipper and the Saviourgate car park offered homeless colleagues basic shelter from rain (*physical well-being*). In Jane's case too, she felt that she was *warm* at the Hot Skipper. But let us go back to Joanne Neale's combination of charac-teristics that commonly comprise home, introduced earlier in this chapter. These are: '... privacy, space, control, personal warmth, comfort, stability, safety, security, choice, self-expression and physical and emotional well-being' (Neale 1997: 54).

In each case, homeless colleagues arguably had some *privacy* and *space*, certainly more privacy than was available to them on the street or in a more visible place, such as a doorway. Each site offered space in the sense that colleagues could spend time away from other people. To a degree, each site described here offered the user some *control* and *choice* – control over where in the space they slept, what time they went to sleep, when to leave and return, some autonomy. It is hard to argue that either Jane or Jacko felt *comfortable* at the Hot Skipper or the Saviourgate car park but they each told me that they were able to lie down and use cardboard and sleeping bags to make their respective spaces comfortable enough to sleep. Both colleagues perceived the spaces they showed me to offer them *safety* and *security* – not security of tenure but security from immediate personal danger. Both colleagues mentioned that the site offered them *emotional well-being* to some degree. In Jane's case, she told me that it was a 'good' thing that she shared her space with a pigeon and it clearly cheered Jane to know that someone at the pizza restaurant authorised her use of the skipper by leaving her food and cigarettes. Equally, the security guard who chose to turn a blind eye to Jacko's illicit use of the Saviourgate car park helped to make a gated boundary porous and the proximity to 'Care Bears' contributed to feelings of well-being. To those of us lucky enough never to have experienced homelessness in Britain, the sites described here are inadequate, miserable and wholly unsatisfactory as places to sleep for the night let alone to call home. But homeless *habitus* suggests that the sites function as better home-space than, for example, some homeless hostels or other 'spaces of care' (Johnsen, Cloke and May 2005).

Conclusion

In documenting homelessness as it is experienced and perceived by home-less people the Homeless Heritage project sought to use archaeological and ethnographic methodologies to better understand and interpret why homeless people often 'choose' to make home-space in 'unsuitable', 'unau-thorised' parts of the city, opting to live under bridges or in bin-stores. In conclusion, it is suggested that homeless *habitus* reveals some places occu-pied by homeless people to be home like due to their propensity to offer more of the intangible aspects of home – privacy, space, control, personal warmth, comfort, stability, safety, security, choice, self-expression and physical and emotional well-being – than are afforded by places intended for use by homeless people (for example, hostels and night-shelters). At such institutional settings, shelter and access to basic resources (food, hot water) might be guaranteed but access is dictated by staff, behaviour is closely monitored and opportunities for self-expression and autonomy are severely limited. Safety is also often compromised (Johnsen, Cloke and

May 2005). When viewed from the perspective of homeless *habitus*, a quiet space in front of a hot-air vent, where one is free to come and go, where smoking is permitted and dogs are allowed seems more 'homely' than a bed in a noisy and unpredictable night-shelter, surrounded by bedfellows who have complicated problems.

To be homeless has been a criminal offence in Britain since the 1824 Vagrancy Act[3] but criminalising people for their lack of shelter does nothing to address their need for *more than just shelter*. Rather than aggressively tackling the affordable housing shortage that faces the UK, the British government has seen fit to strengthen police powers to arrest people for certain behaviours that are not illegal in other parts of the city. For example, in London, the ironically named Public Space Protection Order enables London councils to stop activities in particular areas that are deemed anti-social and fine those who are found in breach of the law – homelessness is one such 'activity' deemed anti-social.[4] If we want evidence of the ways in which public space is gradually being privatised, we might start by looking at how homeless people try to exist in the city (Mitchell 2003). Homeless *habitus* in twenty-first-century England is ephemeral, transient and creative because, as resistance to institutionalisation, it has to be.

Bibliography

Baudrillard, J. (1981). *For a Critique of the Political Economy of the Sign*. St Louis, MO: Telos Press.
Beier, A. (1985). *Masterless Men: the vagrancy problem in England 1560–1640*. London: Methuen.
Bourdieu, P. (1977). *Outline of a Theory of Practice*. Cambridge: Cambridge University Press.

3   <http://www.legislation.gov.uk/ukpga/Geo4/5/83/contents>.
4   <https://www.theguardian.com/cities/2015/sep/08/pspos-new-control-orders-public-spaces-asbos-freedoms>.

Brink, S. (1995). 'Home: the term and the concept from a linguistic and settlement-historical viewpoint'. In D. N. Benjamin (ed.), *The Home: Words, Interpretations, Meanings and Environments*. Aldershot: Avebury: pp. 17–24.

Caplan, P. (ed.) (2003). *The Ethics of Anthropology: Debates and Dilemmas*. London: Routledge.

Crea, G. et al. (2014). 'Turbo Island: excavating a contemporary homeless place'. *Post Medieval Archaeology* 48(1): pp. 133–50.

Dixon, J. (2009). 'Shopping and Digging'. *British Archaeology*, Issue 105: pp. 32–7.

Fairclough, G. (ed.) (2008). *The Heritage Reader*. London: Routledge.

Fitzpatrick, S., and Jones, A. (2005). 'Pursuing Social Justice or Social Cohesion? Coercion in Street Homelessness Policies in England'. *Journal of Social Policy* 34(3): pp. 389–406.

Fitzpatrick, S. et al. (2015). *The Homelessness Monitor: England 2015*. London: Crisis.

Foucault, M. (1972). *The Archaeology of Knowledge*. London: Tavistock.

Giddens, A. (1986). *The Constitution of Society: outline of the theory of structuration*. Oxford: Polity Press.

Giddens, A. (1995). *A Contemporary Critique of Historical Materialism*. 2nd edn. London: Macmillan Press Ltd.

Gokee, C., and De Leon, J. (2014). 'Sites of Contention: Archaeological Classification and Political Discourse in the US-Mexico Borderlands'. *Journal of Contemporary Archaeology* 1(1): pp. 133–63.

Gosden, C. (1994). *Social Being and Time*. Oxford: Blackwell.

Graeber, D. (2011). *Debt: The First 5,000 Years*. New York: Melville House Publishing.

Graves-Brown, P. (ed.) (2000). *Matter, Materiality and Modern Culture*. London: Routledge.

Graves-Brown, P. (2013). 'Authenticity'. In P. Graves-Brown, R. Harrison and A. Picinni (eds), *The Oxford Handbook of the Archaeology of the Contemporary World*. Oxford: Oxford University Press: pp. 219–31.

Graves-Brown, P., Harrison, R., and Piccini, A. (2013). *The Oxford Handbook of the Archaeology of the Contemporary World*. Oxford: Oxford University Press.

Graves-Brown, P., and Kiddey, R. R. (forthcoming). 'Reclaiming the Streets. The role of deconstructing the myths of contemporary society'. *Archaeological Review*. Cambridge.

Hamilakis, Y., and Duke, P. (2007). *Archaeology and Capitalism: from Ethics to Politics*. Left Coast Press.

Hamilakis, Y., Pluciennik, M., and Tarlow, S. (2002). *Thinking through the Body: Archaeologies of Corporeality*. New York: Kulwer Academic/Plenum Publishers.

Harrison, R., and Schofield, J. (2010). *After Modernity: Archaeological Approaches to the Contemporary Past*. Oxford: Oxford University Press.

Holtorf, C., and Piccini, A. (2011). *Contemporary Archaeologies: Excavating Now.* Frankfurt am Main: Peter Lang.

Horst, H. van der (2004). 'Living in a reception centre: the search for home in an institutional setting'. *Housing, Theory and Society* 21(1): pp. 36–46.

Independent (2015). 'Thousands sign petition calling on London borough of Hackney to stop "criminalising" homeless people'. <http://www.independent.co.uk/news/uk/home-news/thousands-sign-petition-calling-on-london-borough-of-hackney-to-stop-criminalising-homeless-people-10295269.html> accessed 6 June 2015.

Islington Tribune (2012). 'Trauma facing tenants forced to move out'. <http://www.islingtontribune.com/letters/2012/jul/forum-trauma-facing-tenants-forced-move-out> accessed 27 May 2015.

Jung, C. (1967). *Memories, Dreams, Reflections.* London: Fontana.

Kiddey, R. (2014). 'Homeless Heritage: collaborative social archaeology as therapeutic practice'. <http://etheses.whiterose.ac.uk/6262/> accessed 18 July 2014.

Kiddey, R. (forthcoming). 'Hand in Hand: homelessness, heritage and collaborative approaches to the material past'. In S. B. Hyatt (ed.), *The Routledge Companion Guide to Contemporary Anthropology.* London: Routledge.

Kiddey, R., and Schofield, J. (2010). 'Digging for (Invisible) People'. *British Archaeology* (July/August): pp. 18–23.

LASPO (2012). Legal Aid, Sentencing and Punishment of Offenders Act 2012. <http://www.legislation.gov.uk/ukpga/2012/10/section/144/enacted> accessed 6 June 2015.

Lefebvre, H. (1991). *The Production of Space.* Oxford: Blackwell.

Little, B. J., and Zimmerman, J. L. (2010). 'In the Public Interest: Creating a more Activist, Civically Engaged Archaeology'. In W. Ashmore, D. Lippert and B. Mills (eds), *Voices in American Archaeology.* Washington, DC: Society for American Archaeology Press: pp. 131–59.

McGuire, R. H. (2008). *Archaeology as Political Action.* Berkeley, CA: University of California Press.

Martin, P. S. (1971). 'The Revolution in Archaeology'. In M. P. Leone (ed.), *Contemporary Archaeology: a guide to theory and contributions.* Carbondale and Edwardsville, IL: Southern Illinois University Press: pp. 5–13.

Maslow, A. H. (1987). *Motivation and Personality.* 3rd edn. New York: Harper and Row.

Meskell, L., and Joyce, R. (2003). *Embodied Lives: Figuring ancient Egypt and the Classic Maya.* London: Routledge.

Mitchell, D. (2003). *The Right to the City: social justice and the fight for public space.* New York: Guildford Press.

Neale, J. H. S. (1997). 'Homelessness and Theory Reconsidered'. *Housing Studies* 12(1): pp. 47–61.

Olsen, B. (2010). *In Defense of Things: Archaeology and the Ontology of Objects.* Plymouth: Alta Mira Press.

Olsen, B., Shanks, M., Webmoor, T., and Witmore, C. (2012). *Archaeology: The Discipline of Things.* London: University of California Press.

Pels, P. (1999). 'Professions of Duplexity; a prehistory of ethical codes in anthropology'. *Current Anthropology* 40(2): pp. 101–36.

Quilgars, D., Johnsen, S., and Pleace, N. (2008). *Youth Homelessness in the UK: a decade of progress?* York: Joseph Rowntree Foundation.

Rapoport, A. (1995). 'A Critical Look at the Concept of "Home"'. In D. N. Benjamin (ed.), *The Home: Words, Interpretations, Meanings and Environments.* Aldershot: Avebury: pp. 25–52.

Rathje, W. L. (1981). 'A Manifesto for Modern Material Culture Studies'. In R. A. Gould and M. B. Schiffer (eds), *Modern Material Culture: The Archeology of Us.* New York: Academic Press: pp. 51–6.

Reinders, L., and Land, M. van der (2008). 'Mental Geographies of Home and Place: introduction to the Special Issue'. *Housing, Theory and Society* 25(1): pp. 1–13.

Sahlins, M. (2008). *The Western Illusion of Human Nature: with reflections on the long history of hierarchy, equality, and the sublimation of anarchy in the West and comparative notes on other conceptions of the human condition.* Chicago, IL: Prickly Paradigm Press.

Saunders, P. (1989). 'The Meaning of "Home" in Contemporary English Culture'. *Housing Studies* 4(3): pp. 177–92.

Scaare, C., and Scaare, S. C. (2006). *The Ethics of Archaeology: philosophical perspectives on archaeological practice.* Cambridge: Cambridge University Press.

Shanks, M. (2012). *The Archaeological Imagination.* Walnut Creek, CA: Left Coast Press.

Smith, L., and Waterton, E. (2009). *Heritage, Communities and Archaeology.* London: Gerald Duckworth and Co..

Somerville, P. (1989). 'Home Sweet Home: a critical comment on Saunders and Williams'. *Housing Studies* 14(2): pp. 113–18.

Somerville, P. (1992). 'Homelessness and the Meaning of Home: rooflessness or rootlessness?'. *International Journal of Urban and Regional Research* 16(4): pp. 529–39.

Steinbock, A. J. (1994). 'Homelessness and the Homeless Movement: A Clue to the Problem of Intersubjectivity'. *Human Studies* 17(2): pp. 203–23.

Stengers, I. (2005). 'Introductory Notes on an Ecology of Practices'. *Cultural Studies Review* 11(1): pp. 183–96.

Thomas, J. (2004). 'Archaeology's Place in Modernity'. *Modernism/modernity* 11(1): 17–34.

Wikstrom, T. (1995). 'The Home and Housing Modernisation'. In D. N. Benjamin (ed.), *The Home: words, interpretations, meanings and environments*. Aldershot: Avebury: pp. 267–82.

Zimmerman, L. J. (2003). *Presenting the Past*. Oxford: Alta Mira Press.

Zimmerman, L. J., Vitelli, K., and Hollowell-Zimmer, J. (2003). *Ethical Issues in Archaeology*. New York: Alta Mira.

PART IV

Ruptured Habitation

CATHERINE RICHARDSON

10 Continuity and Memory: Domestic Space, Gesture and Affection at the Sixteenth-Century Deathbed

ABSTRACT

This essay explores the spatial impact which death had on the early modern house. It is focused on the depositions given in testamentary cases in the ecclesiastical courts, which explored the legal validity of wills through an investigation of the circumstances under which they were produced, and assesses the way stories told about a death depend upon the physical context of the house to generate their meaning. Death is a moment when domestic continuity is obviously threatened; when the ownership of a property, of the furniture and furnishings with which it is filled and the ways of living which they facilitate and encourage, are disrupted. The death of householders in particular, in a period of patriarchal authority within the household, occasioned concern, scrutiny, and the careful and detailed transfer of possessions and governance from one generation to the next. It was in the early modern period that the saying that 'a man's house is his castle' became current – the household was recognised as an analogy for the state, and a man's rule within it was therefore actively compared to the monarch's over the country and Christ's over his church. Inhabiting, for these individuals, meant organising space, people and possessions in a way which underpinned the social, religious and political stability of the realm. With such high stakes, behaviour around the deathbed was a matter of significant contemporary concern.

The process of death in early modern England was carefully managed to ensure the best temporal and spiritual outcomes, in a set of practices which had changed remarkably little over the course of the Reformation. Instruction was offered through both texts in the *Ars Moriendi*, or the craft of dying, tradition and the services of the *Book of Common Prayer*, to the dying person and their friends, relations and neighbours in their roles around the deathbed.[1] Responsibilities included making sure that they had made their

---

1 For more information on this tradition and its texts see David William Atkinson, *The English Ars Moriendi*, Renaissance and Baroque Studies and Texts, Vol. 5, Peter Lang, 1992.

will so that, their earthy responsibilities discharged, they could concentrate on their soul; and praying with them and questioning them to produce a profession of their faith. Those close to the testator, either through kinship or through physical proximity of living, should spend time with them as they drew towards their end – the parish bell was tolled when this point was reached, and its sound penetrated the houses of those who should know, because of their Christian duty as good neighbours, to whom its peal referred: as John Donne expressed it in his extended meditation on hearing his local bell when himself sick, 'any man's death diminishes me, because I am involved in mankind, and therefore never send to know for whom the bells tolls; it tolls for thee'.[2] Those present at the final expression of a person's wishes might be asked to bear witness to the words of their last will and testament, making a mark or signature on the document which recorded their role as witness, a responsibility which required them to pay close attention to the testator's mental and physical health, to the precise part of the house in which the document was made, to the other people present in the room, their order of arrival and where they were sitting, and to the bequests given within the document, its writer and the time and place in which it was written and read back to the individual whose wishes it recorded. Death was therefore the most prominent extraordinary, legally, socially and personally significant event which fittingly took place exclusively within the house.

This essay begins by exploring the question of the extent of the time spent with the dying person and its links to memory, as the court probes who was there, for how long, how constant was their presence and therefore the quality of their witnessing of the passing on of domestic property. It then considers the relative levels of secrecy and openness involved in the making of the testament: the moments at which information about the transfer of houses and goods might appropriately be widely disseminated, and the way the different rooms of the house could facilitate such concealments and revelations. Finally, consideration is given to the extent of memories about both death and bequests – the way houses and their inhabitants held onto memories of people, things and events over long

---

2   John Donne, *Devotions Upon Emergent Occasions*, XVII. NUNC LENTO SONITU DICUNT, MORIERIS, '*Now, this bell tolling softly for another, says to me: Thou must die*'.

periods of time and the intentions of neighbours and relatives claimed a purchase within the houses of the living. In doing so, it seeks to identify the roles which the house itself played in mediating and shaping continuity and memory around the early modern deathbed, and to explore the extent to which material culture and written texts structured the nature of these domestic events.

This study is based on an analysis of 175 testamentary cases heard in the Archdeaconry and Consistory Courts of Canterbury between the 1540s and the 1580s which make it possible to construct a sense of typicality in the use of domestic space, although the qualitative detail needed to analyse domestic continuity and memory necessitates a focus on three cases in particular. Historians have identified a significant increase in the business of the church courts in the sixteenth century, demonstrating their influence on the development and promulgation of appropriate domestic processes (Houlbrooke 1979; Sharpe 1980; Ingram 1987; Gowing 1993). Houlbrooke specifically identified a rise in testamentary disputes, suggests that the legal proceedings around such cases would be familiar within local communities (Houlbrooke 1979: 39).[3] The depositions do not involve either the most wealthy or the poorest in Kentish society, but taken as a group the deponents, if not the testators themselves, do represent a considerable proportion of the social scale from poor nurses to local gentry. As a result, it is possible to examine a widely shared contemporary perception of the relationship between memory and domestic continuity through this evidence.

Houlbrooke identified those parts of the death process which could cast doubt upon the validity of the will, the most important being its witnessing, the testator's sanity and freedom from undue influence, and the question of whether or not the document represented the final expression of the dead person's wishes (Houlbrooke 1979: 98). As areas of contention, these aspects of the deathbed scene were the ones on which deponents were required to concentrate in detailed descriptions which provided implicit answers to the broader question behind the case, 'did this individual make

3   For further details of the testamentary process, see T. Arkell, N. Evans and N. Goose (eds), *When Death Do Us Part, Understanding and Interpreting the Probate Records of Early Modern England*. Oxford: Leopard's Head Press, 2000.

a valid will?'. The majority of depositions, therefore, relate events in the room in which the death took place, and record in considerable detail the speech, movement and gestures through which the dying person expressed themselves to those present.

The court's interest in the proper witnessing of the testament leads many deponents to list those who were in the house at this point, and explain the manner in which they themselves, if not others as well, were called to the scene. To fulfil the requirements of legal proof, testators had to provide two, or at the most three witnesses, although in practice they often looked for more to ensure wider knowledge of the provision they had made for the future (Houlbrooke 1979: 98). Witnesses might arrive as one of a group of men found in the close proximity of the house either by servants or relatives looking for those of good reputation as quickly as possible. Those at work on nearby houses were called away, from tiling for instance (PRC 39.10.1, Nether Hardres, 1581), and those at the plough might be asked to down tools too (PRC 39.9.114, Woodnesborough, 1579). Some people were sent for explicitly, for instance those perceived to have special skills of benefit to the smooth running of the testamentary process, relatives of the testator not already present, or those with whom it was necessary to put the record straight before death (Helen Forde of Tenterden calls her neighbour to her on account of 'certen unadvised wordes spoken', that they might 'be friends and forgyve one an other of us', PRC 39.5.78, 1567). In general terms, then, at the point at which the will was witnessed, the testator was likely to be surrounded by a mixture of close friends and relatives, and those members of his local community who were reasonably upstanding, preferably male, and in the right place at the right time. Provision of more of the former rather than the latter category of witnesses indicated better forward planning and a more stable familial situation. In any case, at this moment, the household was potentially much more open than usual to a wider range of individuals, and it was this openness that translated memory of the event from a domestic to a communal level.

The death of John Williamson affords an opportunity to look in detail at the dynamics of such groupings in the death-room, by using record linkage to give a further depth of meaning to the deposition material (X.10.12.65v, ff.). The case, Cock and Donney vs. Awgar, contested by

three litigants who were the testator's sons-in-law, revolves around whether
or not he made a nuncupative, or spoken, will on the afternoon in which
he died. Identifying who was there during his final hours was therefore
crucial. The thirty-year-old wife of Launcelot Vanderpyer came to court on
3 May 1564 to testify that, 'she this deponent diverse and sondrye tymes did
com to the said John Williamson in the tyme of his seeknes who lay in the
house of John Cock within Christchurch gate', in other words within the
precincts of Canterbury Cathedral in Kent.[4] She came, she said, 'partely to
visite hym and comfort hym as an neighbour'. The court's interest in how
long she stayed with the dying man is occasioned by a previous testimony
by John Awgar, in which he stated that, 'John Williamson, about three
houres before his death declared his will by word of mouthe' in front of
Awgar and his wife, John Elvy and his wife, Thomas Donney and his wife,
Stephen Fletcher and Richard Wolflete, John Cock and his wife. Against
this picture of the testator's daughters, sons-in-law and associates ranged
around his bed listening to his last wishes, Mrs Vanderpeer states that 'she
this deponent was with the said John Williamson the testator all the same
day in which he dyed for the moost parte coming and going and tarryed
with hym and in the house ... And saith she cam to hym a litill afore the
tolling of the bell for hym tarrying till the tyme he died', all of which time
she saw only another woman, Williamson's wife and the householders, and
'hard not the said testator make any disposition of his goodes by word of
mowthe or other wise'.

In addition to denying any event at which he might have spoken his
will, Mrs Vanderpeer also calls into question the testator's children's performance of their Christian duty. She goes on to state 'that at suche tyme
as when she percyvid that the said John Williamson was drawing to thend
of life, the same day that he died which was about iiii or v of the clock at
night this deponent spake to the goodwife Cock saying that she marvailled
where the goodman Elvye goodman Donney and goodman Auger were

---

4   In quotations from primary sources, contractions have silently been expanded, use
     of i/j and u/v and capitalisation regularised, and a minimal amount of punctuation
     added to aid comprehension of the sources.

because they were not at the same tyme there with the testator lying so neere
apon deathe'. Once she had mentioned this glaring omission, 'goodman
Ely, Donney and Auger cam unto the testator and none other at that tyme,
at the which tyme of their coming the said testator lay at point of death
and was speacheles'. When they did arrive, she has to admit that they did
their best: 'the said Elvy and the others at their coming did aske how he
the said John Williamson did who could make no aunswer to them and
thereupon they exhorting hym to have in remembrance the passion of
Christ and to dye in the faith of Christ the said testator for all that could
make no aunswer but lifted upp his hands in token that he had the same in
remembrance, and incontinently therapon he dyid'. Even her assertion of
their fulfilment of the duty of exhortation to prayer, however, implicitly
denies any equivalent encouragement to testamentary provision.

Also in the house at that time, although not mentioned by Mrs
Vanderpyer, was Nicholas Young, servant to John Cock for seven years,
but by the time of the court case in service elsewhere.[5] He was, he says,
'with the said John Williamson the same day that he died, in thafter none
a litell before he died, whan he was in reading of a prayer after a preest
as he thincketh, which did reade the same unto hym in the presence of a
greate many being their at that tyme', although he cannot remember who
they were. 'And shortly after apon the reading of the said prayer the said
John dyed sone after, this deponent departing out of the chamber before
he died, and that apon tolling of the bell for hym'.

Nicholas's partial view and understanding of events expresses the spatial and temporal positions of service. More explicitly, in a different case,
when Arthur Chamber of Lydd heard that his master Richard Hardiman
was at the point of death, he 'came unto his master's chamber doore and
there standing lokd into the chamber and harkened what was there in doing'
(X.10.6.51, case of Richard Hardiman of Lydd, 1554). He stands just outside
the door throughout the will-making process, where he is later joined by a
fellow servant. Both of them are noticed by those in the room, but neither

---

5   F.74. Now twenty-four years of age, he has been servant to Hugh Jones of St Andrew's
     parish for four years.

are invited nor feel able to enter it. There is a strong sense here of the door to the room as a threshold between the death and the rest of the house, one which reinforces the social hierarchy by allowing servants to watch, but not to enter the space at key moments. Such liminal individuals are rarely asked to bear witness.

Revealing as these testimonies are about the relationship between household space and status, servants offer problematic testimonies to the court precisely because their presence is not constant. Young denies any knowledge of Williamson's visitors at any other time of the day, or of the making of the will, as 'he did but goo to and froo apon errauntes in and out as he was sent'. Vanderpyer, who may partly have been acting as his nurse, was also present 'two tymes in the least severally, every tyme an hour or an houre and an half and aslong tyme hath been away from hym the same aft noone at tymes'. Elizabeth Hallam notes that 'Women acted as constant attendants [at the deathbed] providing daily support, whereas men's contributions figured more strongly in terms of specialised services provided on particular occasions' (Hallam 1996: 68). Although they may have been present with testators over a longer period of time, however, their attention was fractured by the nature of the tasks they had to perform and it is service (permanent or temporary), rather than gender per se, which divides these testimonies. This type of long-term but partial presence produces a particular quality of disjointed and piecemeal domestic memory.

In contrast, experiences like that of William Austen of Woodnesborough indicate a different purpose and quality of attention: coming with the vicar to the bedside of Jervase Brooke, he was required 'to sitt downe in the meane season and to heare hym make and declare his will' (PRC 39.9.115v, Woodnesborough, 1579). His acceptance of the invitation signals his commitment to the ensuing ceremonies, and to the coherence of attention which is perceived to be necessary for all those in such a position. Two different time scales are thus presented as operating at once within the houses of the sick: household routines must go on, and people executing them will be constantly on the move, in a pattern of behaviour against which death is set as a rupture. At the deathbed, stillness is the normative pattern of behaviour, and mental concentration, as opposed to physical ministration, are needed to note and interpret every gesture. The court prioritises such focus, and denigrates constant activity, partly because the former belongs to the key textual processes of the deathbed, and partly because it leads to a different quality of memory – an ability to appreciate events in their entirety.

Considering the relationships between those present at the deathbed in more depth makes it possible to reconstruct the social and familial patterns into which such an extraordinary event fitted. Williamson's sons-in-law had clear business ties to one another, in addition to their familial connexions. Thomas Donner, shoemaker, took two apprentices who received their freedom in 1559/60, four years before this case (Corpe and Oakley 1982: 73). His inventory, made in 1577 (thirteen years later), was taken by four men, including a saddler (a profession related through raw materials) and a William Cock, possibly John's son (PRC 10.9.303v). It shows a hall, parlour and buttery with two chambers above. A standing bedstead with featherbed in the parlour, worth £3, makes up a considerable proportion of the £14 2s which his possessions were worth, suggesting that he had at one time been of rather higher status.

Augar, who gives his occupation to the court as shoemaker, was overseer of John Elvye's will in 1560 (PRC 17.35.72). We do not know exactly when John Williamson died, but his wife is said by Mrs Vanderpeer to have 'lyvid after the space of vi or vii yeres', and Richard Wolflete considers it has been 'a long tyme sithen the death of the said Jo Williamson', for which reason 'all thinges was not than freshe in his remembrance' (f.66), so Elvy's death between Williamson's demise and the court case explains the fact that he is not a party on either side of the case. In his will, he gives Augar his best gown and jacket, and also his child to look after, suggesting the closeness of their brotherly ties. When Elvyn's servant Henry Lawrence appeared as a witness in another court case, his master's occupation was listed as tanner and saddler. First his apprentice (1553–4) and after his death his son (1572), entered the ranks of freemen (Corpe and Oakley 1982: 78).

Augar's own will, stating his occupation as cordwayner, and his location as St Margaret's parish, was made in 1565, in other words the year after this case was heard (PRC 17.39.270). His inventory describes a house with hall, parlour, little and great butteries, a kitchen with two spinning wheels for wool and linen, chambers over a shop, buttery and hall door (in other words the porch) (PRC 10.2.119). In the shop were seven pounds-worth of shoes, and the whole was priced at £26 5s, including signs of comfort such as cushions and a carpet in the parlour. His son entered the freemanship between 1571 and 1572, after his death, and had an apprentice from 1559 to 1560 (Corpe and Oakley 1982: 11).

These men belonged to a broad status group of relatively prosperous tradespeople, all establishing themselves with apprentices around the time of their father-in-law's death, on the lowest rung of middling status but obviously intending to rise, and putting down further strong roots by apprenticing their sons. They appear from this additional evidence to be men tied not only by marriage, but also by a common trade and occupation, all working with leather and therefore able to help one another in business in the town. The closeness of business ties are revealed by Vanderpyer who, when asked about the likelihood of bias, says that Stephen Fletcher, one of the other witnesses to Williamson's supposed testament, 'hath been a long tyme the curror of the said Augor's lethers, and thereby he gayneth a great part of his lyving ... by reason wherof this deponent thinccketh in her conscience that the said Steven Fletcher will be the rather persuadid by the said Augor to depose according as the said Augor wold have hym' (f.73v). These men's closeness to one another in this evidence, in relationships which are both professional and familial, shows the wider family of the testator capable of forming an effective business unit, which exploits complex ties of obligation and affection.[6] Such groups as these were undoubtedly very different to the pragmatic assembly of witnesses mentioned above. The presence or absence of such a tight-knit group at Williamson's deathbed would indeed be a significant matter for familial continuity.

We can also reconstruct the material details of Williamson's death space, within the house of his son-in-law John Cock, and thus discover more about the domestic location of his death. Cock was a barber – Mrs

---

6   For more on these functions of the extended family see Ilana Krausman Ben-Amos, *The Culture of Giving; informal support and gift-exchange in Early Modern England*, Cambridge University Press, 2008; Catherine Richardson, 'Shakespeare's Siblings', in Stanley Wells and Paul Edmondson (eds), *The Shakespeare Circle*. Cambridge University Press, 2015.

Vanderpyer states that he told her 'how that the said Steven Fletcher had
been with hym at his house washing or shaving hym and asked the said
Cock how he did with the writinges that was made by his father deceased'.
He owned property in St Alphege parish, just outside the precinct walls,
but he asked to be buried in Christchurch (church)yard, beside his first
wife, when he died fourteen years after this court case (in 1578), leaving
four daughters and four sons (PRC 32.34.40; inventory PRC 21.3.200). The
house in which Williamson apparently died, then, lay behind a barber's
shop in the precincts of the Cathedral. At the front, there was a window
with four feet of glass in it and a shop door, as well as boards and a lattice
which indicate an alternative selling space that may have been let out to a
grocer, as the inventory mentions a frame and stall made for one, with the
boards belonging to it. Cocks' own sales area included a crystal looking
glass for the use of customers (although only valued at 12d), and painted
cloths of white and black which advertised his trade. Behind was a hall
with a table 2.75 yards long, with six stools around it, and a bench 3.5 yards
long with a seeled back (made of wainscot boards) and a painted cloth
hanging over it. A round table and little square one with a cupboard in
it, and a carved cupboard with a press in it, offered space for the playing
of the virginals, clavichords and lute which were kept there, as well as the
playing tables and chess board.

As this wide range of items for leisure suggests, the house was an
impressive one, its hall apparently ceiled over to provide living accommodation above, even at this early date.[7] But the dying man was, according to
the deponents, lying downstairs in the parlour in another standing bed with
joined tester, bolser, dornix coverlets and trucklebed, a room also containing
a tressle table, a joined form and a carved cupboard (which had four cloths

---

7   For the ceiling over of Kentish properties, see Sarah Pearson, *The Medieval Houses of
     Kent*, Royal Commission on the Historical Monuments of England, HMSO, 1994.
     Upstairs in Cock's house there was a great chamber with standing bed, joined tester
     and accompanying trucklebed, the former furnished with impressive bedding and
     adorned with two frame-work cushions (probably made by Cock's wife, as there was
     a frame to make cushions in the kitchen), plus Cock's own bedchamber with slightly
     less impressive bedding and the children's chamber.

specifically belonging to it, two of diaper and two fine ones fringed at the ends). As Williamson and his wife apparently lived with the Cock family, they may well have occupied this lower room on a permanent basis. Often heated by the chimney stack inserted when halls were ceiled over, parlours frequently contained expensive bedding, and when they were not housing older relatives may well have been used for honoured guests.[8] The provision of such a room indicates a solidly middling status within the town, which afforded Williamson his own comfortable downstairs space at the time when he needed it most. Frequently positioned behind the hall in urban situations where street-frontage was at a premium, these spaces were set back from the entrance to the house, more secluded and only entered by guests of a similar status to the householder. In such a room, the activities of the dying man and his visitors were less likely to be observed.

The position of testators within the house is directly related to the way their will might be witnessed, and further useful information on this question comes from the instances when testators move from one room to another during the process of their will-making. Helen Harris, having washed the face and hands of Robert Randall, asks him 'will you lay downe on your bedd in the chamber. No quoth he I will lay by the fyre. Then they layd hym downe by the fyer in the houll [hall] upon a bedd there readie made' (PRC 39.5.4, Eastchurch, 1567). Similarly, in Tenterden in 1564, Mr Black 'ymediatle was sett by the fyer in his chaier where he then presentlie departed this world' (PRC 39.4.114v, 1564). It seems that these testators moved to be closer to the fire, and the contrast with Williamson's deathbed is palpable: the lack of a heated downstairs chamber means the sick reposition themselves on temporary beds made up for the purpose, rather than staying put in chambers; social status directly shapes the nature of the deathbed scene.

More modern attitudes towards individual sleeping spaces and differing senses of the value of privacy are likely to conflict with early modern ideas about appropriate use of household space here, however. The depositions

<hr>

8   For further discussion of the nature of the parlour in the second half of the sixteenth century see Hamling and Richardson, *A Day at Home in Early Modern England*, Yale, forthcoming 2016, especially chapter 5.

reveal a tension, for those with a choice of rooms for warmed sleeping, between the desire for comfort and the need to make will-making a more public event – chambers are capable of producing privacy, of providing boundaries at which servants must sometimes stop in a way that halls do not, and in early modern England privacy is a fiercely contested and morally suspect term.[9] The tensions between the wish for comfort and the need to extend memory into the community is palpable.

In a case which exhibits similar spatial features, Henry Southouse, vicar of Northbourne, is required to make the will of Henry Smith whom he calls cousin, and whom he believes has possessions worth £2000 (although the testator values himself at nearer £1300). The scale of his assets increases the stakes around his will-making. When Southouse entered the house, 'he founde the sayd testator Henry Smith syttinge upp and leaning his head under the wyndowe agaynst the cupboard in the upper greate chamber' (PRC 39.10.166, Northbourne, 1583). Also present with him were his wife, 'dyvers of his children and Rychard Hudson his servante and Rycharde Smyth the sayd testators brother and one Elizabeth Kecherell one of his mayd servantes'. The identification of this prestigious room, suggesting gentry pretentions, indicates that Smith had positioned himself in a way appropriate to the reception of significant visitors, equivalent to the parlour for those of high status.

When Henry Smith came to bequeath his £1300, however, he moved out of the Great Chamber, and 'wente in to the nexte chamber over the entrye, and there dyd lye down uppon the bygger bedd of the two, his wyef, children and all those before named following hym and this deponent walkyng with him. There being redy provyded penne, Inke and paper'. Chambers over entries were smaller and less likely to be designed for entertaining than Great Chambers. Smith's movement apparently signals spatially that the business for which Southouse had been sent is about to begin: he had previously sent his brother the five miles from Northbourne to Sandwich to buy paper, and all the necessary items had been laid out in preparation in this more secluded chamber. Smith states his concerns to the vicar: 'I would that you sholde make my wyll, but first I doe not knowe

---

9   For more on contemporary pejorative, moralised readings of privacy, see Lena Orlin, *Locating Privacy in Tudor London*, Oxford University Press, 2007.

howe I shall doe, unto whom this deponent agayne answered feare not that for by the grace of god yow shall doe well enoufe'. Apparently comforted, Smith 'commaunded all to goe out of the chamber savyng [Southouse] and his brother ... who departed ymedyatlye' (f.167). The movement from one space to another is presented in terms which appropriate a sense of ritual, setting up echoes with other lines of people who move with priests at their head. By the move itself, and by the heightened nature of it, anticipation is built, and the idea that the testator has a high degree of control over the situation is reinforced. The language of command and instant obedience insists on Smith's authority, even in extremis – the preamble to the still-extant will, conventional in so many ways, sounds particularly meaningful and significant in the light of the court case, and reminds us that these were never empty words 'I Henry Smythe of Norbone in the countie of Kent sicke in bodie yet neverthelesse thanckes be to god of perfect Mynde and memorie doe ordaine and make this my present Testamente and last will ...' (PRC 17.45.207). The smaller audience of men in the room over the entry, all likely to have been of householding age and comparable upper-middling social status, confines knowledge of the detail of bequests, within the overall awareness that a will is to be made – a more intimate space away from the four daughters and five sons whom the will reveals may have followed him from the Great Chamber, and who may have had views on the nature of their portions.

A distinction is often made in these cases between the making and the reading of the will, the former being an occasion where the clarity and single-mindedness most easily found in the company of a small group of people (usually men) is preferable, and the latter the moment for pub-licity to a group of friends, relatives and neighbours who can be asked formally to bear witness. Nicholas Waferer, for instance, found his cousin Thomas Arden lying 'on a pallett bed a long by the Chimnye syde' in the hall in his house in St Mildred's parish in Canterbury, about a week before Christmas, with the parson, George Powell and the testator's son, along with 'diverse of his servantes els' (PRC 39.6.223v-237).[10] The will had already

---

10   His inventory lists two tables, each with a carpet, four forms, six joined stools, a settle, two turned chairs and two matching sets of six cushions each in the hall, PRC 10.3.97v, 1563.

been written, and the testator 'desired this deponent to read it over, and he also desired this deponent and the sayd Mr Hill, and George Powell to be witnes thero, and to testifye the same', at which point Waferer 'read over his sayd will with a loud voyce then and there' (PRC 39.6.223v-224). Waferer is asked to write a list of the testator's debts at the end of the will 'the testator speaking specifying and declaring the sayd debtes him selfe', and the parson then reading 'the sayd will likewise with a loud voyce' and the testator responding to questions by answering 'This is my will I praye you all to beare witnes unto it, and I praye you to sett your handes therto'. The self-consciously ritualised nature of this event insists upon the legality of the testament, and its performance in the hall ensures that it is a more open event than it would be if it had taken place in a chamber, and therefore a part of many more memories.

By imagining this kind of public reading, we can see how gravitas might increase the strength of memory: Arden's will has a lengthy and impressive preamble which at a later point quotes St Augustine, but which begins by stating 'I Thomas Arden of the cytie of Canterbury gent, hole of mynde and of good and perfect remembraunce ordeyne and make this my present testament here in concernynge my last wyll in manner and forme following: first and before all other thinges I commytt me unto god and to his mercy, belevynge with out anny doubt or mistrust that by his grace, and meryttes of Jhesuus chryste, and by the virtue of his passion and resurectyon I have and shall have remyssyon of my synnes and resurrection of body and soule accordynge as it is wryten. I believe that my redeemer lyvethe and that in the last day I shall ryse out of the earthe and in my fleshe shall see my savyor. This my hope is leyde up in my bosome'. As read, this preamble forms an equivalent to the type of prayers and faithful professions appropriate to the deathbed. Reading, listening and bearing witness to such words declaimed within domestic space, to a hope laid up in the bosom but also read and therefore testified to multiple witnesses, animates the text and connects it, through the act of bearing witness, to individuals' memories of particular spaces and audiences. An ideal pattern comes to light across these cases, then, of will-writing in chambers and will-reading in halls. These different kinds of domestic spaces offer the opportunity to pattern concentrated male activity against a wider kind of publicity, and low voices against proclamation.[11] Deponents' sensitivity to the sensory qualities of action within domestic space is an important part of the way they structure their perception of the different types of audience for the events around death.

Household space holds memories of events, intentions and witnesses. Every deposition given in these cases, therefore, indicates contemporary sensitivity to complex relationships between the household, continuity and memory. The potential extent of these memories beyond the will-making itself can be seen in Waferer's record of Arden's testamentary provision and the way it was fulfilled, which stretches back over five years and extends to eight pages (PRC 39.6.223v- 227). He remembers, 'about halfe a yeare ago or there about', the payment of a sum of money for one creditor which took place 'in one Esdayes house a sheareman dwelling in Stowers streate'; another 'about Christmas last was two yeares in the house of the sayd Mris Arden being in the parish of St Mildred in the Cyttye of Cantorberye' when she paid Mr Gardyner £12; another 'abbout two yeares agoo' when he was at 'the flower deluce in the Citye of Cauntoberye', when the widow 'reckened and accompted' with Mr Gardyner for the rest of the money; another four or five years ago, 'in the house of the sayd Mr Drayton in the Cittye of Cauntorberye', when he himself delivered the debt due 'and in token that he was fullye satisfyed, he the sayd Mr drayton delivered to this deponent for the sayd Mris Arden all such plate was was layd to gage for thesame monye';[12] and similar payments made three or four years ago in Mr Furner's house for the mortgage on Arden's house, five and a half years ago to John Wells in his house for broadcloth for mourning gowns, and twice for Mr Swaleman in the Sun Inn on 25 March and 24 June in the

---

11   There are interesting connections here to the type of regular religious reading undertaken by householders in the hall, as identified by Andrew Cambers in *Godly Reading, Print, Manuscript and Puritanism in England 1580–1720*, Cambridge University Press, 2014.

12   His inventory reveals that he died in possession of two salts, a cruse, a mazer and twelve spoons of silver worth £10 in 1569, which gives some sense of the value of the debts which he might have been able to secure against his household goods, PRC 10.3.97v.

twelfth year of Queen Elizabeth. In this latter case Waferer says, as we might guess from the precision and the form of the dates he gives, that he has 'sene the writinges [and]... a bond wherin the testator aforesayd was bounden to the sayd William Swalman ... for the payment of the sayd Cli in fourme abovesayd'. Such documents would be kept carefully in the househ in a personal chest or coffer. Waferer's memory of these events proves his extensive skills at bearing witness, apparently reconstructed through a complex relationship between textual proof and memories of spaces and events, as well as the objects (here silver plate) which they concerned.

Connecting these cases to the wills to which they relate and the inventories of possessions which they occasioned makes it possible to comprehend more fully the extent to which household goods offered the continuity and mediated the memories that most obviously formed a contemporary sense of inhabitation. When pressed in a further set of questions, for instance, John Cock's servant Nicholas Young recalls that when he was once again 'goo[in]g to and fro', he 'chaunced to be in the parlor of the said John Cock where Williamson used to lye', with Williamson himself and his four sons-in-law (ff. 76-v). The men 'had their among them certayn writinges whiche were not there redd, or what the same writinges were or did concerne he cannot depoase nor was expressed by any of them'. Something of their nature is, however, suggested by the presence of 'certayn vessell that he this deponent thincketh was geven among them aforesaid by the said Williamson and to their wifes', and which were intended to be marked with their initials, 'as he herd, for the whiche purpose this deponent was sent for the marking yron who brought it unto them'. Marking items in this way was intended to distinguish between them when they were later given to their new owners, and therefore indicates that the writings involved either a will or a deed of gift, which was often symbolised by the transfer of an individual object in metonymic representation of a larger whole.

The deponents in these cases also left objects in their own wills which would have been committed to memory by their witnesses, demonstrating the overlapping timescales of will planning, writing and witnessing across and between generations. John Augar, for instance, gave his three daughters a silver spoon each after the death of his wife (PRC 17.39.270). Launcelot

Vanderpyer, husband of the first deponent, made a more detailed gift of a featherbed, a joined bedstead, two spoons, a joined cupboard, table and a form to be given to his daughter Anne at her marriage (PRC 32.34.249v). Anne was married to John Lapham in 1600, an event which conferred freedom of the city upon him, in addition to the furniture (Corpe and Oakley 1982: 227; PRC 21.2.220, 1574). However, the bequeathal of objects was not always a matter of sentimental transfer of goods from one generation to the next; the issue is rather the way objects are known to be related to both houses and individuals through their locations and ownership respectively. Thomas Arden's son Arthur was given a harness and dagger by his father, but he immediately put them up for sale.[13] Jasper Nayler of Patrixbourne deposes that he 'hath sene the sayd harnes at one Robert Culters shoppe in Cauntorberye, and this deponent coming by the sayd Robert stall asked him the sayd Robert being in his shoppe what armour the same was, and who sent it or brought it thether and the sayd Robert aunswered that it was the sayd Arthur Ardens, and that he sent it thether to be sold'. He also says that 'he knewe the sayd armour before in the testators life tyme and sawe it in the sayd Testators house in his life tyme' (f.235v). This kind of detailed knowledge of provenance shows how active things were in defining individuals' relationships to their household spaces.

Within these households, then, objects were circulating in different states of ownership – promised to sons, in keeping for daughters, part of dowries and bequest strategies which stretched backwards and forwards across the generations. Along with the memories of deathbeds and their subsequent events held by those formally asked to bear witness and those who happened to be present, coming and going, the links between people, objects and spaces through time formed an important part of peoples' perceptions of the household – early modern men and women's sense of what inhabitation meant.

---

13   Thomas Arden gave his son Arthur his 'harness and dagge', his 'bay geldynge and my gowne whiche I commonly use to weare', and his son John his gown of silk, as well as a grey gelding in his will, PRC 17.40.237.

Bibliography

Since the publication of Ralph Houlbrooke's *Church Courts and the People during the English Reformation 1520–1570* in 1979, interest in the evidence provided by the depositions given in such courts has increased at a rapid pace. The main concern both of his book, and Martin Ingram's *Church Courts Sex and Marriage in England 1570–1640* (1987), was to explain the procedures of the courts, the divisions of work between them and the operation of the most common kinds of cases brought before them.

Arkell, T., Evans N., and Goose, N. (eds) (2000). *When Death Do Us Part, Understanding and Interpreting the Probate Records of Early Modern England.* Oxford: Leopard's Head Press.

Atkinson, D. W. (1992). *The English Ars Moriendi.* Renaissance and Baroque Studies and Texts, Vol. 5. Oxford: Peter Lang.

Cambers, A. (2014). *Godly Reading, Print, Manuscript and Puritanism in England 1580–1720.* Cambridge: Cambridge University Press.

Corpe, S., and Oakley, A. M. (1982). 'Canterbury Freemen: a list compiled from original sources in the Canterbury City Archives', 5 vols. Canterbury Archives.

Donne, J. (1624). *Devotions upon Emergent Occasions*, XVII. London.

Gowing, L. (1996). *Domestic Dangers: Women, Words, and Sex in Early Modern London.* Oxford: Oxford University Press.

Hallam, E. (1996). 'Turning the Hourglass: Gender relations at the deathbed in early modern Canterbury'. *Mortality* 1(1): pp. 61–82.

Hamling, T., and Richardson, C. (2016). *A Day at Home in Early Modern England.* New Haven, CT, and London: Yale University Press.

Houlbrooke, R. (1979). *Church Courts and the People during the English Reformation 1520–1570.* London and New York: Oxford University Press.

Ingram, M. (1987). *Church Courts Sex and Marriage in England 1570–1640.* Cambridge: Cambridge University Press.

Krausman Ben-Amos, I. (2008). *The Culture of Giving; informal support and gift-exchange in Early Modern England.* Cambridge University Press

Orlin, L. (2007). *Locating Privacy in Tudor London.* Oxford: Oxford University Press.

Pearson, S. (1994). *The Medieval Houses of Kent.* Royal Commission on the Historical Monuments of England, HMSO.

Richardson, C. (2015). 'Shakespeare's Siblings'. In S. Wells and P. Edmondson (eds), *The Shakespeare Circle.* Cambridge University Press.

Sharpe, J. (1980). *Defamation and Sexual Slander in Early Modern England: The Church Courts at York.* Heslington, York: University of York, Borthwick Institute of Historical Research.

STEPHEN WALKER

11 Don't Try This at Home: Artists' Viewing Inhabitation

ABSTRACT

This essay will discuss three art projects: *House*, by Rachel Whiteread [1993], *Alteration to a Suburban House*, by Dan Graham [1978] and *Splitting*, by Gordon Matta-Clark [1974]. All are concerned with mass housing typologies rather than bespoke housing. In all three, connection to any real lives is erased and frustrated in various ways, forcibly distancing our consideration from the particulars of previous inhabitants of these places, inviting us instead to project our own sense of home onto these anonymised places. The artists deploy complex dynamics of looking and not looking, seeing and not seeing, the visible, the invisible and the hidden, in order to draw attention to everyday material and spatial frameworks that persist in mass housing. I will dwell on how these projects combine examinations of the invisible relations of power exercised across domestic space with the familiar, visible image of home.

Introduction

> All great simple images reveal a psychic state. The house, even more than the landscape, is a 'psychic state', and even when reproduced as it appears from the outside, it bespeaks intimacy.
> — GASTON BACHELARD, *The Poetics of Space* (1958: 70)

> We must be insistently aware of how space can be made to hide consequences from us; how relations of power and discipline are inscribed into the apparently innocent spatiality of everyday life, how human geographies become filled with politics and ideology.
> — ED SOJA, *Postmodern Geographies* (1989: 6)

With a nod to Bachelard's reverie concerning the great simple image of the house, and to Soja's more incisive warning about the invisible spatial operations of power, this essay will consider the image of home between two conditions, or between two viewing positions, which we might for convenience refer to as the overt – from the outside – and the covert. In combination, Bachelard and Soja, representing overt and covert positions respectively, suggest that within the innocent, intimate image and domestic space of home are hidden decidedly non-domestic forces.

Instead of pursuing their work directly, the essay will discuss how these forces are manifest in various ways in three art projects: *House*, by Rachel Whiteread [1993], *Alteration to a Suburban House* by Dan Graham [1978] and *Splitting*, by Gordon Matta-Clark [1974]. In various ways, these three projects cause us to reflect on what such overt and covert views provide, and what it might mean to disrupt their usual associations with the At Home and the Not-At-Home. All these projects are depersonalised to a degree where observers can appropriate them and project their own lives onto them. Taken separately and together, these project raise questions that reflect on our own situations rather than on the real lives lived there. They invite us to consider how much these associations cross over into each other, how much we presume by taking their separation for granted, how much our feelings of being At Home are underwritten by assumptions of stability and security. Artists can help us to look at the familiar with fresh eyes, and to raise questions about our everyday spaces of domestic inhabitation.

Rather than assuming that one has to be out, away from home, to be Not-At-Home, I want to explore the notion that these two conditions are physically co-extensive. One of the underlying notions that this collection addresses is that to inhabit implies a broad engagement in the world, communal and personal, whereas the term inhabitation carries overtones of everyday and particularly domestic space. At stake in the stability of those places associated with the At Home and the Not-At-Home is (among many other things) our relationship to the culture within which we live. As Soja hints, the capitalist system behind this cultural situation endeavours to maintain the conflation of home with domesticity, by which we usually understand some sort of comfort, safety, not-work, family or private situation. But as he and many other critics have observed, this picture of domesticity is achieved at a price. In other words, the At Home and Not at Home are deliberately kept apart; they are maintained as opposites. But this is some strange accounting: the projects discussed here suggest a different approach to home economics.

The home, or the domestic, has been in and out of fashion as a subject for artistic practice for as long as what we call Western civilisation has been rolling along. In the recent past (at least since the advent of what is generally labeled as conceptual art) there have been many artists, working in many different media, who have produced works that take on 'the home'. Such projects can work to reveal how the political, economic, artistic, symbolic, as well as architectural systems within which they are located function; they can expose the natures of domestic practice, the individual and collective experience and negotiation of identity through spatially differentiated materiality. Despite the apparently everyday or 'ordinary' objects of such work, the sheer range of responses demonstrates that houses are actually the bearers of an overplus of meaning.

The three works discussed here are all concerned with mass housing typologies rather than bespoke (Architectural with a capital A) housing, with suburbia. Connection to any real lives is erased and frustrated in various ways, in contrast to many of the other examples that run through this collection. The artworks forcibly distance our consideration from the particulars of previous inhabitants of these places, inviting us instead towards a more archetypal situation, or to project our own sense of home onto these anonymised places. I will dwell on how these projects combine examinations of the invisible relations of power exercised across domestic space with the familiar, visible image of home. They deploy moments of looking and not looking, seeing and not seeing, the visible, the invisible and the hidden, to draw attention to everyday material and spatial frameworks that persist in mass housing. In various ways, they set up situations where, as viewers or visitors, we encounter moments when two (or more) conditions are experienced together, when the Not-At-Home becomes a dimension of the experience of home, and when this disruptive material or spatial presence has the opportunity to remind us of the complexities of a broader situation. They do this by interrupting the conceit of what is taken to be a homogenous system, demonstrating that At-Home and

Not-At-Home are not necessarily oppositional. To say this in a different way, they destabilise convention, what we take for granted and what we rely on to underpin Bachelard's psychic state of domestic intimacy.

We can think of this relationship in a visual register, with the invisible Not-at-Home being inscribed within the visible At-Home. This over-simplistic approach has many disadvantages, none of which will be outlined, but what it does allow is for the three very different artworks to be discussed alongside each other, and to be brought alongside some of the broader themes and issues addressed in this collection about how people live.

Figure 11.1: Rachel Whiteread, *House*, 1993. Concrete. Commissioned by Artangel. (Photo credit: Sue Omerod. © Rachel Whiteread; Courtesy of the artist, Luhring Augustine, New York, Lorcan O'Neill, Rome, and Gagosian Gallery.)

House, Rachel Whiteread, 1993

House was made at, and from, 193 Grove Road, one house in a row of nineteenth-century terraces in Bow, East London. The terrace had been slated for demolition, making way for an urban park. Rachel Whiteread's project involved casting all the internal spaces this dwelling. The technological virtuosity involved was considerable. Once the concrete had set, the existing building skin was removed, revealing detailed impressions of windows, doors and skirting, as well as the overall arrangement of spaces that made up the house. Opened in October 1993, it won Whiteread that year's Turner Prize, but simultaneously a furious row was played out in the local and national press, leading to the work's destruction early in January 1994.

In the terms introduced earlier, it is tempting to describe *House* as literally concretising the invisible (either private-domestic space, or space-as-not-matter). However, this explanation retains all the stability of the initial situation, and effectively follows an economy of replacement: invisible for visible, Not-at-Home for At-Home. While this may be true for Whiteread's earlier, smaller, gallery-based works, *House* maintained an ambiguity for the observer that developed away from their 'usual' encounter with the domestic. While casting the intangible, invisible space of the house, and thereby allowing its 'discovery', *House* simultaneously excluded the observer (and the past lives of its previous occupants) from the site, covering this realm over. In situ and in photographs, *House* is comprehensible – it is legible as a house, and by extension as part of a Victorian terrace found, in variations of a type, all across Britain – but simultaneously incomprehensible and unfamiliar, reduced to a single unit isolated in park-land, such that its context and domestic scale are not immediately clear.[1]

---

1   Anthony Vidler, an architectural writer well known for his work on the uncanny, has written an essay that situates *House* in this broader intellectual trajectory of the *unheimlich*, where he warns against easy readings of Whiteread's work in Freudian terms, while also using *House* to challenge this aspect of Freud's work. See Vidler (1995).

However, such an explanation retains all the stability of the initial situation, and effectively follows an economy of replacement. Instead, it can be suggested that what *House* did was rather to maintain an ambiguity in the observer that developed from their 'usual' encounter with the domestic. *House* simultaneously blocked out the observer, excluded them from and involved them in the domestic space, demanded that they work to recompose the inverted and fragmented spaces and traces of the former house, and thus return the artwork to the idea and reality of the domestic.

There are many aspects of the work that contributed to this situation; at the overall scale of the piece, there were fragments of wall and floor construction still visible, trapped inside the concrete, evidence of the mold that produced the piece. Their presence juxtaposed the 'invisible' spaces of the house (the floor void, the brick wall) with the 'invisible' spaces of *House*. Two invisibles that nonetheless operated in different registers, a sort of both/and rather than the either/or of simple replacement. It can be observed that the structure of the old house was to some indeterminate extent continuing to provide support for the new. Although the piece had been made by using this structure as a mold, contrary to convention the mold was not removed, at least not entirely, once the fluid concrete had solidified. Rather than disappearing, the structure of the house, the bricks and mortar, became translucent in the cognition process, that is to say that *House* was opened up and covered over by the previous structure.

At a smaller scale, a similar translucent situation arose, inasmuch as a close inspection of any part of *House* could reveal both a firm physical boundary and simultaneously suggest a domestic space, a comfortable corner, a warm fireside or a familiar room. To this extent, the hard surface of the concrete could be penetrated by the spectator's vision in some sort of modern-day extramission, and they could simultaneously gaze on the domestic spaces and have their gaze denied.

The norms that predicate our understanding of home are revealed in this partial blocking, partial yielding. As another dimension of the same interrogation, the distinct boundary of the objective object is made ambiguous. The explanations that might be offered for this failure of the subject and object to connect are conventionally blindness on the part of the subject or invisibility on the part of the object. However, the complex, translucent situation just outlined collapses any distinction between these two poles, and forces the 'subject' – the new, porous subject – into a condition of invisibility usually reserved for the object. It must be emphasised that this is not a situation without vision, where the subject might defer to another mode of perception that deployed the senses of touch, for example, but one in which vision is forced to operate in the spot of total darkness that permits vision to operate. *House* registers a disturbance between perception and congnition, raising questions that can be reflected back At Home. Subject and object here are held in a relationship of reciprocal presupposition, and *House* foregrounded that excessive moment when the gaze operates to maintain the subject outside of the object, with all the attendant anxiety that this involves.

Coincidentally, the relationship between mind and matter, knowing subject and external object, had during the Enlightenment been given one explanation based on the metaphor of the domestic interior, where the dark room – camera obscura – represented the mind of the subject, into which rays of light were permitted to enter from the outside world. Jonathan Crary remarks on the epistemological shifts that took place in the early part of the nineteenth century in terms that echo the ambiguity between outside, surface and interior that *House* set up. 'What begins in the 1820s and 1830s is a repositioning of the observer, outside of the fixed relations of interior/exterior presupposed by the camera obscura and into an undemarcated terrain on which the distinction between internal sensation and external signs is irrevocably blurred' (Crary 1990: 24). Although such an overcoming of transcendence may be taken as 'progress', what is suggested by Crary is that (in addition to 'progress' being a suspect term) this new mode of vision is allied to capitalism, with demands of standardisation, rationalisation, management, attentiveness, and so on: 'Once vision became located in the empirical immediacy of the observer's body, it belonged to time, to flux, to death. The guarantees of authority, identity, and universality supplied by the camera obscura are of another epoch' (Crary 1990: 24). Looking at the ambiguous surfaces and decontextualised whole of *House* produced in the epoch of late capitalism can set up and unsettle resonances with our everyday acceptance of domestic space understood as a realm apart from public life. This separation is explored with different techniques and consequences by much of Dan Graham's work from the 1960s onwards.

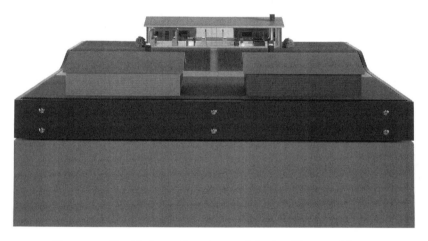

Figure 11.2: Dan Graham, *Alteration to a Suburban House*, 1978/1992.
Wood, felt, plexiglass. Dimensions: 11 x 43 x 48". (Collection Walker
Art Center, Minneapolis Justin Smith Purchase Fund, 1993.)

Alteration to a Suburban House, Dan Graham, 1978

Dan Graham produced his proposals for an *Alteration to a Suburban* House in 1978. Although never realised as a project, his descriptions and models have been circulated widely and much discussed. As with much of his work, *Alteration* addressed moments of separation, the politics of space, and individual agency, and reinforced his interest in the production and consumption of the mass housing that had been produced in the Unites States since the end of the Second World War, and announced in early projects such as the conceptual piece, which was positioned in the large circulation magazine, *Homes for America* (1966).

Graham's unrealised(-able) proposal for *Alteration* was to replace the front facade of a typical single storey North American suburban tract house with a sheet glass curtain wall, and then to clad the middle internal wall (parallel with the façade) with mirror. Describing the proposal and the dynamics of vision it would set up, Graham writes: 'The entire façade of a typical suburban house has been removed and replaced by a full sheet of transparent glass. Midway back and parallel to the front glass façade, a mirror divides the house into two areas. The front section is public, while the rear, private section is not disclosed. The mirror as it faces the glass façade and the street reflects not only the house's interior, but the street and the environment outside the house. The reflected images of the facades of the two houses opposite the cut-away "fill in" the missing façade' (Graham 1981, 35).

As a strategy, his gesture might appear to be the opposite of Rachel Whiteread's: rather than denying the observer access to the space of the house, either physically or via the various visual means just mentioned, Graham's *Alteration* denies the observer leave to leave. There is no escape, no objective distance for the observer or casual passerby. However, both projects, *Alteration* and *House* operate at that moment when the mechanics of viewing are revealed, when a gap is opened in the 'normal' field of vision and the invisible spills out, revealing vision's contingency and inherent instability, as well as questioning our assumptions about the protection afforded by the domestic interior.

Whereas *House* foregrounded such instability by juxtaposing various registers of invisibility, *Alteration* incarcerates the observer within a suffocating expanse of the visible. The conventional or convenient realms of public and private are forced together in the working of the mirror, which denies the spectator any distance from the occupant of the house or the domestic space (and vice-versa) instead forcing both to occupy the same visual field. Domains that are usually maintained as separate, if not as polar opposites, are thrown together and become continuous in the reflection of the mirror.

The suburban home, whether the Victorian British terrace or the mid-century tract house, is a product and key component of capitalist society, and usually figured as being apart from the urban realm. However, both are integral to the system of production and consumption, which as Guy Debord observed, was not without its dangers for those in power, as it would concentrate workers together to meet the demands for labour in the processes of production. Debord refers to capitalist strategies of urbanism such as housing estates, and suggests that these fulfill a need that 'requires that isolated individuals be recaptured and *isolated together*' (Debord, 1967, #172). Moreover, he argues that one of the principal devices deployed to bring about this collective isolation was 'the spectacle' which pursues 'the isolated individual right into the *family cell*, [where] the widespread use of receivers of the spectacular message enables the individual to fill his isolation with the dominant images – images which derive their power precisely from this isolation' (Debord, 1967, #172). Within the homes that Graham's project addresses, the widespread take-up of television was significant, and one can imagine the front room of *Alteration* (now the 'public' section of the house) arranged around the television set, with members of the family gathered around watching while themselves being watched as a spectacle.

The system that Debord criticises requires a social masquerade to maintain the artificial isolation on which it depends (the promise of a better life in suburbia), a masquerade which observes that home is a long away from work, or that home is safely removed from the machinations of power. Graham's project refuses to play along, introducing the optical device of the mirror, which sees all and blinds all with its excess of sight.

Viewing from one domain into another (staring into a house from outside) is no longer underwritten with a guarantee of not being seen; the introduction of the mirror deep in the domestic space of the suburban house has the effect of removing the opportunity of invisibility on the part of the spectator, whose eye coincides twice over with the mirror (witness, and witness to this witnessing, both Not-at-Home and At-Home). The passerby/spectator (and inhabitant in the fuller, slippery sense of this term) can only experience the potential trauma of self-revelation within the system from a viewing position within that system. The asymmetry required by the masquerade is not supported by the mirror, which simultaneously gives back both domains, public and private, to the spectator, who occupies both within the dynamic of this particular visual field.

Some have read this as a profoundly pessimistic work, one that locks the observer into a fatalistic acknowledgement of nihilism, but it could be suggested instead that the realisation that *Alteration* brings about could provide a disruptive dimension to experience that could act to maintain a more fluid and complex relationship between these places or states of mind. What is important to emphasise is that this gesture does not involve a simple reversal of the At Home and the Not-At-Home, but that it brings these two together, cancels their usual asymmetry, and reveals their interconnectedness.

In contrast to the (albeit temporary) concrete materiality of *House*, it is worth remembering that *Alteration* was only ever a model conveying an idea (albeit a very powerful one), a model into which viewers had to project themselves from an architect-like position outside. As Roland Barthes has argued, this is not a weakness of the model, but in fact it is a great strength: 'Models allow full perception of many architectural contradictions, they allow the imitated object to reveal something which remained invisible or even more incomprehensible with the mere object ... intellect added to the object' (Barthes 1964: 216). The final artwork to be discussed here operates on a house as if it were a model, revealing something that had remained invisible (or only seen by the mind's eye of the architect) to those that experienced the project.

Splitting, Gordon Matta-Clark, 1974

Of the three projects presented here, Gordon Matta-Clark's artwork *Splitting* remained closest to the house it was made from, it remained most recognisable as a house (if not a home). As with *House*, where Whiteread was able to take possession of a building scheduled for demolition, Matta-Clark was given the property that became *Splitting* shortly before it was demolished to make way for new development. It had been a servant or

Figure 11.3: Gordon Matta-Clark, *Splitting*, 1974. Collage: four black and
white photographs mounted on separate board. (Courtesy of the
Estate of Gordon Matta-Clark and David Zwirner,
New York. © ARS, NY and DACS, London 2016.)

chauffeur's home in the grounds of a large residence in New Jersey. Matta-
Clark produced the piece by cutting through the house vertically (it was
made of timber, and he made one continuous vertical cut one inch wide
through all the structural members, interior and exterior walls, floors

and roof). He then removed a section of the masonry foundations and eased one half of the house into a new position. Anticipating Whiteread's work, this project also received a hostile reaction in the press, precipitating a broadside against artists 'wasting' valuable homes while overlooking the fact that both projects worked with buildings that were about to be demolished.

Whereas *Alteration* operated at a moment of excessive vision (amplified with the Barthes' consideration of the model), and *House* operated at a moment of excessive blindness or invisibility, *Splitting* held these two moments together in a different operative relationship. One of the demands this work made was that it couldn't be seen in a single view; the experience of *Splitting* would change as an observer moved around the dissected building, stepping over the split as the passage was made from room to room and from storey to storey. This movement through the house, horizontally and vertically, would have been interrupted by the presence of the cut, the (usually invisible) section.

This encounter would have foregrounded the architectural conventions of orthographic drawing, which involve the static mapping of architectural space (usually associated with its design and production, rather than its 'use'), and turn it back upon itself. It would have foregrounded an invisible framework within the normal visual field and domestic spaces of the house. Parallel to the way that *Alteration*'s mirror would bring together realms that are usually kept apart, *Splitting* revealed the Not-at-Home – here, architectural convention – within the domestic. Both these situations presume a dominant system, an omnipresent view, one that can look without being seen, and that seeks to penetrate into domains within which they would claim to be invisible.

To make more of this comparison, *Splitting* maintained a juxtaposition of invisible and visible, while *House* and *Alteration* forcibly moved the spectator to occupy a position that was excluded from or captured by domestic space. For visitors to *Splitting*, the presence of the 'whole' or recognisable building would never have been allowed to slip too far out of sight or to become too foregrounded, which has several consequences. The chance of obtaining an overall view (albeit impossible) would have been denied to the visitor, because the architectural convention that would claim this view from nowhere is demonstrated to be contingent, written into the material fabric of the structure. Also, the viewer (more generally, the subject of architecture) would have been maintained in a position between two mutually exclusive systems of representation, namely the invisible material and spatial make-up of architectural elements that are only usually 'seen' by the architect (as a drawing) or builder (as work-in-progress), or by the occupants as the inhabited, personalised and particular domestic spaces of the home. There are parallels with the simultaneous exclusion and inclusion observed regarding Rachel Whiteread's *House*, where the spectator remained physically outside the space of the home while projecting their own experiences into the concrete spaces of the work, and with Dan Graham's *Alteration*, where spectators would be visually incorporated within the home while remaining physically removed from the building.

However, *Splitting* adds to these two viewing situations: rather than just being a 'snapshot' work available for consumption from a single, overt point of view, and rather than allowing observation 'from nowhere' that the privileged, covert architectural system of orthographic drawing presumes, Matta-Clark's project would have demanded what we might call an operative viewing, a mobile observer, and one that acknowledged that the dimensions At-Home and Not-At-Home were not held in a stable opposition but that both must be addressed together.

Don't try this at home

Artistic work on the home – particularly that which co-opts the physical structures that really were once homes, such as *Splitting* or *House* – can prompt us as observers to reflect on our own particular domestic situations as much or more than we might speculate on the individual and family lives that were lived out in these particular places. As other essays in this collection also suggest, this mode of reflection calls this 'we' into question. To what extent can similarities and differences of domestic life be related across geographical and historical examples? How much does this 'we' take the notion of 'common experience' more or less for granted? To what extent are these particular homes any more anonymous or particular than that of the surgeon in Pompeii?

Whiteread's *House* points to the state of inhabitation – its architectural provision – being mutable rather than static or permanent. Graham's *Alteration* points to its involvement in broader machinations of power, within which 'inhabitation' plays a more oppressive role. Matta-Clark's *Splitting* can be considered more directly as a viewing device, through which the observer was able to position the building – the home – as well as themselves, in a broader schema. Considering this range, we might ask what is at stake in these artworks. Mindful of the hostile reaction that the 'alteration' of real houses carried out by Matta-Clark and Whiteread provoked in the popular press, it is worth emphasising the almost visceral connection that such work can bring about in a wide audience, connected perhaps to an individual and group memory and identity that is often related to the notion of *habitus*.

Amongst many associations, *habitus* has been related to the acquisition of ways of knowing, understanding, acting, and relating, and has been closely (but not exclusively) related to domestic space and the relationships that occur there. The artworks discussed here precipitate a reaction precisely because they invite, or force, spectators to view not only the artworks, but to reflect on their own identities and needs as these are compressed into the habits and *habitus* that write themselves into, are written into, the forms of their 'house' in its broadest sense. These artworks actively precipitate their audience to consider the contradiction that emerges between overt and covert views of the domestic, adding an extra temporal position from which it might be considered that we are always already within the *habitus*, not simply constituted and structured by it as individuals. Georges Teyssot has argued that 'For both Benjamin and Deleuze, it seemed that the humanistic category of *Habitus*, defined as the embodiment of conventions, concordance and style, should be led toward its own dissolution, to force "the foundation of habit into a failure of 'habitus'", making it the thought and the production of a new kind of repetition, which becomes "difference in itself"' (Teyssot 2013: 19, citing Deleuze 1968: 94). Although Teyssot's address was to the thinking of Benjamin and Deleuze, it resonates with the artworks discussed here, and returns this discussion to the

252 STEPHEN WALKER

distinction between the overt and covert approaches of Bachelard and Soja. What are the dangers of being outside the *habitus*? As Teyssot observes at a later point in his argument, architecture 'can be transformed into a device that participates in th[e] staging of [a] novel situation, [where] an architectural design no longer simply leads to something to look at (such as an object or building), but rather becomes an apparatus that allows the viewer – that is, the user – to behold something other than the thing itself' (Teyssot 2013: 250)

Bibliography

Bachelard, G. (1958/1964). *The Poetics of Space*. Translated by M. Jolas. Boston, MA: Beacon Press.
Barthes, R. (1964). 'L'Activité Structuraliste'. In *Essais Critiques*. Paris: Gallimard.
Crary, J. (1990). *Techniques of the Observer: On Vision and Modernity in the Nineteenth Century*. Cambridge, MA: MIT Press.
Debord, G. (1967/1983). *Society of the Spectacle*. Detroit, MI: Black and Red.
Deleuze, G. (1966/1968). *Difference and Repetition*. New York: Columbia University Press.
Graham, D. *(1981)*. *Dan Graham: Buildings and Signs* exhibition catalogue. The Renaissance Society at the University of Chicago.
Lingwood, J. (ed.) (1995). *Rachel Whiteread: House*. London: Phaidon.
Soja, Ed (1989). *Postmodern Geographies: The Reassertion of Space in Critical Social Theory*. London: Verso.
Teyssot, G. (2013). *A Topology of Everyday Constellations*. Cambridge, MA: MIT Press.
Vidler, A. (1995). 'A Dark Space'. In J. Lingwood (ed.), *Rachel Whiteread: House*. London: Phaidon, 1995: pp. 62–72.[2]

FRANCES F. BERDAN

Afterword

There are few things more basic in human life than habitation. Humans everywhere define meaningful spaces for themselves. They construct spaces. They embellish them, and they place values (positive, negative, or more nuanced) on them. People carry out activities in and around these spaces. People establish, cement and nullify relationships, go through prescribed life cycles, and amplify their own idiosyncracies ... all in the context of natural and constructed habitations. Throughout prehistory and history we have occupied and transformed spaces. In turn, these transformed spaces have delineated and influenced our movements, activities, relationships and outlooks. In the broad view, human-built and human-occupied spaces embody our amazingly diverse ways of looking at the world as well as facilitate (or constrain) our strategies for surviving and thriving in it.

From the perspective of an anthropologist, an exploration into the nature, structure, meanings and dynamics of habitation is a particularly worthwhile, intellectual and practical pursuit. As explained by the editors in the introduction to this volume, habitation consists of the complex and mutable interplay among place, objects, actions, relationships and values. It is culture in its physical and ideological context, echoing the subtitle of this book, 'people, places, and possessions'. Sometimes habitats emerge as harmonious and rational, sometimes confusing and jumbled, sometimes contradictory. It's complicated. It's human. But it is not unfathomable.

This brings us to the substance of the several contributions to this intriguing volume. *InHabit* connects with some fundamental anthropological ideas huddled under the umbrella of habitation, most notably a focus on culture, an appreciation of diversity, a recognition of dynamics and change and the application of a holistic and encompassing perspective. This book also contains an unusual and engaging potpourri of case studies that collectively demonstrate the value of focusing on habitation as a productive realm of study. I am a big fan of case studies. To me, case studies have the potential to shed light on broad cultural propositions at the same time as highlighting nuances that may be missed or overlooked in more general presentations. With these few little words at the end of this wide-ranging and thought-provoking collection, I would like to briefly stress a few salient points that derive from and unify these diverse contributions.

Some key themes

Several key themes that pique the interest of an anthropologist recur throughout this volume: variation, adaptation, relationships and context, and dynamics and agency.

Variation and diverse expressions. Understanding, explaining and appreciating cultural diversity is at the heart of anthropology. In this book we see habitation examples ranging from early Roman England, an upscale London street, English country houses from the fifteenth to the nineteenth centuries, narratives in *Playboy* magazine, shipboard domestic spaces, sixteenth-century Canterbury deathbed sites, created house sculptures, and, as an interesting contrast, homeless locales in Bristol and York. Together, these offer a hint of the wide-ranging ways that humans have devised to satisfactorily occupy and creatively modify physical spaces. Wholesale diversity is far too immense and unwieldy to consider here. Nonetheless, it is worthwhile reflecting on a few dimensions of cross-cultural diversity that pertain directly to habitation and which are exemplified in this book's chapters. First, *functional suitability* frequently plays a part in habitation creation, modification, and use. This is demonstrated in virtually all of the chapters, but especially in the discussions of rural domestic assemblages of Late Iron Age/Early Roman England (Chapter 4), shipboard life (Chapter 8) and homeless strategies (Chapter 9). The idea of function frequently revolves around efficiency, utility and comfort, and is probably a universal (or near-universal) consideration in habitat choices and creation across cultures. Yet on-the-ground practicalities are not the entire story, and a second consideration is *social status and image*, exemplified in the chapters on elite social status in English country houses (Chapter 6), shipboard living arrangements (Chapter 8) and deathbed customs in sixteenth-century Canterbury (Chapter 10). We see here, and in other worldwide examples, how human actions are embedded in egalitarian or hierarchical societies (and others ranging in between these poles), and how they take place in physical settings that facilitate these societal and cultural proclivities. Third, *ideology and worldview* play important parts in habitat structures and dynamics, as habitats embed and emit cultural meanings right alongside idiosyncratic inclinations. This can be readily seen in the chapters on *Playboy* narratives (Chapter 7), deathbed customs (Chapter 10) and the artistic projects creating disorienting perspectives on habitations (Chapter 11). A fourth widespread consideration in habitations is *safety*, especially noted by Damian Robinson for shipboard residents (Chapter 8) and by Rachael Kiddey for homeless individuals (Chapter 9). Less fully represented here, but a recurring dimension of habitations worldwide, is the explicit expression and exercise of power related to habitation.

Beyond broad considerations of cross-cultural diversity, variation was (and is) also prevalent *within* specifically defined cultures and societies. While this aspect of variation is highlighted less often than broader comparisons, it is considerably revealing of human behaviour. Some of the chapters here lead us to think about this. What about the urban dwellers on London's Tilney Street (Chapter 5), where individual tastes can be seen to override fashion conventions? What about cultural constraints and personal preferences surrounding spatial arrangements tied to food choices in Late Iron Age/Early Roman England (Chapter 4)? Other examples of internal cultural variation are legion, and remind us that recognising variation, while always interesting, is one thing. Explaining it is quite another. For that, we can look to additional themes.

Adaptation

Human habitation is a cultural phenomenon, and as such encompasses ways in which humans express their ways of life in their use of space. While perhaps sounding simple and straightforward, this is a complex matter and involves structures, relationships and meanings. Habitation is related to cultural proclivities, social and economic realities and political imperatives. Well-formulated models and conceptual frameworks can help unravel these complexities. One option, ecological, points to cultural adaptations to site and situation that can be combinations of responses to physical, economic, social, political and religious considerations. A few brief examples: The traditional nomadic Dobe! Kung of the Kalahari Desert construct small temporary huts from local materials at their frequent stopping points – these can be constructed within one to four days. These hasty structures are not really intended for occupation (except for catching a brief afternoon nap), but serve primarily for storage and to symbolically stake out living spaces for their occupants. They serve both practical and symbolic purposes. Medieval European castles were perched on hills for sensible defence and to project military and political might as well as ideological superiority. The single-family houses of the Peruvian Jívaro are situated on small hillocks for defence, and their quality reflects the household head's personal status and powers. Examples of complex ecological adaptations in habitations are legion, and additional insights might also emerge from viewing the case studies in this volume from this perspective: adapting to the constraints and social hierarchy of shipboard life, finding suitable and safe homeless settings, creating idealised spaces based on *Playboy* narratives, and so on.

This is only one way of looking at adaptive strategies. Andrea Placidi (Chapter 3) describes the most suitable buildings as adaptable, flexible and capable of change, and his concept of 'furnitecture' as mediating between the external structure and the internal constellation of furnishings allows for these elasticities. Interesting. It reminds us that habitations can be intentionally flexible settings: for example, the Kalapalo of central Brazil create a temporary wall across part of their open household living space to seclude a mother and newly born child for up to a year. Situational adjustments, intended or serendipitous, are part of the adaptation scenario. Other approaches help us understand habitation strategies. Matthew Jenkins and Charlotte Newman (Chapter 5) apply a biographical approach (material, human and household life histories) to fine effect and Rebecca Devers (Chapter 7) brings narrative techniques to the table to spotlight idealised mythic or fantasy spaces, certainly an approach that could be used more widely on the cross-cultural stage.

A focus on adaptation and attendant ideas helps us understand some fundamentals such as nomadic versus sedentary (or temporary versus permanent) adaptations, communal versus isolated spaces, or uniform versus diversified habitations. What about 'divided habitations' reflected in statements such as the commuter's lament 'I live in my car' and the workaholic's installation of a home-like environment in his or her workspace?

But much more can be said, beyond adaptation. What about other salient aspects of habitat, especially interpersonal relations, dynamics and agency?

Relationships and context

At one point, during an ethnographic fieldwork season in a small fishing village in eastern Mexico, I was invited to a wake for a small child. Upon arrival I was directed to the door of the one-room house to offer my condolences to the child's mother. I was not invited inside. Instead, I was asked to join the men and children assembled on the house's outdoor patio where we shared a curious but potent drink and passed the afternoon in increasingly amiable accord. Although I remember little else (!), what struck me most was the prescribed use of household space to identify and segregate people in this ritualised event, and my own ambiguous status (being neither man nor child). This sort of thing (arranging people spatially) is more the rule than the exception across cultures, and highlights the importance of focusing on relationships when discussing habitation. People animate places.

The concept of *habitus* pops up here with its emphasis on habitual actions carried out in defined spaces, with objects and embellishments as supporting actors. The idea of habitus opens the door to viewing habitations as networks of interpersonal relations. And these relations extend beyond individual habitation; they have broader contexts. The very process of constructing dwellings can tell us a great deal about more encompassing people–place relations. For instance, the making of the Cheyenne tepee was the responsibility of the woman of the house, who enlisted the aid of other women to process the hides. The tepee also required the skilled input of a female expert lodge-maker as well as the formal dedication by a courageous

warrior; none of these were to ultimately occupy the tepee. Among the
Zinacanteco Indians of southern Mexico, extended families were collectively mobilised for house-building, the new house and its site claimed
by its young family and sanctified by the erection of a house cross. These
examples illustrate that from its very conception a new dwelling embodies
practical, social and ritual-symbolic elements tying each domestic setting
to the larger social and ideological milieu. Such considerations of broader
contexts resonate well with Antony Buxton's discussion of English country
houses (Chapter 6), where status-laden spaces in these grand houses have
shifted over time, depending on internal and external priorities of social
relationships. Once established, people engage in culturally prescribed
and socially expected activities in and around their dwellings, modifying
and personalising their spaces as conventions, taste and economics allow.

People are more than social creatures – the lives they build are also
shaped by worldviews and beliefs. This tension between behaviour and belief
as prescribed and personal, or conventional and innovative, is addressed in
Wendy Morrison's application of Mary Douglas's culture theory grid to
questions of consumer preferences in Late Iron Age/Early Roman English
domestic assemblages (Chapter 4); against Douglas's model, Morrison
suggests that more nuanced interpretations can be made of archaeological
data. In another vein but still in the realm of the more abstract, Catherine
Richardson (Chapter 10) offers an interesting perspective with the idea
that houses and their residents hold onto memories of people, events and
things, and the realisation that stories told about a death are set within
the physical context of a house. Rebecca Devers's treatment of idealised
'fantasy' living spaces published in *Playboy* issues also squarely addresses
worldview issues (Chapter 7). In each of these cases, we are reminded that
human relationships have broad contexts and complex but patterned ties
to worldviews and ideologies.

Dynamics and agency

Almost all of the chapters in this book embody or at least recognise some
aspect of change, over short and long spans of time. Some of the case studies

are set in transitional times to intentionally highlight transformations over time: the Late Iron Age/Early Roman setting, the eighteenth- and nineteenth-century houses on London's Tilney Street, four centuries of English country house evolution and historic and contemporary shipboard habitats. Once laid out, spaces are potentially mutable. Some, indeed, are designed with flexibility and multiple uses in mind: deathbed customs in Canterbury entailed short-term adaptations and emphases within dwellings, and Kalapalo post-partum customs partitioned existing house space (as mentioned earlier). Among these cases, perhaps flexibility is most vividly expressed in the lives of homeless people, who often face conditions requiring alterations or movements in their domestic settings. Habitations are not static entities, but undergo changes, adjustments and transformations on daily, life-cycle, generational and longer bases. What might be at the core of the dynamics of something as fundamental as one's habitation?

A recurring theme in this book is the matter of agency, basically addressing the question of what animates or motivates change and facilitates adaptations. Humans are typically considered the agents of change, but Jane Anderson (Chapter 2) turns this on its head by also examining how inanimate buildings and objects shape the lives and perspectives of human beings (as inhabitants and also as architects and archaeologists). In other words, in the context of habitats, inanimate spaces we live in, and the inanimate objects we fill those spaces with, produce meaningful influences on us. In this frame, Linda Hulin (Chapter 1) seeks the relations between built forms and social action by looking at buildings as agents of social change within specified domestic contexts. Andrea Placidi (Chapter 3) suggests that change can be effected by 'furnitecture', and Catherine Richardson (Chapter 10) broaches these dynamics in asking about the roles played by houses themselves in reinforcing hierarchy and shaping domestic memory. Stephen Walker (Chapter 11), through his visually disorienting architectural projects, resonates with these thoughts by suggesting that houses bear meanings. Taken together, these cases highlight complex interrelationships, worthy of heightened attention. The question, 'what aspects of space do we value the most?' comes to mind; its answer is likely to draw on both animate and inanimate domestic dimensions.

The value of interdisciplinary approaches

The editors in their introduction express the hope that this book's multifaceted chapters may stimulate further discourse on the wide-ranging
topic of habitation. They stress that advances in this arena can be most
productively explored through interdisciplinary methodologies, teasing
out shared concepts through the application of complementary methodologies. This multidimensional approach is central to understanding the
diversity, complexity and dynamics of human habitations, and to gener-
ating interesting questions, holistic interpretations and insightful results.
Unravelling the many dimensions of habitation is made realistic through
the variety of approaches exemplified in this volume: archaeology, history,
architecture, interior design, linguistics, social geography, literary texts
and theory and ethnography; several of the chapters merge two or more
of these approaches, enhancing interdisciplinarity.

As the chapters of this unique volume demonstrate, the spaces that
people carve out for themselves, through time and across the globe, are
varied and creative. And not only is habitation universal (or very close
to it, as even the homeless devise homes), it also staunchly celebrates a
particularly clever side of humanity – the ability to modify and manipulate surroundings into myriad settings, be they temporary or permanent,
isolated or communal, functional or whimsical, comfortable or dreary,
accommodating or menacing, personally indulgent or socially crowded.
In the words of the editors, this book serves as a 'platform' for specialist
presentations – case studies – that exemplify broader themes in the realm
of habitation. I find all of this anthropologically captivating and energising.

Notes on Contributors

JANE ANDERSON is an architect and Principal Lecturer at Oxford Brookes University where she is the Programme Lead for Undergraduate Architecture and runs OB1 LIVE, a programme of live projects designed and implemented by students in collaboration with the local community. She is the author of *Architectural Design* (AVA, 2011). Her research interests include the relationship between reality and imagination in architecture; interdisciplinary connections and collaborations between art, literature, music and architecture; the work of John Hejduk; live projects and the pedagogy of architectural design. She is co-founder of the Live Projects Network, an online resource to connect students, academics, practitioners and clients involved in live projects. In 2014, Jane was awarded a National Teaching Fellowship.

FRANCES F. BERDAN is Professor Emerita of Anthropology at California State University, San Bernardino, USA. She received her BA degree in Geography at Michigan State University and her PhD in Anthropology at the University of Texas, Austin. Her research focuses on ethnohistorical, archaeological, experimental archaeological, linguistic and ethnographic approaches to Aztec, colonial and contemporary native Mexican economies, societies and cultures. Her interdisciplinary works include a four-volume edition of *The Codex Mendoza* (1992, co-authored), *Aztec Imperial Strategies* (1996, co-authored), *The Postclassic Mesoamerican World* (2003, co-edited), and *Ethnic Identity in Nahua Mesoamerica* (2008, co-authored). Her most recent book is *Aztec Archaeology and Ethnohistory* (2014, Cambridge University Press).

ANTONY BUXTON lectures on design history, material and domestic culture at Oxford University Department for Continuing Education. A first degree in archaeology and anthropology and an early working life in furniture design, making and conservation generated an interest in people, their possessions and surroundings, the subject of doctoral research (Oxon), on which *Domestic Culture in Early Modern England* (Woodbridge: Boydell Press 2015), a study of the practice of non-elite dwellings is based. He was a co-convenor of the Oxford Centre for Research in the Humanities (TORCH) inHabit seminar programme. Continuing research interests embrace human habitation, the making and consumption of commodities and the range of contexts in which they are employed.

REBECCA DEVERS is Assistant Professor of English at New York City College of Technology (City Tech). She also serves as Co-Coordinator of Writing across the Curriculum at City Tech and Assistant Editor of New American Notes Online. Her research interests lie in the intersections among fiction, culture, and domestic architecture, as seen in her 2014 article '"You Don't Prepare Breakfast … You Launch It Like a Missile": The Cold War Kitchen and Technology's Displacement of Home', published in *Americana: The Journal of American Popular Culture 1900–Present*.

LINDA HULIN is Research Officer at the Oxford Centre for Maritime Archaeology in the School of Archaeology, University of Oxford. She is a supernumerary fellow at Harris Manchester College and tutors in Archaeology there and in Magdalen College. Linda Hulin received a degree in Archaeology of the Eastern Mediterranean from the University of Liverpool, and at the University of Reading wrote a doctoral thesis on the social function of Cypriot fine wares in Egypt and the Levant during the New Kingdom. This prompted an interest in the ways in which objects work together, and this runs through her subsequent academic work. Linda Hulin has excavated at sites throughout the eastern Mediterranean and directed field survey in eastern Libya.

MATTHEW JENKINS is Teaching Fellow in the Department of Archaeology, University of York. He is a historical archaeologist, with a specialism in buildings and urban landscapes. His research focuses on the creation of buildings biographies and social narratives surrounding domestic living and consumer culture, particularly in the long eighteenth century.

RACHAEL KIDDEY is Editorial Assistant at the Independent Social Research Foundation where, among her responsibilities, is the production of the interdisciplinary *Bulletin* <http://www.isrf.org/bulletin>. Kiddey worked as a radio and television documentary producer (BBC Radio 4 and Channel 4 television) for several years before returning to academia. She received her PhD from the Department of Archaeology at the University of York in 2014. The chapter produced for this volume is based on her doctoral research, which involved developing methodologies for working archaeologically with homeless people and documenting how heritage can function in socially useful ways. Her PhD research was shortlisted for the Times Higher Education Award for Widening Participation Initiative of the Year 2012. She is currently completing a monograph on her 'Homeless Heritage' work for Oxford University Press.

WENDY MORRISON (DPhil Oxon) is Researcher at the University of Oxford's Institute of Archaeology and Assistant Director of the Dorchester Research Project. She has worked extensively in both commercial and research archaeology. Her current research project is mapping and characterising the metallurgy of Harappan bronze materials. She has a particular interest in the use of grid/group classification to understand individuality of ancient worldviews.

CHARLOTTE NEWMAN is currently the curator for English Heritage's archaeology collections in the London and East Territory and Architectural Study Collection. She is a historical archaeologist specialising in post-medieval buildings and associated material culture. She is particularly interested in institutional buildings and the interactions between people and space.

ANDREA PLACIDI graduated with a distinction in Architecture in 1992 with studies in both Rome La Sapienza and Copenhagen Kongelige Kunstakademi. He has worked as Construction Coordinator for the International Red Cross in the war-torn regions of ex-Yugoslavia between 1993 and 1997, specialising in the rehabilitation of educational buildings for the disabled. Since 1998 he has been a senior lecturer in the School of Architecture at Oxford Brookes University, and since 2004 the Subject

Coordinator for the BA Honours Degree in Interior Architecture. As a practising architect, he has designed and built several educational facilities in the United Kingdom and abroad, as well as numerous residential buildings. In 2014, he attained a PhD with a thesis on 'Bruno Zevi's legacy for the definition of architectural space'. His research and publications focus on themes connected to the experience of architecture, and have been published in the proceedings of international conferences since 2009.

CATHERINE RICHARDSON is Reader in Renaissance Studies at the University of Kent. She studies the literature and history of early modern material culture, and has written books on *Domestic Life and Domestic Tragedy in Early Modern England* (Manchester, 2006), *Shakespeare and Material Culture* (Oxford University Press, 2011) and, with Tara Hamling, *A Day at Home in Early Modern England, The Materiality of Domestic Life, 1500–1700* (Yale, 2016).

DAMIAN ROBINSON is Director of the Oxford Centre for Maritime Archaeology in the School of Archaeology at the University of Oxford. He conducts field research at the submerged port-city of Thonis-Heracleion, Egypt, in conjunction with the European Institute for Underwater Archaeology, where he is currently excavating an Egyptian river-going *baris*-ship. He is particularly interested in issues related to maritime domesticity and the ways in which seafarers create their homes either at sea or on land and the formation of specific maritime sub-cultures.

STEPHEN WALKER is Reader in Architecture at Sheffield School of Architecture (SSoA), where he is Director of the Graduate School. His research broadly encompasses art and architectural and critical theory, and examines the questions that such theoretical approaches can raise about particular moments of architectural and artistic practice.

Index

CULTURAL INTERACTIONS
Studies in the Relationship between the Arts

Edited by J.B. Bullen

Interdisciplinary activity is now a major feature of academic work in all fields. The traditional borders between the arts have been eroded to reveal new connections and create new links between art forms. Cultural Interactions is intended to provide a forum for this activity. It will publish monographs, edited collections and volumes of primary material on points of crossover such as those between literature and the visual arts or photography and fiction, music and theatre, sculpture and historiography. It will engage with book illustration, the manipulation of typography as an art form, or the 'double work' of poetry and painting and will offer the opportunity to broaden the field into wider and less charted areas. It will deal with modes of representation that cross the physiological boundaries of sight, hearing and touch and examine the placing of these modes within their representative cultures. It will offer an opportunity to publish on the crosscurrents of nationality and the transformations brought about by foreign art forms impinging upon others. The interface between the arts knows no boundaries of time or geography, history or theory.

Vol. 1   Laura Colombino: Ford Madox Ford: Vision, Visuality
          and Writing
          275 pages. 2008. ISBN 978-3-03911-396-5

Vol. 2   Graham Smith: 'Light that Dances in the Mind':
          Photographs and Memory in the Writings of E. M.
          Forster and his Contemporaries
          257 pages. 2007. ISBN 978-3-03911-117-6

Vol. 3   G.F. Mitrano and Eric Jarosinski (eds): The Hand of the
          Interpreter: Essays on Meaning after Theory
          370 pages. 2009. ISBN 978-3-03911-118-3